2.⁵⁰

SHALLOW WATER DIVING
AND
SPEARFISHING

SHALLOW WATER DIVING AND SPEARFISHING

By

HILBERT SCHENCK, JR.

and

HENRY KENDALL

Illustrated by

VINCENT VITALE

CORNELL MARITIME PRESS

Cambridge, Maryland

1954

Library of Congress Catalog Card Number: 53-9687

Manufactured by
Universal Lithographers, Inc.
Baltimore 2, Md.
U. S. A.

DEDICATION

To the Frogmen of the Allied Navies who developed and perfected Shallow Water Diving techniques.

INTRODUCTION

In our first book on the general subject of shallow water diving we tried to discuss the state of the art as it appeared up to that time (1949). Now, in the ensuing three years, this original volume has become obsolete, due primarily to the tremendous upsurge in interest in underwater sport and particularly underwater spearfishing. It therefore seemed necessary to rewrite the first book completely, adding much new material on fishing and on the wealth of new equipment that is now flooding the diving market. At first we desired to include in this single volume a complete survey of underwater activity, including a comprehensive chapter on undersea photography. But it became apparent that this would create too expensive and bulky a volume, if all the necessary data were to be included. Therefore, the reader will find in this book a complete survey of shallow water diving, except for photography, which subject will be discussed in a companion volume entitled, *Underwater Photography*.

As in the previous book, we have divided the consideration of diving equipment into separate chapters, four in number. This information has been expanded considerably to include more data on methods of diving, since it was felt that the first book was weak in this direction. New chapters have been added on general diving science, on spearfishing, on the ocean sciences, on special applications, and on underwater vacations. Also, a fairly complete bibliography of diving has been added in an effort to collect basic information from many sources under one cover. We have tried in the equipment and methods chapters to include a picture of every available diving product on the current market. While this is not entirely possible, the reader will find a large majority of the equipment pictured.

While the surplus diving market is no longer as full as in 1949, there is still equipment available if the reader will search for it. But to replace the surplus has come much new gear from several manufacturers, at lower prices than were available three years ago. All the equipment problems are not yet solved by any means, but more people are working on these problems and more soundly engineered gear is being produced as a result.

In spite of the ever increasing numbers of rank amateurs venturing underwater, there has been no corresponding increase in diving accidents, which are still practically non-existant. This contradicts the fears and claims of many so-called experts who have repeatedly presented diving as an extremely hazardous occupation. What accidents there are, are generally the result of lack of knowledge rather than malfunction of equipment. We urge all divers who have this book to read it thoroughly from cover to cover, and not just in scattered sections. If this is done carefully, and the precautions and suggestions followed, we believe you will be able to get out of any situation that you may get into.

Above all, keep cool and calm when diving. Enjoy the new dimension of the undersea, and you will have found a last frontier of adventure in this all too civilized world.

ACKNOWLEDGMENTS

The line drawings in this book have been done by Vincent Vitale, a young commercial artist on his first book assignment. Their clearness and simplicity of execution have, we feel, contributed much towards amplifying the text and assisting the reader. We wish to express our appreciation to Mr. Vitale and will hope to see more of his work in the future.

Mary-Low Schenck has rendered invaluable assistance in the preparation of the manuscript, the reading of proofs, and in the large volume of correspondence necessary for a book of this sort. To her our sincerest thanks and best wishes.

Many firms and individuals have generously supplied illustrative material, advice, and encouragement during the preparation of the book. We would like to thank: René Bussoz and the U. S. Divers Co., Max Gene Nohl and Desco, Lewis Maxwell and The Florida Frogman, H. S. Moncrief and Fenjohn Co., Jim Auxier and "The Skin Diver," J. B. Dunne and Mine Safety, H. S. Barrada and Bel-Aqua, Lee Bright, D. F. Comstock, James Dugan, R. T. Keagle, Woody Dimel and the Los Angeles Neptunes, Roderick White and the Santa Barbara Seals, Ed Sutherland and the Neptune Club, Aqua Sports Inc., The Spearfisherman, Aqua-Lung Inc., La Spirotechnique S. A., The Cornelius Co., The Sea Net Manufacturing Co., The Morse Diving Equipment Co., Marine Studios, Metal Formfab Corp., The United States Navy, The United States Coast and Geodedic Survey, The National Safety Council, Dr. Harold Edgerton, Burton McNeeley and the Tampa Tridents, The Engineering Development Corporation, Gustav Dalle Valle.

CONTENTS

Chapter I

DIVING SCIENCE

The problems encountered in underwater exploration, sport, and scientific investigation are problems of many sciences. Physics and Physiology play leading roles, as do Mechanical and Electrical Engineering, Acoustics and Optics, the ocean sciences of Marine Biology and Oceanography, and many other specialized fields of technical knowledge. Yet even the simplest of underwater expeditions may require a full understanding of all phases of undersea problems lest the diver arrive at his place of diving with dangerous and ill-formed opinions on the proper use of his gear. Also, the diver may travel many thousands of miles for sport or scientific purposes and find himself improperly equipped and unable to accomplish his objectives underwater. No one can know all of modern technology, not even all in a single, small field such as diving and underwater work, but all interested in diving can understand and use basic principles which are often inflexible in application. To depend unthinkingly on popular misconceptions or half-formed guesses is unwise and unsafe.

HYDROSTATIC PRESSURE—BOYLES LAW

Hydrostatic pressure is simply the pressure due to the weight of a fluid upon a body immersed in it. Air is a fluid and at sea level a column of air extending upwards to infinity (empty space) exerts a pressure of 14.7 pounds on every square inch of surface. Pressure has no special direction but acts normal (at right angles) to any surface immersed in the fluid. Common sense tells us this. If it were not true, a body placed in the air would have unequal forces on its various sides and would move in some direction. Since this does not occur in still air, we know that the pressure forces on the body's sides balance out and that the pressure is acting normally over the whole body. Although the air is of such low density that it requires a thickness of many miles to cause a pressure of 14.7 psi (pounds per square inch), water weighs a great deal more for a given volume than air and 33 feet of sea water produces the same pressure as the entire extent of the air over the Earth. Thus, descent underwater places a human being in a region of suddenly increasing pressures and introduces him to an environment that is abnormal and seldom encountered in everyday life.

(1)

Boyles Law, Figure 1, states that the volume of a given mass of gas is inversely proportional to its absolute pressure. All diving equipment is affected and controlled in its operation by this basic principle. If we consider, for example, one pound of air at sea level, tables tell us that this air occupies a volume of 13.3 cubic feet. Now if this air is placed in a rubber bag and forced downward through the water, its volume will decrease and the bag will shrink. At sea level the air was under a pressure of 14.7 psi. For every foot underwater, the weight of the water above it will add something less than one half pound per square

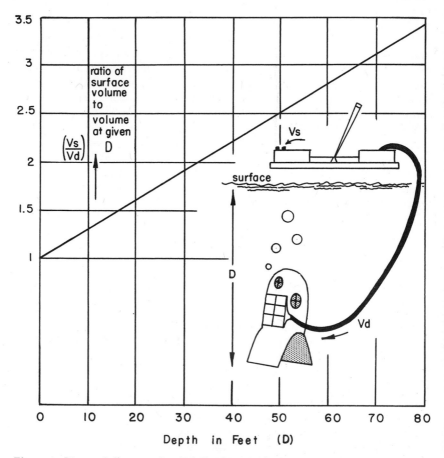

Figure 1. Plot and diagram showing the decrease in gas volume due to an increase in depth as governed by Boyles Law. At thirty-three feet the surface volume of a given mass of gas is twice that at the depth, at sixty-six feet the surface volume is three times, and so on.

inch until when it is 33 feet down in sea water it will be under a total pressure of 29.4 psi, half of this pressure being due to the weight of the atmosphere, and half being due to the weight of the water. Boyles Law tells us that the bag, which had a volume of 13.3 cubic feet at sea level now has half that, or 6.6 cubic feet. Going down another 33 feet triples the pressure and reduces the volume to one third its sea level value, and so on. Notice that each unit increase in water depth does not decrease the volume of the bag by a unit amount. At 33 feet the reduction from surface volume is 50 percent, while at twice this depth, 66 feet, the reduction is only 66⅔ percent. This means that submergences near the surface have more effect volume wise, than equal submergence deeper under water.

A simple example will make this clear. Consider a diving helmet, open at the bottom, seated on the diver's shoulders. The helmet is filled with air at sea level and the diver is walking just underwater breathing from the helmet. Now supposing the diver falls suddenly to 33 feet. His surrounding pressure has doubled, so his air volume has halved and the water level in the helmet is probably up at his nose or higher. Now consider the same diver in a completely air filled helmet walking at a depth of 66 feet. Again the diver suddenly falls 33 feet deeper underwater to the 99 foot level, but this time his helmet held air at a pressure of three times atmospheric or 44.1 psi and he fell to a region of 58.8 psi. The pressure increase in this second case is only four-thirds rather than twice as much, and the helmet air volume is decreased to only three-quarters rather than half what it was before the fall, though the distance fallen was the same in each case. Obviously, in this example, a fall from close to the surface is more dangerous than one from deep underwater. This is often true in diving as will be discussed in a later section.

Boyles Law can be expressed in the following formula,

$$\text{Volume at (2)} = \text{Volume at (1)} \times \left\{ \frac{\text{Pressure (absolute) (1)}}{\text{Pressure (absolute) (2)}} \right\} \qquad (1)$$

The pressure at any depth is easily found from the formula;

$$\text{Pressure (psi)} = .445 \times \text{Depth (feet of sea water)} \qquad (2)$$

where for fresh water the constant .445 becomes .433. Equation (2) gives pressures in *Gage Pressures*, that is, it does not include atmospheric pressure but considers sea level as a zero reference. To get *Total* or *Absolute* pressure, simply add 14.7 psi to the result found from (2). At times it is useful to express pressures in *Atmospheres*, that is the number of times 14.7 psi can be divided into the total pressure. Pressure at sea level is one atmosphere, at 33 feet in sea water two atmospheres, and so on. To relate the number of atmospheres with water depth use;

$$\text{Pressure in atmospheres} = .0304 \times \text{Depth in sea water} + 1$$

$$\text{Pressure in atmospheres} = .0295 \times \text{Depth in fresh water} + 1 \tag{3}$$

which gives the total or absolute pressure in atmospheres. Gage pressures are usually not expressed in this manner.

One important consequence of hydrostatic pressure is the effect of bouyancy. If an object immersed in a fluid weighs less per cubic foot than water (which weighs about 64 pounds per cubic foot) then it will float, while if its density is higher than that of water it will sink. This is the well known *Archimedes Principle* which is very important in diving work since many materials such as wood, plastic, rubber, etc. are lighter than water. An air space, such as that enclosed by a mask or helmet, or the chest cavity, is essentially weightless and will require added weight if it is to be sunk in the water. Should an object have exactly the same density as water, it will have neutral bouyancy and be able to float at any position underwater that it happens to be in. Since water is very incompressible, it is not likely that an object will sink to 'denser' water and then float suspended in mid-ocean.

PARTIAL PRESSURE

The concept of partial pressure is extremely important in understanding most of the physiological effects of underwater work and in the design and use of self-contained equipment. A law of physics states that each kind of gas in a mixture of gases exerts a pressure which is independent of the other gases. Air is a good example of this. The atmosphere at sea level contains many gases including oxygen, nitrogen, water vapor, carbon dioxide, argon, neon, etc. All but the first two are present in tiny quantity. If we take a sample of sea level air in a tight box and completely remove the oxygen, we find that the pressure exerted by the sample is no longer atmospheric, but somewhat lower. In fact, the total pressure in the box is now roughly 11.7 psi. Ignoring the rarer gases in the atmosphere, it can be deduced from such an experiment that the *nitrogen partial pressure* is about 11.7 psi and the *oxygen partial pressure* is around 3 psi. *The total pressure equals the sum of the partial pressures.* If the air is compressed to two atmospheres both these figures will be correspondingly doubled, and so on. In diving, one other gas is important besides nitrogen and oxygen. This is carbon dioxide, which is produced by the lungs as a waste product in respiration. In normal outdoor air the partial pressure of carbon dioxide (CO_2) is vanishingly small, but in a confined space where respiration is taking place, the partial pressure of carbon dioxide may reach values of one half psi or more.

In any mixture of gases, the relative amount of each gas can be expressed in several ways. The amount can be specified by *partial pressure*, by *volume*, or by *weight*. Each has its utility and it should be noted that for a given mass of gas in a mixture, the percentage of the total expressed by volume and partial pressure is different from the percentage expressed as a weight fraction. Again, air is a good example of this. If we separate the oxygen and nitrogen into two separate boxes and note what fraction of the total pressure each has, we find that oxygen is 21% of the total and nitrogen is 79% of the total. The same figures apply if we allow each gas sample to be placed under the same pressure and we measure the volume of each. But if we weigh each sample, we find that by weight the oxygen percentage is 23.2 and the nitrogen 76.8. The two cases would only give the same numbers if the nitrogen and oxygen had equal molecular weights.

In diving, partial pressures are significant for most problems so that where percentages are given, they will be partial pressure percentages. The following formulas may prove useful:

$$\text{Partial pressure of gas} = \text{total pressure of mixture} \times \begin{cases} \% \text{ gas by volume} \\ \qquad\qquad (\text{or}) \\ \% \text{ gas by partial pressure} \end{cases} \quad (4)$$

and:

$$\% \text{ gas by weight} = \begin{cases} \% \text{ gas by volume} \\ \qquad\quad (\text{or}) \\ \% \text{ gas by partial pressure} \end{cases} \times \begin{cases} \text{Molecular weight mixture} \\ \text{Molecular weight gas} \end{cases} (5)$$

FLUID RESISTANCE

A car traveling through air is partially retarded in its motion by the resistance of the air flowing around it. So a submarine or diver traveling underwater is also retarded by water resistance, and water being some 900 times denser than air, it will be much more difficult to move through the undersea.

The resistance to motion of any fluid stems from two effects. One is the friction of the body's surface against the fluid molecules, while the other is the formation by the body of whorls and eddies of fluid which, by their internal frictional effects, use energy and limit the velocity of the body. This second cause of resistance is often the predominant one, and can be minimized by streamlining, thereby resulting in the formation of smaller fluid eddies, or none at all. The prediction of the resistance or *drag* of a non-streamlined body is a most difficult problem which as yet admits no complete mathematical solution.

However, certain facts can be deduced regarding fluid resistance which may be of use to divers.

The drag on an underwater projectile, such as a shot fish spear, is a function of its geometrical shape, its velocity, and the density of the fluid in which it is traveling. In comparing ranges and impact power of a spear fired in air with one in water, one can generally state that the drag will be 900 times greater in the denser water, if the two leave the gun with the same velocity and have the same shape. The com-

Figure 2. A shallow water diving dress is very bouyant when filled with air. Here the diver floats comfortably on the surface after 'blowing up'.

putation of range in each case is complex, but it may safely be stated that there is no possibility of a water-fired spear having half the effective range of an air fired spear. In all probability, the underwater effective range is a very small fraction of the air effective range.

Aside from underwater missiles, it is of interest to consider the power requirements of a body to achieve a given velocity underwater, since this is the case of a swimmer. This problem is easily solved and results in the expression;

$$(Vf/Vw)^3 = Pf/Pw \qquad (6)$$

where the symbol (V) is velocity, (P) is power, and (f) and (w) refer to two different methods of swimming. In our case we will take (f) to mean swimming with fins, and (w) to mean without fins or with the bare feet. Now if we take Vw arbitrarily as 1, then a 30% increase in swimming speed due to the addition of fins will give a Vw value of 1.3 and a 40% increase a value of 1.4. Then (6) says that the resulting necessary increase in power transmitted from the body to the water will be, respectively, 1.9 and 2.75. What happens is that the fins do not actually increase the bodily power output, but rather permit a more efficient utilization of body energy in swimming. Note that to increase speed 10 percent in this example, the power increase is much larger, almost 30 percent. To double speed through the water by the use of fins would require a transmitted power increase of eight times over non-fin swimming. The conclusion is that the difference in swimming speed between well designed and badly designed fins is not great, since the body is probably transmitting power fairly efficiently in either case. Any improvement in fin design that will give substantial increase over present speeds does not appear likely.

HEAT TRANSFER

The temperature range of ocean and lake water runs from just around freezing, 32°F, up to 90°F or so. If the reader has had any diving experience, he knows the effects of being under in cold water. Respiration is quickened, the body chills, and fingers and toes may turn white and become numb. A diver under such conditions is taking grave chances, for his mind is often so preoccupied with trying to stay warm that he is careless and unable to do much useful work. The solution, of course, is to wear some form of protective covering that will stop, or at least slow the loss of heat from the body.

Like a machine, the body operates at a certain best temperature, about 98°F. The outer layers of skin may not be at this temperature, and can be much colder for long periods of time without discomfort. Water over 80°F is very comfortable for a bathing-suited diver. Periods of immersion of one or more hours are possible without chilling or excessive loss of heat. We may therefore take 80°F as the 'normal operating temperature' of the skin. Now the rate at which heat is lost from a warm body is easily described. The rate will be rapid when the temperature difference between the body and its surroundings are large. The rate will be slow when some resistance to heat flow is placed between the warm body and the cold surroundings. These obvious facts are expressible in a basic law of cooling;

$$Q \quad = \quad 1/R \quad x \quad (T_{hot} - T_{cold})$$

$$\text{(rate of heat flow)} \quad \text{(resistance to flow)} \quad \text{(temperature difference)} \quad (7)$$

This formula is applicable to diving. We have said that roughly 80°F is the surrounding temperature at which little body heat is lost. Thus if we lose Q heat at 70°F we will lose 2Q heat at 60°F, 3Q heat at 50°F and so on. But we have at our disposal the design factor, $1/R$. Supposing we wear a tight fitting rubber suit, or a set of thick underwear, what effect will these have? First we must consider the value of $1/R$ for bare skin. As it happens, the resistance to heat flow from a surface (skin) to water is dependant on the velocity with which the surface moves through the water. To simplify the analysis we will ignore any body movement through the water, remembering at all times that a swimming body will lose heat more rapidly than is predicted here. Considering the factor $1/R$ for skin to water with heat transferred under stagnant conditions, the following table compares heat loss from various parts of the body, for various temperature differences between surface and water;

TABLE I

($T_{surface} - T_{water}$)	10	20	30	40
$1/R$ arms (4″ diameter)	50	56	62	65
$1/R$ legs (8″ diameter)	35	43	51	56
$1/R$ torso (15″ diameter)	30	36	44	47

(where for those interested in numerical calculations, $1/R$ is in the units, BTU/hr. °F ft.²).

Now, remembering that the larger $1/R$, the quicker heat flows from the body, Table I gives some interesting facts. First, the smaller the member, the faster heat is lost. This is justified by experience which tells us that fingers and toes grow cold most rapidly. Second, the greater the temperature difference, the more rapidly heat is lost per degree difference. Thus, cold water gives a double bonus of trouble. Not only is more heat lost because ($T_{skin} - T_{water}$) is greater, but $1/R$ is greater as well so that Q in (7) will be much greater for cold water.

But insulating the body is most beneficial in preventing heat transfer as can easily be shown. Consider Table II;

TABLE II

Substance	$1/R$ for one foot thickness (in BTU/hr. °F ft²)
Air (stagnant)	.015
Helium (stagnant)	.090
Hydrogen (stagnant)	.110
Oxygen (stagnant)	.015
Rubber (gum)	.100
Kapok	.020
Water (stagnant)	.350

All these insulating materials are considered on a one foot thickness basis whereas in a diving dress the thickness is much less and the $1/R$ greater. Let us consider the following insulated divers. a) no suit (bare skin), b) Rubber suit form fitted to skin, c) Rubber suit with ¼ inch stagnant air space between skin and rubber formed by underwear, d) ¼ inch thickness of stagnant water formed by wearing underwater with no water proof covering over it. In all cases take rubber ⅛″ thick.

For case (a), Table I gives the answer directly. For arms with 40°F differential we have a $1/R$ value of 65. For case (b) there are two resistances in series to heat transfer, the skin-through-rubber resistance and the rubber-surface-to-water resistance given by Table I (it doesn't matter what the surface is as long as it is smooth). We use the following formula to obtain the total value of R.

$$R_{total} = R_1 + R_2 + R_3 + \text{etc.} \qquad (8)$$

For ⅛″ rubber, the $1/R$ value will be 96 times that given in Table II since these table values are based on a foot thickness. Then $1/R$ for skin-through rubber is 9.6 which is added to 65 as specified in (8) giving an overall $1/R$ of 8.3, about seven times smaller than bare skin alone. Following along with (c) and (d) cases in the same manner we can draw up Table III for the various conditions specified.

TABLE III

Insulation Conditions	1/R total (arms)
Bare skin:	65.00
Tight fitting ⅛″ rubber:	9.60
¼″ underwear (air) plus ⅛″ rubber	.68
¼″ underwear (helium) plus ⅛″ rubber	3.00
¼″ underwear not waterproof (stagnant water)	13.40

Table III shows quite graphically the advantages of an insulating layer of air as compared with other methods. When helium is used in the diving dress in place of air (for very deep water work), heat is lost five times as fast. With underwear wetted over the body the heat loss is over twenty times greater than the lowest case.

HUMIDITY

Nowhere is there higher humidity than at the bottom of the sea, so it would appear at first glance that the diver could hardly have any real interest in humidity when underwater. The diver, and most of his tools, however, must be, in part or entirely, surrounded by air and air that has amounts of water vapor suspended in it. A simple mask slipped over the nose and eyes contains some air from the surface and some air from the lungs. The mixture is very humid for exhaled air is always saturated with moisture. The low temperatures of the surrounding water will cool this trapped air until it can no longer hold all its moisture, causing dew to form on the glass which fogs over, obstructing vision. All divers and spear fishermen know the remedy for this condition. They spit on the glass facepiece and rub the saliva over it. Saliva acts as a wetting agent and permits the moisture to run clean from the glass rather than forming fog. If this is not completely successful, various companies, such as the Mine Safety Appliance Company, sell so-called fog-proofing compounds which are applied to the inner sides of glass facepieces. In the case of an inclosed underwater camera box or in a recirculating diving apparatus some moisture may condense. If, in the camera box, fog forms on the lens window, expensive film may be ruined during exposure and small bags of a moisture absorbant, such as silica gel, may be placed in the mechanism. This is more likely to occur in cold waters since the interior air is cooled and cannot hold much moisture. In a recirculating self-contained apparatus the circulating air is fully satuarated from the lungs and the amount of moisture condensed per unit time can be predicted from psychometric charts. This is considered in a latter chapter. Generally, the formation of fog is not too troublesome except under extreme conditions, i.e. a very humid day when diving is done in very cold water.

OPTICS

Underwater optics is a complex and neglected field. It encompasses the absorption, scattering, and refraction of light and the design of optical systems that must include both water and air in their optical paths. Most of these problems are mainly applicable to undersea photography, which is considered in detail by the authors in a companion volume, *Underwater Photography*. A few introductory remarks may be of interest to all divers. As everyone knows, light coming from a dense medium (water) into air is *refracted* or bent. Spearing a fish that is lying underwater is most difficult for a man in air, for the fish appears to be where he isn't and the spear usually goes wide of the mark. This is due to the differing value of the velocity of light in water as compared with air. A man underwater does not have the same trouble although he does see things displaced in a direction directly towards him. That is, he sees all objects to be larger than they actually are and his eyes focus at a closer distance than they would in air. The brain interprets this sense data to mean that the object is closer than it actually is. The distortion ratio is a factor of ¾, that is, a fish

Figure 3. A diver in full deep water dress walks along the bottom at Silver Springs, Florida. The water here is some of the clearest in North America. (Official U.S. Navy Photograph)

20 feet away by tape measure appears to be 15 to all divers. This poses no real problems except for the spear fisherman who usually quickly learns to comphensate for his misinformed senses.

ACOUSTICS

Unlike the optical properties of the sea, underwater acoustics is the object of wide and frantic investigation, for undersea sound is one of the best ways of locating hostile submarines. Most work of this sort is being done in the ultra-sonic or high frequency range of the sound spectrum, but certainly the current emphasis on underwater demolition by self-contained divers must mean that work in the audible range is also going forward. Actually, sound communication between divers is, at first glance, a simple matter, for the attenuation of sound in water is much less than in air. Unfortunately, man is unable to utilize water in his vocal mechanism so that a spoken or shouted sound must begin in air and then be transferred from the diving helmet or mask to water. It is in this transferrence of sonic energy across the air-water interface that the great losses of energy come, for the *impedance match* (the matching of pressures and displacements of a sound wave in the two mediums) is so bad that at the interface only one-ten-thousandth of the sonic energy gets through. What is required is that the low pressure, high amplitude waves of air-borne sound be re-modeled at the interface to high pressure, small amplitude waves which are necessary for water travel. This can be done in part by placing a metal diaphragm in the front of a diving mask or helmet that will vibrate when sound waves impinge on it. There is, however, no simple method for underwater spoken communication that is really excellent, although, as noted classified work is undoubtedly being done. Several interesting acoustical phenomena occur in the sea, and they will be considered in detail in a later chapter.

UNDERWATER RADIO

The problem of locating objects, particularly metallic ones, under-water has fascinated men since the first treasure ship went down. With the advent of electronics it appeared that radio waves might be used for the detection of underwater objects in the same manner that radar is used to pick out objects at night or in a fog. Unfortunately, such has not proved to be the case. The conductivity of the sea is sufficiently high (1.6 mho per foot) so that a radio wave projected underwater loses its energy in a very short distance. Thus, Sonar, or high frequency sound, has received the major share of attention, since, as has been pointed out, a sonic wave that starts in water is not dissipated to any extent over long distances.

A close examination of the problem indicates that, in spite of the high losses of radio energy underwater, radio or magnetic waves are the only medium that will differentiate metallic objects from rocks, sand bars, and other discontinuities on the ocean bottom. Sound waves from a Fathometer or depth finding device will indicate a lost ship if it is large and intact, but it will also pick out rocks as well. Also, most ships are flattened by storms so that they seldom project more than a few feet above the surrounding bottom and in many cases are actually buried. Normal 'treasure finders' and mine detectors operate on high frequencies in the one meter or less range, but a one meter wave in normal sea water loses 999/1000 of its energy in four inches of water. As the wave length is increased (lower frequencies are used) the situation improves. For 1000 meter radio waves, 999/1000 of the energy is lost in 5 feet, while for 10,000 meter waves 999/1000 is lost in 33 feet, which begins to look like a practical distance. But a quarter wave antenna for projecting such a long wave would be a mile and half a long. It might be possible to use a ⅛ wave or shorter antenna in the form of a long wire trailing behind the search ship but the water would have to be shallow and the receiver sensitive.

One other possiblility remains. A coil and condenser placed to form a resonant circuit and pulsed at resonant frequency would be dragged by paravanes (surfaces which hold an object at any desired depth when in motion) as close to the bottom as possible. When a metallic object came near, the coil would act like an air core choke that has had a piece of iron thrust into it. Its inductance would change and thus the resonant frequency of the entire circuit would change. Since the pulsing frequency remains unaltered, the circuit as a whole would go out of resonance and a drop in voltage across the circuit could be detected on a meter. If the surface operator could steer the paravane from the ship's stern, he could manouver the whole rig to port or starboard to give maximum meter fluctuations and thus fix fairly well the location of the metallic object. This scheme appears to be the most feasible of any for locating sunken ships.

DIVING PHYSIOLOGY

In this chapter the physics and engineering aspects of diving have been breifly noted since they form a needed background for the important subject of underwater physiology. Man is not really equipped for abnormal pressures so he must take certain precautions in his new environment. But in spite of his rather second rate equippage for pressure, he can do quite well, providing he understands his own deficiences. More than this, diving equipment and the subsidiary gear that we must take underwater are too complex to trust to a mind that is hampered by a body uncomfortable or in pain. A proper dive should be effortless, the whole mind being devoted to the sights of the undersea, the correct use of the diving gear, and the accomplishment of whatever tasks are required.

General Remarks: Respiration supplies the body with part of its fuel, namely oxygen. A deep breath takes from the atmosphere some 1/9 of a cubic foot of air of which 21% by partial pressure is oxygen. On exhaling, only 16% of the oxygen comes back out, the remaining 5% having been replaced by carbon dioxide, a waste product, and water vapor. Carbon dioxide is not a poison in the sense that carbon monoxide, cyanide, etc. are poisons. Since it is a waste product, it is useless for fuel and occupies space that otherwise might be taken by oxygen. But more important, an excess of carbon dioxide has a catalytic effect on respiration. Lungs operating in an atmosphere containing four or five percent CO_2 increase their respiration rate enormously. As the CO_2 partial pressure continues to increase, the breather may collapse and die unless the CO_2 concentration is decreased. But once revived, the breather usually suffers no disabling effects, while if he had collapsed under the action of carbon monoxide or other poisons, he might suffer permanent brain damage. Thus carbon dioxide is, in a sense, a blessing in disguise, for it warns the breather that his air is impure and gives him sufficient time to correct the situation. Since carbon dioxide regulates breathing, a little is often desirable, except under certain special diving conditions which will be discussed later in the chapter. The concentration of carbon dioxide in certain types of diving equipment is the determining factor as to how much air must be supplied to the diver so that he feels no distress.

When men first considered respiration underwater they often proposed a helmet connected to the surface by a long tube through which the diver would breathe air by lung power alone. All divers now know that three or four feet is the maximum depth underwater that the lungs will operate in drawing air from the surface and that even at these depths it is extremely difficult. This idea is useful to consider, however, since any equipment that has an air reservoir attached to the diver is more or less operating at the same condition. If the reservoir of air is not at the chest level, breathing will not be effortless and, like the man underwater sucking air from the surface, the diver will be exerting himself unduly. A one foot difference in water is equivalent to a pressure difference of .445 psi. Taking the chest area over the lungs to be one-half square foot or 72 square inches, breathing against a one foot water differential would be breathing against a force of 33 pounds. Even four inches of water is the same as breathing with an 11 pound weight on the chest. Therefore the proper placement of air reservoirs is very important for effortless respiration.

If a man underwater with a tight fitting mask suddenly had his hose to the surface cut, he would be in the same position as our early diver who planned to suck air down to great depths. But rather than drawing air through the hose, this diver would feel a part of his face try to go up it, for the air in the mask would rush to the surface until the pressure in the mask was at surface pressure, while the pressure on the diver's body was much higher. To prevent this unpleasant occurrance, all diving equipment has one-way valving attached firmly at the diver which will hold air in the equipment should something happen to his air lines.

Bends: When we breath a mixture of nitrogen and oxygen, part of the oxygen is used as fuel while the nitrogen is almost completely exhaled. Some of the nitrogen is always present in the body, dissolved in the blood and tissues, the amount depending on the pressure of the atmosphere surrounding the breather. As pressure is increased, more nitrogen goes into simple solution in the body, but this condition is not harmful if the breather's surroundings do not undergo a sudden pressure reduction. If pressure should suddenly be decreased, the blood and tissues will no longer hold as much nitrogen in solution and some of it will escape and form bubbles. Stoppages of circulation occur with accompanying pain, itching skin rash, paralysis, and, in severe cases, even death. This disorder is the 'Bends' or 'Caisson Disease'. To prevent its occurance, the diver leaving a region of increased pressure should *decompress* (procede to a region of lower pressure in slow stages). This permits the dissolved nitrogen to come out of solution, find its way to the lungs, and escape from the body. Some shallow water divers may disregard the possibility of bends, a dangerous oversight if any diving is done in water over 36 feet deep. Appendix A of this book gives standard tables of decompression to 150 feet. Also, the self-contained chapters have short-cut data on decompression.

Air Embolism: This is an extremely dangerous diving disorder. Consider the lungs at 33 feet. They use compressed air at twice atmospheric pressure. If the diver should fill his lungs, throw off his helmet, and swim up, the air would expand and at the surface would exert a pressure of 14.7 pounds above atmospheric on every square inch of lung surface. Since a pressure rise of three psi in the lungs is dangerous, this foolish diver would be quite dead. The only possible excuse for coming up without the helmet or mask is failure of equipment. In this case it may be done safely by *rising slowly* and *allowing air to escape from the lungs* during the ascent. Naturally, air embolism can happen with the equipment on if the breath is held while rising.

For this reason all ascents should be made at a moderate rate, 25 feet per minute, with the diver breathing naturally.

Squeeze: A diver completely encased in a rubber suit and metal helmet must be careful that he does not descend or fall too rapidly into deep water. As the pressure increased, his suit would begin to press in upon him since, following Boyles Law, the volume of air trapped in the suit will grow smaller. Should the surface pump fail to send down more air rapidly enough to counteract this loss in volume, the diver will be *squeezed* by his suit and pressed upward into his helmet. Since the helmet is rigid, it's volume cannot change and in order that pressure equilibrium be maintained, something must give. In a bad squeeze this something is the diver who may be so badly compressed that his lungs collapse and hemmorage.

The squeeze is one of those occurances which is most dangerous in shallow depths. Since the violence of the squeeze depends on the amount of volume change inside the diving suit, falls in shallow depths, as we have noted, will produce the greatest effect. The inflated suit diver who blithely jumps over the side and plummits to the bottom is thus taking the gravest risk, for if his compressor should stop he would be falling in the region of greatest volume change per foot fall, and might end more inside his helmet than out. Another easy way to get squeezed in an enclosed, inflated suit is to have the air line cut with no one-way valve at the diver. This is exactly equivalent to falling instantaneously from the pressure at the point of severance of the line to the depth of the diver.

Obviously, if there is any place where water may enter a helmet, the squeeze is impossible. In that case, when pressure suddenly increased, water would come into the dress to equalize the unbalanced pressure on the rigid helmet. This is what happens in a shallow water helmet in which squeeze is impossible.

In a close-fitting, Frog Man type rubber suit, squeeze is also, very unlikely since in this case the rubber suit becomes as an outer layer of skin and the body is simply compressed from all sides. When a mask is worn over the face of a suit, slight squeeze effects can be noticed, but they are never serious due to the small volume of the mask. The swimmer who uses diving goggles will definitely be squeezed around the eyes in any deep ascent. The fairly rigid goggles do not change their volume much so that the eyes bug out to try and equalize pressure. For this reason, the authors reccomend that goggles never be used, but rather a mask covering nose and eyes together be substituted. Then lung air can be snorted into the mask and squeeze will not occur.

Ear Pain: Pain in the ears due to increased pressure is probably the oldest complaint of undersea divers. Aristotle mentions it as do other early writers on diving. Since it has been known for some twenty-five-hundred years, it would be thought that by now the problem would be clearly understood by all divers. Such is unfortunately not the case. Of some 3000 submarine trainees placed under pressure at New London, one third complained of ear pain in varying degrees of intensity. Thus it is worth every diver's time to study carefully this section and learn about the mechanisms in his ears and how they respond to pressure increases.

The total make up of the ear may be described as follows (see Figure 4): The *outer ear* is simply the channel leading from outside the head to the *ear drum*. This drum is a taut membrane which completely blocks the ear passage and vibrates when sound waves im-

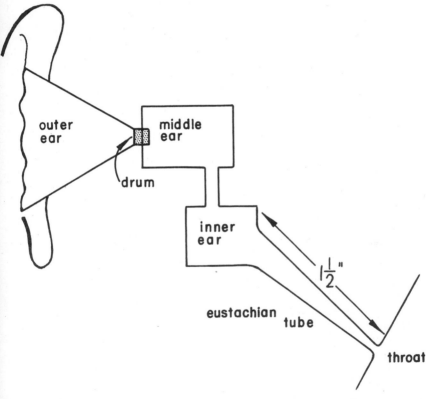

Figure 4. A schematic diagram of the human ear. The throat and outer ear are always at the same pressure, and if the eustachian tube is open, so are the middle and inner ears. If not, the external pressure presses on the drum. Should the outer ear be blocked, a pressure equalization between throat and middle ear will force the drum outwards.

pinge on it. On the other side of the drum is the *middle ear*, which contains three bones which transmit the vibrations from the drum to the *inner ear* and the nervous system. The middle and inner ears are connected by an open channel so that gas passes freely between them. The inner ear is connected with the throat by the *eustachian tube*, which is an opening in the tissues about an inch and a half long. Since the throat is always at the same pressure as the outside, which includes the passage of the outer ear, this completes the gas 'circuit', so to speak. *All parts of this circuit must be at the same pressure.* This is fundamental in all diving physiology. All pressures everywhere in the body must be equalized or pain and tissue destruction will result.

In the case of the ear, the eustachian tube is the trouble maker. The tube is designed by nature to drain pus and infectious material from the middle and inner ear to the throat, but to prevent any reverse transfer of fluids from the throat up into the ear. It is thus a crude one-way valve, and in the descent underwater, this one-way feature can be a nuisance. The tube is like a soda straw that is rigid at one end, but flattened and soggy at the other. If you blow on the rigid end the air whistles right through, but if you blow on the soggy end, the straw may flatten even more and very little air will get through. Using this analogy, the open end of the tube is at the inner ear and the flattened, 'soggy' end is at the throat. Any excess of air in the inner ear escapes quite easily, while a lack of air which must be replenished from the throat may be difficult to remedy. As a diver descends, his outside pressure is increasing which means that the pressure in the outer ear channel and in the throat are also increasing. If no air gets through the eustachian tube into the inner ear, the excess pressure on the ear drum will distend it inward and cause pain. This condition is known as *Aero-Otitis Media* in the medical literature. Fairly severe pain is experienced at a submersion of two and a half feet with no equalization through the eustachian tube. Continuation of the descent with no air movement into the inner ear will result in drum rupture at 5 to 20 feet under water. Unfortunately, the throat end of the eustachian tube will block if the diver descends four feet without equalizing and further descent will simply rupture the drum since the tube is now tightly shut and *no amount of swallowing or other tricks will open it.* This suggests that the greater the pressure differential between the inner ear and the throat end of the tube, the more difficult equalization becomes. Thus, when a diver experiences pain, he should rise a few feet until the pain disappears and try to equalize. Forcing open the lower end of the tube is done by swallowing, yawning, moving the back of the jaws freely about, or pressing the nose tight against the diving mask or helmet and blowing hard to force air into the passages. The rising when pain occurs is important.

If done properly the tube may open as the diver goes up and the familiar click or pop of air traveling through the tube will be heard without resorting to other methods. All this sounds quite simple on paper, but underwater it can be a painful and annoying matter. By descending slowly, trying all combinations of swallowing, blowing, etc. and by rising when pain occurs, the great majority of people can generally 'pop' their ears when using diving apparatus. Everyone, even the most experienced, finds at one time or another that his ears simply will not clear. This is usually due to an excess of mucus in the throat and the only solution is to give it up for the day. Anything that forms mucus, such as a cold, sinus and hayfever, or even drinking milk just before diving, will make the ear equalizing harder.

Several companies and some books on underwater work still suggest ear plugs, wax, or ear muffs to, as they put it, 'lessen pressure effects on the ears'. This sounds most attractive to one who has trouble with his ears, *but is actually an extremely dangerous procedure.* Plugs and wax may be forced deep into the ear by pressure, requiring surgery to get them out, even if nothing else happens. But all ear stoppers have a basic deficiency which can be shown by the application of a little logic. Consider two cases. Case one assumes that the ear stoppers, whatever their nature, do not keep out the water. If they don't then they are no more than useless encumbrances and should be discarded. Case two assumes that they actually do keep out water. Then, as the diver descends, the outer ear will have air at atmospheric pressure, since no water can enter. But the inner ear and middle ear are getting new air through the eustachian tube and roughly paralleling the overall external pressure increase. Now the ear drum is bulging outward into the low pressure region of the outer ear and at from 5 to 20 feet underwater the ear drum will most certainly rupture outwards. Damage is inevitable in this second case, since the plug or muff, unlike the eustachian tube, offers no possibility of equalization. Therefore, ear plugs are most dangerous items except in certain specific cases where their use is recommended by a doctor. If the reader has an open ear drum as the result of disease or previous diving work he should consult a physician before continuing with the underwater work. For normal ears, *never place anything in the ears before diving.*

Two other complaints similar to ear pain are occasionally experienced by divers. One is sinus pain, a particularly unpleasant ache in the forehead or under the eyes. Like ear pain, this occurs primarily on the descent and is due to mucous clogging the tubes leading into the sinus air spaces. It is difficult to equalize pressures here except by descending very slowly and rising whenever pain occurs. A slow descent may allow air to seep into the sinus spaces and equalize their internal pressure with outside pressure. Fortunately once the sinuses are pressure equalized, the ascent often blows them clear of mucous. On reaching the surface, the diver may find himself coughing up thick, yellow phlegm. Rather than a cause for worry, this is a most beneficial occurance since it means that the sinus spaces are clear, perhaps for the first time in months. This does not mean that diving is a cure for sinusitis, and in fact, those with sinus troubles should consult their doctor before taking up diving.

The second complaint similar to ear pain is pain in the teeth. Commercial divers having spent a long time at great depths occasionally have a tooth explode on ascending. This disorder is different from ear and sinus troubles in that it almost always happens on the ascent, indicating that gases produced by bacterial action and decay are expanding inside the tooth and pressing on the nerve. Since this never happens in healthy teeth, a diver who experiences tooth pain should see his dentist.

Nitrogen Narcosis: The effects of nitrogen in the body are two fold at great depths. The first effect, the bends, has already been considered. The second, nitrogen narcosis, or the 'divers' sleeps' does not ordinarily occur at depths shallower than 150 feet. Nitrogen under such high pressures has curious effects on human beings. Sometimes the diver is exhilarated and drunken in his actions, while other times he may curl up and take a nap. The reason why nitrogen causes this is still not fully understood, but it is thought to be due to the great weight of gas in the lungs and its inhibitary effect on the body's metabolism. Naturally, a diver in such a condition is in a most dangerous position. His judgement may be so impaired that he will simply not come up at all, or he may do foolish things on the bottom. Since the onset of nitrogen narcosis is often quite unnoticed, diving to 150 feet is unwise for any but the most experienced diver. Helium substituted for nitrogen in air completely stops this diving disorder and dives to depths of 550 feet have been made without noticeable narcotic action. Modern diving equipment such as the Aqua-Lung has given the amateur and inexperienced diver useful tools for undersea work, but they have also presented technics that can kill if carelessly used. In Europe, a number of senseless attempts at 'record' depths using air have resulted in dangerous or tragic outcomes. In one case a young diver got down to close to 400 feet before nitrogen narcosis overwhelmed him. He was not using a safety line or any connection with the surface nor was he accompanied by anyone else. His death under such circumstances was inevitable. The good diver does not take needless chances. *He stays in shallower water than 150 feet unless he is firmly connected by lines to the surface.*

Anoxia: This is simply the condition of too little oxygen for life. It is ordinarily most dangerous for aviators and mountain climbers in the rarified atmosphere of high altitudes where the oxygen partial pressure is far below its normal value of 3 psi. Anoxia or 'oxygen want' is a most serious condition since it appears to produce serious damage to the brain after the patient recovers from a prolonged lack of the life-giving gas. It cannot ordinarily occur in diving except in one special case. This is with a recirculating self-contained apparatus which has nitrogen in the system. In recirculating apparatus the carbon dioxide is continually removed and new oxygen supplied. If there is an appreciable amount of nitrogen also present and the oxygen should no longer be admitted due to failure of the equipment, the atmosphere of the breathing bag would grow progressively richer in nitrogen, but the breather would not notice the change due to the removal of carbon dioxide, the 'warning gas'. Since anoxia, like nitrogen narcosis, can be very stealthy in its approach, the diver could collapse before he realized his danger since he would be breathing mainly nitrogen. Even if he should recover he might be permanently injured. For this reason, no equipment that uses carbon dioxide absorbant should ever contain nitrogen. Certain war time British equipment violated this rule, but only under the stress of military necessity. It should be noted that anoxia is not possible in any equipment with continually entering fresh air since the oxygen concentration will never drop low enough to endanger the diver before the CO_2 concentration has risen to uncomfortable levels. Thus, CO_2 will warn the diver of impending danger. Keeping recirculating gear free of residual nitrogen will be discussed in the chapter on this type of equipment.

Oxygen Poisoning: At high pressures pure oxygen is a poison. An oxygen partial pressure of around 30 psi or greater will produce tremor, irritability, tingling of the body, nausea, and muscle twitching. If the breather returns *at once* to atmospheric pressure and breathes air he will undergo no harmful effects, but if he remains under oxygen pressure, convulsions will follow. These preliminary symptoms do not occur as soon as high pressure oxygen is breathed, but (in 40 feet of sea water) one to four hours after onset of high pressure oxygen in the lungs. The safe period is quite variable and is shortened greatly by heavy exertion. If the diver goes deeper than 35 or 40 feet, the symptoms will occur more quickly. It can be seen that oxygen poisoning is somewhat like the bends in that its occurance depends on the degree of pressure and the time spent under pressure. As already noted, pure oxygen must be used in recirculators to forstall any chance of anoxia, so it is with this type of equipment that oxygen problems occur. A pressure of 30 psi (total) which corresponds to a depth of around 35 feet must be considered the maximum depth for all but the shortest dives. The authors have used oxygen equipment to this depth for periods exceeding an hour on many occasions and suffered no ill effects.

One consideration that has been brought out in this connection by the Bureau of Mines is that the onset of symptoms occur more rapidly if there is CO_2 in the oxygen system. Thus, a well designed recirculating unit should have as low a CO_2 concentration as possible so that the diver can remain under for the maximum amount of time. Hard exertions under oxygen pressure also bring on symptoms more rapidly and may cause headaches even at less than the danger pressure of 30 psi. Fortunately, oxygen poisoning is an obvious symptom and the diver can readily surface before serious effects occur.

DROWNING

Although it is possible for shallow divers to fall victim to several of the more exotic diving diseases such as Air Embolism, Bends, etc., this is highly unlikely. Those few divers who get into real trouble will, for the most part, swallow too much water and be pulled from the water in a semi-asphyxiated condition requiring immediate artificial respiration. It is therefore the responsibility of every diver to learn the proper methods for resuscitation of the drowned and practice these methods.

In the past few years it has been established beyond question that the Schaefer method of artificial respiration does not ventilate the lungs as well as other techniques, notably the Neilsen method or *Back-Pressure*, *Arm-Lift* method. With the kind permission of the National Safety Council, the following section on this method is quoted verbatim from a paper on the subject by F.A. Van Atta, Ph.D.

General Instructions: 1) When a person is not breathing time is of prime importance. Do not wait and look for help, to move the victim to a more convenient place, to give stimulants, to loosen tight clothing or for anything else. The important thing is to get the resuscitation started at once, so get to it.

2) Put the person in the prone (face down) position, with the head turned to one side and the cheek resting on the hands, or one hand.

3) Open the mouth and sweep your finger through to pull the tongue forward and remove any obstruction.

4) Begin artificial respiration and continue without interruption until the patient is breathing spontaneously or is certainly dead.

5) If the subject begins to breath on his own but still requires help, adjust your rate to his breathing rate; do not attempt to force your rhythm upon him.

6) When help is available or when the victim is breathing without help get the clothing loosened and supply warmth and other measures

as needed. Do not interrupt the artificial respiration for any of these purposes.

Arm-Lift Back-Pressure Method: 1) Carry out the first three steps under the general instructions. Note: In carrying out the Schaefer method it was quite necessary to raise the arms in order to have the chest at maximum expansion. In this method this is not necessary and

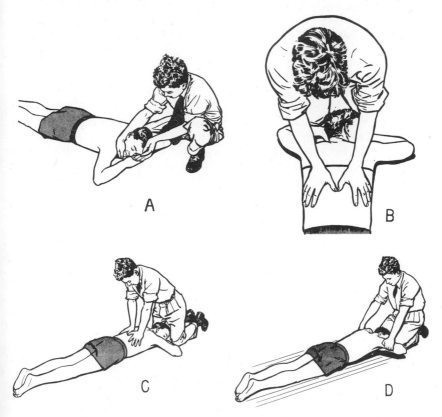

Figure 5. A sequence of drawings showing the correct application of the Arm-Lift, Back-Pressure method of artificial respiration. (Courtesy of the National Safety Council)

the only reason for having the hand or hands under the face is to keep dirt out of the mouth. In soft ground this is very important. (see A in Figure 5).

2) Kneel at the head of the victim on one or both knees.

3) Place your hands on the victim's back just below the shoulder blades and rock forward to exert a steady gentle pressure on the back

to force air out of the lungs. Keep your elbows straight and let the weight of the upper part of your body do the work. (see B in Figure 5).

4) Release the pressure quickly but without giving any extra push at the release. (see C in Figure 5).

5) Rock backward running your hands along the victims back and arms till you pick up his arms at a point just above the elbows. Continue rocking back, taking the arms upward and towards you. Use just enough effort to feel resistance and tension in the victim's arms. This lifts and expands the chest to permit air to enter. (see D in Figure 5).

6) Rock forward again, placing the victim's arms on the ground and sliding your hands down the arms and back until they come to rest again at the proper pressure point.

7) Repeat the cycle rythmically at a rate of 10 to 12 complete cycles per minute. Each phase of the cycle should take about 1½ seconds. The rocking motion helps to keep the steady rythm. The position may be changed from one knee to the other or to both during the operation but it should be done without breaking the rythm.

The above quoted instructions plus Figure 5 should enable the reader to learn the method quickly. If you needed this help, you would certainly hope that someone with you could administer it. Therefore, learn it yourself in case you are called upon for assistance.

Chapter II

HELMET DIVING

Of the various kinds of air-supplied diving equipment, the rigid helmet, fitting over the head and shoulders, is the least complicated, requires the least air, and is most easily made by the rankest amateur. Possibly many readers have attempted their first dive in a modified five-gallon oil drum supplied by one or two ineffectual bicycle pumps, and seen a little of the undersea before impending suffocation forced them to the surface. Certainly, any history of diving will indicate that the helmet has been used since the Middle Ages, becoming more and more popular as better air pumps were devised. William Beebe, whose descriptions of diving in Bermuda and the Carribean still stir many to sample the sights beneath the oceans, used a simple helmet in all his shallow water wanderings.

The helmet is now a generally outdated piece of equipment, except for specific uses which will be thoroughly discussed in this chapter. But since many readers may have access to helmets, or may desire to use a helmet for one reason or another, a discussion of the capabilities and principles is necessary. Through an understanding of helmet diving, many basic physical principles of diving as a whole can be easily grasped, so even those readers who wish to use only self-contained equipment or masks should peruse this chapter carefully. It might be noted that when an engineer is trained in school, he does not simply take one series of courses which relate to a single specialty such as internal combustion engines or bridge building. Rather he is forced to carry many other courses, some of which (perhaps to the young engineer's disgust) have nothing whatsoever to do with his favorite field. But when he begins to work, he finds that he actually did not have enough different courses, and wishes he knew more about everything. The same thing applies to the diver. He cannot become an expert on one piece of equipment and one method of diving without knowing the entire field. Someday he may require knowledge not immediately connected with his own narrow skills, and be incapable of action.

HELMET PRINCIPLES

The fundamental advantage of helmets over all other types of gear is the fact that they require the least air supplied. As noted in

Chapter I, the deeper a diver goes, the more the air being delivered to him shrinks in volume, (Boyles Law). Thus, as depth is increased, the surface pump must handle greater volumes of air as well as greater pressures. Since every pump has a maximum capacity in cubic feet per minute, this means that there is a certain depth for a given pump beyond which it is dangerous to go. Most manual pumps can meet the pressure requirements of 100 feet or so of sea water, but few can pump a sufficient volume of air to keep a diver alive at such a depth. Therefore, the air requirements set a depth limit on all dives, and

Figure 6. Homebuilt plexidome helmet constructed by authors and Miller-Dunn #1 handpump.

the establishment of this limit is of utmost importance. A rule of thumb long used in diving says that a man must have one and a half cubic feet of free air to breathe at the surface. At 33 feet where the pressure has doubled, this means three cubic feet of surface air pumped down to maintain the one and a half cubic foot minimum at the diver's depth. Small diving hand pumps cannot meet such requirements, and it is evident that this is too crude a criterion on which to base a dive.

In the helmet, open at the bottom to the water, the entering air has two functions. The most obvious one is to replenish the oxygen that is burned by the body. But if we were to supply only enough additional air to provide 'make up' oxygen, we would find that the diver was soon unconscious, for we would have overlooked one basic consideration. The buildup of carbon dioxide in the helmet would have knocked the breather out. Thus the fundamental purpose of the entering air is to flush the stale air, polluted with carbon dioxide, and to insure that the concentration of the CO_2 does not reach dangerous values. What we wish to know is, how much air at the diver's depth is needed?

A simple mathematical analysis of this problem was undertaken in the authors' first book, and the resulting formula proved:

$$\text{Surface \% of CO in helment} = \frac{\text{Cu.ft./min. Oxygen converted to } CO_2}{\text{Cu.ft./min. air entering helmet}} \tag{9}$$

This formula may cause some confusion unless the reader follows carefully the ensuing explanation. In the first place it is desirable to express the concentration of CO_2 on the basis of surface or sea level conditions, since it is in this manner that the danger concentration is always given. Now the volume of oxygen converted to CO_2 is the same for all depths, so that the numerator of equation (9) is a constant throughout the dive. Supposing we consider 5% as the maximum sea level concentration of CO_2 that can be tolerated by a man. If the man is in an enclosed space with air entering at the rate of 1 cubic foot per minute, the formula says he can safely produce one twentieth (5%) of a cubic foot of CO_2 per minute. Now suppose he goes to a higher pressure region 33 feet underwater. He is still producing one twentieth of a cubic foot per minute of CO_2 since the rate of conversion is undisturbed by pressure, but he is receiving at this depth only half a cubic foot of air whereas before he received one cubic foot. The formula now tells us that the concentration has risen to 10%, twice the toleration limit. In other words, for a given pump, as pressure on the system is increased, the numerator remains constant and the denominator decreases. Actually, on the basis of partial pressure of the gases at sea level and in deep water, the permissable partial pressure percentage decreases with depth, but since the above formula was derived on the basis of air volume entering the helmet, the expression gives equivalent sea level concentrations. Essentially what happens as the diver descends is that the entering air volume gets less and the flushing action is less.

It is necessary to specify the proper values for use in equation (9). The crucial quantity is the oxygen to CO_2 conversion which is variable depending on the diver's exertions. The following table is from the work of J. S. Haldane, the pioneer of diving physiology.

TABLE IV

Type of Exertion	(1) Oxygen Consumption cu.ft./min.	(2) CO₂ Production cu. ft. /min.	(3) Volume of breath cu. ft.	(4) Cubic feet breathed/ minute
Resting (prone)	1/100	1/150	1/50	1/4
Standing	1/70	1/100	1/40	5/14
Walking				
2 mi./hr.	1/35	1/40	1/22	5/7
3 mi./hr.	1/28	1/28	1/18	25/28
4 mi./hr.	1/18	1/18	1/14	37/28
5 mi./hr.	1/11	1/11	1/4	15/7

Although only column (2) is of interest in the present discussion, all these values will prove useful in considering other equipment later in the book. We will take the 3 mi./hr. column as average exertion underwater, and 1/28 of a cubic foot per minute as a typical value of CO_2 production. This allows a slight margin of safety in the calculations. The next question is how great a percentage of CO_2 is permissible for comfort. Another table can be given for this quantity.

TABLE V

Surface percentage of CO₂	1-3%	3-5%	5-10%	10-25%
Physiological Symptoms	No effect	Deeper breathing is noticed	Confusion, severe panting	Death

Now, using Tables IV and V, and Figure 1 in Chapter I, we can specify the best surface air supply for the type of work being done by the helmet diver. As an example, supposing we have a pump capable of pumping three cubic feet per minute at the surface. Consider further that the diver will be doing average work (use 1/28 cu. ft.). Then we wish to know at what depths this diver can operate safely without undue panting. First we can set the permissible CO_2 percentage at 5% as absolute maximum. Then substitute into the equation (9) along with the 1/28 figure and get the minimum delivered air which is .72. Now from Boyles Law, (Figure 1) find the depth at which 3 cu. ft. at the surface will give .72 cu. ft. delivered. It turns out to be 135 feet of sea water which is then the maximum depth allowable for this case. To save the reader such computation, Figure 7 has been prepared on the basis of 1/28 cu. ft. per min. for the various CO_2 percentages. This gives directly the surface air volume requirements for various depths. Figure 7 is suitable for average conditions. If the diver is only going to sit on a rock and make notes, he can use less air than is specified. On the other hand if he is going to do heavy work, the predictions of Figure 7 will be too small.

Although equation (9) is the most important conclusion from this analysis of diving helmets, several other interesting facts can be mentioned. When a diver goes underwater with an essentially pure atmosphere in his helmet he begins to build up CO_2 concentration immediately, the concentration growing larger until it reaches the

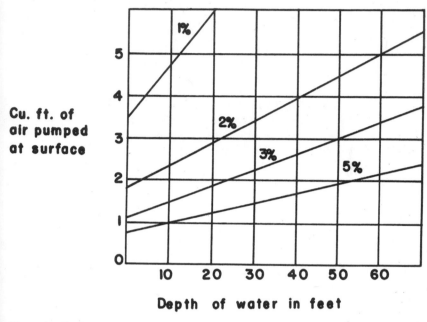

Figure 7. Cubic feet per minute of air pumped at surface necessary to maintain various CO_2 percentages in an open helmet. Notice that to maintain the level in the region of one percent, great volumes of air must be supplied. In the five percent region a slight volume change will make a large percentage change. Therefore with minimum air, great care must be taken lest the concentration rise suddenly due to over exertion or relaxation of pumping.

limiting value as predicted already by equation (9). Now supposing we consider a helmet of one cubic foot air capacity, how long will it take the concentration to build up? The answer depends on the rate of entering air. For an inflow of one half a cubic foot per minute, the time required to approach equilibrium is over four minutes, while with one and a half cubic feet per minute, inflow time is only 1.3 minutes. But it must be remembered that the final concentration value reached is greater for the lower flow rate as noted already. The larger the helmet volume, the longer it takes equilibrium to be reached. One interesting fact is that the time needed to reach limiting equilibrium conditions does not depend on the CO_2 production rate, so that an exerting diver's helmet will reach equilibrium in the same time as a resting diver's helmet, but the final concentration will, of course, be higher for the exerting diver.

A very practical case of an emergency nature may be suggested in the event of pump failure. Supposing the diver is wearing a helmet of one cubic foot capacity (a good average for most helmets) and the pump suddenly stops. What we wish to know is how long he has before bad gasping sets in. The answer depends on what equilibrium concentration was in the helmet at the time of failure. If it was high, around five percent, the safe time is very short. Taking the best case of a pure atmosphere (zero CO_2 concentration) it is easy to calculate the time before gasping. Taking 1/28 cubic foot per minute as the change from oxygen to CO_2, we can see easily that in one minute, 1/28 of the helmet air, or 3.6% has been converted to CO_2, the five percent point being reached in a little under one and one half minutes. Starting with two and one half percent CO_2, the safe or 'emergency' time is reduced to ¾ of a minute and so on. If the diver stays very quiet, he may raise his safe time considerably as can be seen from Table IV, while excitement and panic may cut it to almost nothing. In every case it will be noted that the diver cannot possibly suffer from anoxia or oxygen want. The total oxygen in the helmet begins at roughly 21%, and by the time 5% of it has become CO_2 there is still 16%, plenty for life. Thus, the CO_2 concentration governs the system and knocks out the diver before oxygen want can occur.

All diving equipment can be classified on the basis of its air supply governing mechanisms. The helmet air supply is governed by the concentration of CO_2 as we have just discussed. Thus, the method of air supply determination which operates in this manner will henceforth be called the 'helmet principle'. Equipment operating on the helmet principle requires the least amount of surface supplied air as will be noted in future chapters.

HELMET AIR SUPPLIES

Air supply for all types of diving comes from three primary sources: From a surface pump of some sort, from compressed gas carried by the diver, or in the case of short 'skin dives', from the diver's lungs alone. Helmets are usually supplied from surface pumps which are often hand driven. Now that we have established the rules governing the maximum air supply for helmets it is possible to consider the general nature of air pumps as they relate to helmets. From Figure 7 it is apparent that .75 to 1 cubic feet a minute is required for each

atmosphere of pressure for a normal dive. Thus, for a helmet dive to
33 feet, 1½ to 2 cubic feet per minute are needed as the barest minimum. Most commercially built hand pumps will supply this much
air without too tiring exertion on the part of a single pumper. But
before buying any pump, it is wise to compute the necessary pumping
rate in the following manner. First find the total volume of free air
compressed per stroke of the pump. Take the internal radius in inches
of the pump piston, square it, and multiply by 3.14, giving the cylinder
bore. Then multiply this times the inches the piston travels in com-

Figure 8. Morse #15 shallow water pump. A well-made single-acting pump for
helmets of somewhat greater air capacity than the Miller-Dunn #1.

pressing the air (the stroke) giving the total volume of air compressed per stroke of a single piston. Multiply this by the number
of cylinders used in one stroke. Most of the pumps discussed in this
chapter have either one or two cylinders which are compressed one
each per stroke. Larger, old fashioned pumps used in deep water work
are double acting, that is, each piston compresses air twice per stroke,
giving double the capacity. Now, knowing the required cubic footage
capacity for the desired depth it is possible to use the following
formula to find the strokes per minute.

$$\text{Strokes/minute} = \frac{\text{Cu. ft./min. at desired depth}}{\text{Cu. in. displaced by pump/stroke}} \text{ x 1700 x 1.2} \qquad (10)$$

The factor 1700 converts cubic inches to cubic feet, and 1.2 corrects
an ideal pump (volumetric efficiency 100%) to an average pump
(volumetric efficiency 80%).

As an example, let us consider the worth of an average tire pump for helmet diving. The average tire pump has a piston area of about 1 square inch, and a stroke of about 15 inches, giving a volume per stroke of 15 square inches. At 33 feet we require 1.5 cubic feet per minute minimum air so these figures can be substituted in formula (10) to give a strokes-per-minute figure of 204, or over 3 strokes per second. Even three bicycle pumps in tandem require a rate of pumping of better than one stroke per second. This example then shows not only the use of the formula, but the ill fitness of such small pumps for diving work.

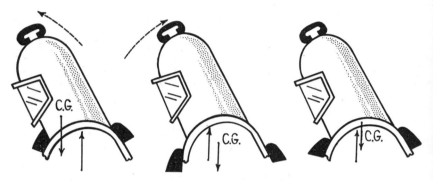

Figure 9. Helmet stability with various center of gravity (C.G.) positions. Dotted arrows show direction of couple force on helmet.

Motor driven compressors can be used for helmet diving in place of hand pumps, and these will be considered in the next chapter. Generally, if a compressor is used the greater air supply available makes the more versatile and lighter mask a better bet. However, very small, lightweight compressors can be used for helmets that are unsuited for mask diving, and if the reader has one available, or desires to use a helmet for other reasons, the motor driven feature is attractive, at least to those left on the surface.

VISION AND STABILITY

Turning to the helmet itself, we can immediately see its greatest drawback, namely weight and awkwardness. The large weight of the average helmet (usually 50 or 60 pounds) is a direct result of Archimedes Principle. Since the helmet displaces a large volume of water, on the order of one cubic foot, weights equal to the volume displaced must be hung around the helmet to keep it underwater. With this much bulk resting on the diver's shoulders, it is important that the whole system be balanced underwater so that it stays firmly, but not uncomfortably placed. There are two main forces acting on a helmet underwater. One is its weight which acts through the center of gravity of the helmet, and the other is the upward thrust of the diver's shoulders which always acts on the helmet-shoulder point of contact. If weights are mounted on the headpiece high up, the center of gravity will be higher than the shoulders and the helmet will be unstable as shown in Figure 9. As the diver leans over, the two forces do not cancel each other, but rather produce a couple which tends to throw off the helmet. Similarly, when the weights are low, the C.G. is well below the shoulder blades, this same couple tends to right the helmet and

Figure 10. Miller-Dunn Shallow Water Helmet. Air enters at the right side of the large facepiece and is forced over the glass to keep it clear. An excellent helmet.

makes bending over difficult. Obviously the best C.G. position is at the shoulders as shown, although it is perhaps best to put the C.G. slightly low so that a small righting couple is always present for safety.

Actually the problem is complicated by the free water surface at the bottom of the helmet which changes the boyancy and the C.G. of the helmet in various positions. However, a helmet designed with a small righting couple will be safe except when the helmet is filling with water, at which point stability becomes only of academic interest.

Most old helmets have flat glass windows protected by a grillwork of bars, since it was thought that curved windows underwater produced seasickness. This has not proved to be true, and new helmets have one piece windows of curved plastic which offer an almost 180 degree view. Curved windows may produce a certain amount of distortion, but this is usually not serious and is compensated for by the panorama viewed from a large window. Unless the window is made of plastic or safety glass, a protecting grillwork still seems desirable as a protection against encounters with rocks or the bottom of a boat. Helmets not so protected must be handled with care in the boat and at the beginning of a dive in rough seas, for the cracking of plastic or safety glass may mean an expensive and time consuming replacement.

COMMERCIAL EQUIPMENT

Very little of what is on today's diving market could be called inexpensive, and it is well worth every potential diver's time to consider carefully the pros and cons of each type of diving gear, and each brand made. Helmets are not the most modern type of diving equipment, but in certain cases which will be mentioned, they still have their place. Once the reader has completed this book and decided on his type of outfit, he may then give a thought to what company he will patronize, and what items he will need for his outfit. Compared to other diving outfits such as compressor-mask outfits and self-contained rigs such as Aqua-Lung, helmet outfits purchased new are somewhat overpriced, considering their limitations and deficiencies. But helmets can be made or bought second hand and small compressors or pumps may be available cheaply, thereby cutting the outlay for a helmet system well below that of any competing gear.

Helmets: If the helmet is to be used frequently, it is recommended that one be purchased rather than made. Only those with extensive shop facilities can hope to match the commercially built shallow water helmets for ruggedness and all-round service. Morse, Miller-Dunn, and Desco are companies that manufacture copperspun shallow water helmets. Unfortunately, diving equipment has a rather set demand regardless of price, and the cost of new gear is high for the average amateur. It might be that the placing of a really cheap ($20 or $30) helmet on the market would result in a large sales increase, but this has yet to be done. If the reader is lucky, he may be able to procure a helmet on the surplus market or from a marine second-hand dealer, but no money should be paid until the condition of the helmet has

Figure 11. Morse Shallow Water Helmet. Notice the fine visibility and construction of this helmet. Weight is between 60 and 65 pounds.

been noted. Helmets with cracked face pieces are to be avoided unless they are practically given away, since replacing the glass may prove difficult and expensive.

Hand Pumps: This is an item that ordinarily must be bought. Bicycle pumps singly or in tandem, do not give sufficient air and are hard on the pumper's muscles. Morse and Miller-Dunn manufacture hand pumps of excellent quality, the Miller-Dunn pumps being in a lower price range. The Morse pumps may prove to be more rugged, although this is not too important a consideration. Most shallow water pumps have two cylinders and a vertical handle between them. Moving the handle back and forth compresses the air in each of the two cylinders in turn. The Morse pumps, #17 and #15, Teco #805, and the Miller-Dunn #1 are single acting, and use each cylinder once per stroke. The Teco #600 is a single cylinder, foot operated pump.

Here again the price of new equipment is high but the buyer may be able to find a surplus pump without too much trouble since a great many were released for sale by War Assets in 1946.

As was noted before, many hand pumps do not deliver 1.5 cu. ft. per min., the specified minimum, at depths of 30 or 40 feet. The reader should remember that a pump whose capacity is 1.5 cu. ft. per min. on the surface gives only half this amount at 33 ft. However, all commercial pumps will meet the air needs at such depths required to maintain the CO_2 concentration at a comfortable level, providing the diver does not overexert himself. Hand pumps are generally unsatisfactory for diving masks unless the mask is modified. Mask diving is fully covered in the next chapter. Motor driven compressors are also discussed in Chapter III, and it suffices to say here that any compressor suitable for mask diving is also suitable for helmets.

If there is any doubt concerning the capacity of either a hand pump or compressor, and equation (10) does not seem to give correct values, the following procedure may be followed to determine air volumes directly. Procure a standard 12 quart pail of the type sold in all hardware stores. Invert the pail off the edge of a dock or in shallow water and hold it just beneath the surface completely filled with water. Now start the compressor or have the pumper begin at his normal speed, and place the hose beneath the bucket so that all the air is going into it. Have an assistant start a stopwatch at this moment. Continue allowing all the air to be collected in the pail until the first bubbles begin to foam up around the sides of the pail indicating it is filled with air, and stop the watch. In the time elapsed, the air will have displaced 3/7 of a cubic foot of sea water, so that the volume capacity of the pump is easily found by multiplying 3/7 by 60 over the time in seconds which gives the air capacity per minute in cubic feet. For example, a pump takes twenty seconds to pump 3/7 cubic feet of air. The capacity per minute is 3/7 times 60/20 which equals 9/7 cubic foot per minute. If a 12 quart pail is not available, any reasonably large container can be used, knowing that a quart is one twenty-eighth of a cubic foot. Should the result derived in this manner be considerably less than that predicted by equation (10) the pump is in bad shape and should have its leathers greased or replaced. In the case of a compressor, the rings may need replacement.

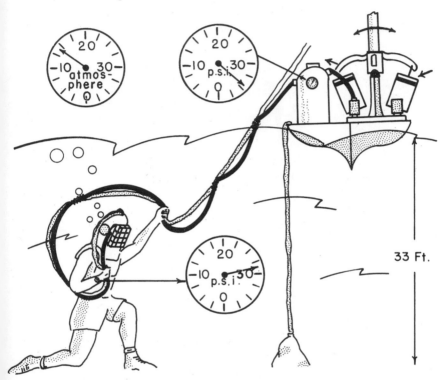

Figure 12. Non-scale diagram of equipment in use with typical pressures for 33 ft. depth. Note 5 lb. drop in hose. This is assuming 100 ft. of standard shallow water hose with a flow of between 2 and 3 cu. ft. per minute. Actual gauges read atmospheric pressure as zero, not as 14.7 psi.

Other Equipment: Besides the helmet and pump, a number of other items are needed to round out the basic helmet outfit. These are: hose, lifeline, valves, and a pressure tank.

Shallow water diving hose comes in fifty foot lengths with female couplings on each end. It can be purchased new from the manufacturer, surplus, or may be replaced by ordinary low pressure welding torch hose which may be cheaper and easier to obtain. Keeping track

Figure 13. Morse Shallow Water Wader for use with a helmet. This diving suit is intended to keep all water from the diver. It cannot be used with the diving mask. Notice the air escape valve on the left cuff. This is used to keep the suit deflated.

of thread and coupling sizes can become involved if equipment is purchased from a number of different manufacturers who make products for various industrial uses. In order to keep confusion to a minimum, a summary of the various air and oxygen fittings, their sizes and threads is herewith considered.

The hose used in diving is the vital link between the diver and the surface and, for this reason it and the associated fittings should be chosen with some care, to insure that no failure can possibly occur. Hose is usually measured by internal diameter. It is manufactured with one or more internal weavings of cotton called plies. For a given internal diameter, the hose may vary greatly outside depending on the number of plies. Standard shallow water hose is ordinarily two-ply, although the best grade may have as many as five. It has been found that one-ply synthetic hose of the type used for flexible water conduit can withstand a direct pressure of 125 psi. This is satisfactory for shallow water diving, although if kept coiled it may kink when straightened out. The advantage of five-ply hose is that it is almost impossible to kink. Welding and cutting hose of the proper internal diameter is also satisfactory. Two sizes of hose are generally used in shallow water work. One quarter inch I.D. (inner diameter) is satisfactory in lengths of not over fifty feet, but with its associated fittings, it tends to restrict the flow of air when used in longer lengths. This adds unnecessary burden to the task of the pumper when a manual pump is used, but with motor driven compressors, it is less important. Most manufacturers of commercial shallow water equipment use hose of 5/16 I.D. Even two or three 50 foot sections coupled together give no unreasonable resistance to air flow. Using larger hose than this makes little further improvement unless very large flow rates are to be handled. Welding oxygen hose is ordinarily 5/16 I.D., although other sizes are used. This is probably the most practical size from an all-round point of view, since the fittings are most easily available. High pressure deep water hose is thick and too unwieldy for shallow diving.

Fittings are used in connecting and assembling the compressor, tank, hose, and mask or helmet. There are fittings intended to connect pipe to hose, hose to hose, copper tubing to pipe, and many other combinations in a bewildering array of sizes. It is hoped that the following will help clear the picture for the potential diver at least. Pipe fitters, when threading and coupling pipe sections, employ the so-called pipe thread. This gets its name from being the thread cut in the end of a pipe when it is desired to screw the pipe into an elbow or coupling. It is, however, not limited to pipe alone, but is used extensively in tank connections. This type of threading is distinguished by the fact that it is tapered. Unlike a bolt whose threading is cylin-

Figure 14. Navy diver using the Miller-Dunn Helmet. Notice the care with which the helmet is placed on the diver's shoulders. This point of the dive demands caution since the helmet is heavy and awkward out of the water. (Official U.S. Navy Photograph)

drical (the nut screws on indefinitely), the pipe thread is something like a wood screw. When screwed into a matching hole, it will eventually bring up by jamming. This is an advantage, since there is no shoulder to bring up, necessitating a gasket. A tapered threaded piece of metal, i.e., a pipe, is screwed into a tapered threaded hole until it simply will go no further. If pipe compound is smeared on the threads first, the resulting joint is strong and air and water tight. Compressor inlets and outlets are invariably pipe threads as are guages, valves, and all orifices in pressure and volume tanks. Pipe fittings come in standard sizes, ¼, ⅜, ½, etc. Most valves, tanks, and compressors used in shallow water diving require ¼ inch pipe fittings, although some compressors may use ⅜ inch or larger. Adapters are readily available. When ordering such a fitting, it is necessary only to specify the size and that it is a pipe fitting, male or female.

Air hose requires a different type of fitting known as an air fitting. These are not tapered, but are cylindrical and resemble garden hose connections, except that they are smaller, and air hose is generally made up with a female coupling at both ends. Hose fittings do not use a gasket, the nut on the end of the hose being firmly taken up. This brass seal will not leak air when tight. Air fittings come in standard sizes, ¼, ⁵⁄₁₆, and so forth. While a ¼ inch male air fitting will screw into a female ¼ inch pipe fitting and vice versa, they are not intended to be used together. These sizes, incidently, are not the sizes of the fittings themselves, but the sizes of the hose or pipe with which they are used. A hose coupling used to couple sections of hose together, is a small piece of brass with an external air thread at each end. This matches the female couplings on each piece of hose. It is not intended to be screwed into a tank or compressor to connect hose to one of these units. For that purpose use a hose-to-tank adapter which has a male pipe thread on one end and a male air thread on the other. There are two standard adapters of this type used in both diving and welding, namely ¼ inch pipe to ¼ inch air, and ¼ inch air to ⁵⁄₁₆ inch air. (There is no ⁵⁄₁₆ inch pipe fitting.) These adapters are easily obtained from welding supply houses. Another coupling having male pipe thread at both ends is called a nipple, and is used to connect valves to tanks and pipe to tanks or compressors. It is found at the local plumber's. The best way to avoid fitting confusion is to standardize on one size throughout. The authors have found that standardizing on ¼ inch pipe fittings, and ⁵⁄₁₆ inch air fittings give good results, and no procurement troubles of any consequence appear when these two sizes are used.

Good half-inch manila is satisfactory for a lifeline, and if possible, a rope that has been 'broken in' should be procured since it will ease the job of line handling. A good way to keep snarling to minimum is to seize the lifeline and hose together with tough seizing cord every foot or so. There should be slack hose between each joining so that, when the lifeline is pulled taut, the hose hangs beneath it in shallow loops. This takes any strain off the hose and couplings. If the rope is new, allow for shrinkage when the seizing is done.

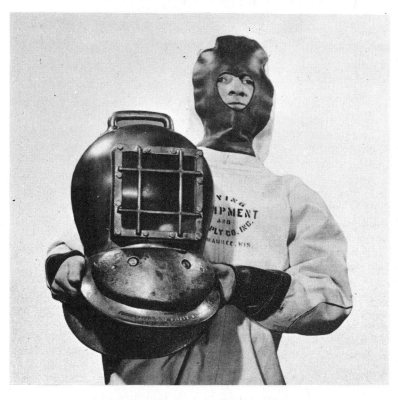

Figure 15. The Desco shallow water open helmet. A somewhat less expensive helmet compared with Morse, but with less visibility. (Courtesy Desco)

A one-way non-return valve is usually essential for any shallow water equipment. Almost all helmets have the air inlet at the side to ensure thorough mixing and the one-way valve keeps the air from escaping if the air line is cut. Most commercially built helmets come equipped with such valves, but if they do not, one should be purchased and attached at the air inlet on the helmet. The Morse Company makes a simple, foolproof, non-return valve with a threaded male coupling at each end, and most diving supply companies stock the item or one similar to it.

A surface pressure tank is useful in absorbing pump pulsations and in action as an air reservoir in the event of pumping failure. Good lightweight tanks, designed for shallow water diving, can be purchased new, surplus, or can be replaced by a surplus low pressure (400 psi) oxygen cylinder with an internal volume of .5 cu. ft. or more. A pressure tank must have inlet and outlet fittings and, if possible, a pressure guage. Thus the oxygen cylinders will require some machining to make them servicable. Figure 12 shows a diagram of the complete outfit in action with typical pressures at various points.

The equipment listed above is all that is required to make safe dives up to 40 or 50 feet. However, the diver in northern waters may find himself uncomfortably cold after a few minutes of submersion. The cold can be partially alleviated by wearing a shirt, pants and sneakers. For better protection, some sort of diving suit may be used. A noninflatable suit specifically designed for shallow water diving is manufactured by Diving Equipment and Supply Co. (Desco). This is the Desco back-entry dress designed for the diving mask, but which will work satisfactorily with a helmet. Morse sells a similar outfit designed primarily for helmet diving. A discussion of the Desco dress is given in the next chapter. If the diver does not anticipate anything more than underwater sightseeing a surplus submersion suit, purchased from almost any surplus outlet for four or five dollars, may solve the cold problems. These suits are made of black rubber and completely cover the wearer except for mouth, nose and eyes. Since they were designed to be donned by a man wearing a standard life jacket, they will prove too large for diving unless they are cut down and patched by rubber scraps and cement. Such a suit is bulky and somewhat awkward, but will at least keep the diver warm for a considerable length of time.

HELMET CONSTRUCTION

Materials: Wood, plastic, or metal may be used, or a combination may offer the best possibilities. Wood is the easiest to work, and a waterproofed, heavily-built wooden helmet can be made very cheaply. Wood has buoyancy however, and is difficult to form into curves; and a wooden helmet tends to be bulky and heavy. Plastic is tricky to work with, and its brittleness makes it susceptible to mechanical shock. Great visibility is its main advantage. Metal is the most widely used and is, of course, strong, tough, and has the highest density. Since 40 or more pounds of weights must be mounted on a helmet to sink it and the diver, metal is usually the choice for breastplates where the weights are hung. Commercial helmets are usually formed out of spun copper, but the amateur will find copper a nasty metal to work.

The Headpiece: The cardinal rule in building the container for the head is: Keep it small. Every cubic foot of helmet volume needs 64 lbs. of weights to sink it in sea water, and while a 100 pound helmet may be roomy, it requires two men to manhandle it onto the diver's shoulders.

While it may be possible to work up a headpiece from flat stock, a much easier solution is to procure some ready-shaped object and adapt it for the job. A few suggestions are: large surplus low pressure oxygen bottle, ten gallon milk can, a suitably sized hot water tank.

If wood is to be used, half inch oak planks can be screwed together to form a box for the head, and the entire assembly painted inside and out. Painting is a necessity for any equipment not made out of copper, brass, plastic, or rubber.

The authors constructed a satisfactory helmet from a surplus aircraft plexidome. The plexi-glass formed the front half of the head-piece and heavy rubber sheet formed the back. The whole assembly was bolted to steel strap, bent to the contour of the shoulders, and weights were hung on the strap, front and back. The helmet has much greater visibility than any commercial helmet made, and weighs only 40 pounds. The average commercial job weighs 70. Plastic is fragile and cannot bear much strain, so such a helmet must be handled with some care on the surface. Even smaller helmets could be constructed with the accompanying decrease in weight, but too small a helmet fed by a low capacity air pump is unsatisfactory due to the rise in water level in the helmet when a quick, deep breath is taken. If a small shallow water pump is used, a helmet with a volume of ½ cubic foot will be about minimum.

Unless the headpiece is made of transparent material as described above, a window will have to be fitted in the front. It is important that the seal between window and headpiece be as airtight as possible, but this is not too difficult since the pressure differential between inside and outside is usually not more than two or three psi.

If a cylinder of metal is to form the headpiece, a curved window will be the easiest to insert. Since bending glass may prove difficult for the home craftsman, thick, transparent plastic sheeting may be bought and bent to fit. This is accomplished by soaking the plastic in boiling water and moulding it, using the helmet itself as the form. If this operation is not performed with care, the plastic will distort. Auto safety glass makes a good flat window. Ordinary window or other shatterable glass is dangerous in diving equipment and should never be used.

The completed window can then be bolted or otherwise affixed to the headpiece. Thick rubber cement makes a good seal, and the window should be fastened so that the sealing compound is forced into the joint by inside pressure. Many beginners are confused into thinking that the highest pressure is on the outside of the glass. If this were true, the open helmet would rapidly fill with water.

Breastplates: Here again, wood is the easiest to work and is the least satisfactory. Heavy steel strap can be bent when hot quite easily, and then bolted or welded to the headpiece which is cut to shoulder contour. Since water will rise in the helmet to the highest exposed portion, a snug fit will give the best results. If strap is used, the ends hanging down over the chest and back should be connected by horizontal braces on which weights can be mounted. If good machine shop facilities are available, it may be possible to make a professional breastplate from flat steel or copper.

Weights: Lead is commonly used, but is expensive. If the builder does not wish to spend $10 or more on weights, he can purchase some cast iron scrap at a junk yard and have it sawed into blocks of the proper size. Cast iron is roughly one third more bulky than lead of the same weight. A good estimate of the weight required can be had by filling the inverted helmet with water, and adding about five pounds to the weight of the water for body bouyancy. If a suit is used, 15 pounds added will be a better estimate. In mounting the weights, remember to get the center of gravity at the shoulder, or slightly below. (see Fig. 9).

A one-way valve is absolutely essential for all normal helmet work as explained previously. In the event of an emergency far from sources of supply of this item, or the necessity of converting to a homebuilt helmet on the spot of diving operations, it may be impossible to procure the valve, or repair it. Diving may continue only if the following precaution is observed. The air hose must be affixed at the very bottom of the helmet so that the air entrance point is below the mouth when the diver stands upright in normal working position. If the hose should be cut at any point, water will instantly rise to the end of the hose where air is entering the helmet. Should this point be midway up the helmet, the diver will probably drown. Mounting the hose at the bottom is very unsatisfactory since the face piece will cloud over easily, and a one-way valve should always be used.

USING THE HELMET

Whether a small compressor or hand pump is used, a good sized boat should be procured for helmet diving. A small skiff or rowboat is generally not suitable in any but the calmest water since the pumper must stand to work effectively, and the hoisting of a heavy helmet in and out of the boat may tip a small one over. Once the equipment has been assembled and the boat anchored at the diving area, a decending line is put down. This is simply a 10 or 20 pound weight on the end of a stout rope which stretches from the stern to the bottom as verticle as the tide and current will permit. The diver then climbs into the water and hangs onto the stern completely submerged except for his head. The pumper begins to work (or the compressor is started) and the tender carefully lifts. the helmet off the deck and onto the diver's shoulders. Gripping the decending line with both hands, the diver then sinks a foot or two underwater so that the helmet is fully submerged, and thinks over the situation for a moment. The lifeline and air hose, seized together as described, come from the boat, under one arm from the diver's rear, and up to the air inlet one-way valve. The lifeline is naturally fastened to the handle or other projection on the top, and is tauter than the air hose at all times. If everything feels and sounds all right, the diver now begins his descent. If there is only a light current, he can hold onto the lines with his right hand and guide his descent on the descending line with his left, but usually both hands grip the descending line, and give the diver complete control over his downward motion. With a manual pump in operation on the surface, it is important to sink slowly to give the pumper a chance to keep the helmet filled. Supposing the helmet volume is one cubic foot and the diver descends rapidly to the ocean floor at 33 feet. Since the pressure on his helmet air has doubled, the headpiece will be half filled with water, and at the rate of one cubic foot per minute of new air entering, it will take half a minute to clear the helmet out. A good rule is to take one minute to go down each 25 feet, since this will give even the most meagre air supply a chance to keep up with the descent. Of course if the surface pump can only just equalize the pressure increase with new air, and not flush any old air out, the CO_2 concentration on the descent can be building up quite rapidly so that even slower descents than this may prove necessary. Only a fool goes down without a descending line of some sort to guide his rate of travel.

Once on the bottom, the diver is free to wander wherever his lines permit. Unless he is actually working or just sitting, one hand should always be kept on the lines to receive any signals from the surface, and to keep the lines under one arm in the proper fashion. It is very easy to get lost underwater, but this is no cause for alarm. The lines always lead to the boat, and they should be reasonably taut at all times. Reasonably taut means that looking back at his lines, the diver should see them rising toward the surface in a sweeping curve behind him, and not lying in coils and snarls on the bottom. The tender must take this responsibility and must at all times be letting line out or hauling it in to maintain the correct tension for good signalling. For simple dives and preliminary equipment testing the following set of signals will be satisfactory:

TENDER TO DIVER	DIVER TO TENDER
1 pull: Are you all right?	1 pull: I am all right.
2 pulls: Am hauling you in.	2 pulls: Haul me in.
3 pulls: Repeat your signal.	3 pulls: Repeat your signal.
4 pulls: No more line left.	4 pulls: Give me more air.

It is important that the same signal for 'pull me in' be maintained throughout all diving experience. Any changes in signals should leave this one as is.

The diving helmet user must be careful at all times that he does not lean over too far and loose air from his helmet, or worse yet, dump the helmet off completely. This should not occur with a well designed, snugly fitting helmet, but under no condition should any helmet be fastened to the body as some open British helmets have been. Since the open helmet can loose air if the diver should trip or bend sharply, a heavy helmet fastened to the body would surely drown the diver and prevent his escape to the surface. Should water fill the helmet however, there is still no need for panic, providing the pump is still working. With an average air supply it should not take more than 30 seconds to clear sufficiently a full helmet down to nose level and give the diver relief. Since it will usually take at least this much time plus strenuous activity to leave the helmet and swim to the surface, it is better to stay with the unit if possible and stay calm and quiet.

As the helmet diver goes deeper and deeper underwater, he notices that a deep breath causes the water level in the helmet to rise appreciably, since the lungs are removing some of the entrapped air which is instantly replaced by water. A maximum deep breath is around one ninth of a cubic foot, so for a one cubic foot cylindrical helmet with an air column inside 15 inches high, the rise in water level will be about one and a half inches, insufficient to cover the mouth, though the water may lap up to the chin. The greater the rate of delivered air, the less the water will rise on inspiration.

When it is time to come up, the diver may either find the descending line and climb it, the tender hauling in the lifeline as he rises, or he may signal the tender and be pulled directly up to the boat. When being hauled in, the diver should grasp the lines with both hands and staying erect in the water, be pulled smoothly upward. One interesting physiological symptom is sometimes noted on the ascent. This is a sudden feeling of giddyness and light-headedness which reaches its peak as the diver breaks surface and then quickly subsides. This is apparently due to the increased ventilation of the helmet on the ascent, for the volume of air in the helmet expands and during the short period of the ascent washes out the CO_2 vigorously. Also the delivered air from the pump is increasing in volume as well. Thus the effective flushing air rate may be on the order of three or four cubic feet per minute and the CO_2 concentration correspondingly less. Since the body has become acclimated to a fairly high concentration, this sudden change appears to cause the slight nausea which some divers notice. The rate of ascent should never exceed 25 feet a minute under any but the most stringent emergency conditions, and of course the breath is *never held. Breathe normally when rising.* When he reaches the boat, the diver waits in the water until the helmet is removed by his tender, being extremely careful to hold onto the boat firmly. If his hands should slip on a slimy gunwhale, he might plumit to the bottom with no descending line and no one on the pump, a most dangerous procedure.

Diving in rough water or in strong currents requires extra precautions, particularly on the surface where conditions may be choppy and unpleasant. Should the tender slip when getting the helmet over the side, a dangerous accident can occur, either to the diver, helmet, or both. Also violent surges close to the surface can upset a helmet diver easily unless he grasps the descending line firmly and keeps the line between himself and the current. The open helmet diver is particularly prone to accidents due to high speed currents and wave action, since he can not afford to fall or lose his balance at any time during the dive lest the helmet topple off. Novice diving teams should never attempt rough water operations since these require maximum efficiency and care in the boat and in the water. The good diver and tender must also be good seamen. Nowhere is this more true than in rough and turbulent water.

Before actually going underwater, the novice should reread carefully the portion on ear pain in Chapter I, since this will be the first unpleasant symptom he undergoes. Once the ears are cleared however, the remainder of the dive should go smoothly providing everything has been prepared carefully and all those concerned with the dive understand their functions. The diver should never stay down when shivering begins, since a serious cold can result. In any case, the tender and pumper will usually be impatient for their turns underwater.

A SUMMARY OF HELMET DIVING SAFETY

To the Tender

Don't hesitate to ask the diver if he is all right.
Give crisp, short jerks for signals on hose.
Don't allow any slack line on the descent.

Maintain line taut enough to receive and send signals at all times.
Keep track of the diver's bubbles.
Keep snarls out of hose and lines in boat during dive.
Keep power boats clear of diving area.
Keep watch of time and depth when diver is over 40 feet down, and
    decompress if necessary.
Never pull the diver up faster than 25 feet a minute except in urgent
    emergencies.

To the Diver

Descend slowly and relax.
Never descend with ears hurting, but rise as outlined in Chapter I.
Keep one hand on lifelines at all times unless actually working.
Keep lines under one arm at all times.
Don't get cold.
Never hold your breath on any ascent, emergency or otherwise.

HELMET USES

By now the reader should have a pretty good idea as to the general
utility of the open diving helmet. It has the serious disadvantage of
lack of flexibility in underwater work, since it requires the diver to
remain erect at all times. Also, it is heavy and cumbersome, requiring
a tender's help before the descent, and effort on the part of all concerned if much carrying is to be done to the diving area. The main
advantage is its minimal air requirements allowing dives to over 30
feet using the smallest hand operated diving pumps. The entire diving
outfit is therefore free from any mechanical trouble which may beset
small gasoline driven compressors, and can be taken anywhere in
the world with the complete assurance that lack of mechanical facilities, gasoline, etc. will not prevent diving activities. The hand pump-
helmet combination is thus most attractive for minor diving operations
far from civilization such as might be desired by scientific groups,
cave investigators, or other specialized people who want a little
diving with a minimum of fuss. For serious and prolonged diving
activity, the mask-compressor outfits described in the next chapter
are more practical.

Many helmets have been made and sold in the past years, and
since a good helmet is fairly indestructible, many readers may have
one available. In this case helmet diving is justified if for no other
reason than convenience of equipment, and the advantage of not
having to spend any money on different gear. Helmets are perfectly
suitable for the underwater sightseer, and many excellent photos
have been taken underwater from helmets. Doctor William Beebe did

all his shallow water work with a helmet, writing several books and papers, and making a great many observations of marine life during his years of diving. One particular advantage of the helmet for naturalists is that telephones are easily used in it, so that notes may be taken on the surface, or tape recordings made. An underwater movie narrated by the diver making the pictures would indeed be both interesting and novel.

Chapter III

MASK DIVING

The diving mask is a fairly recent development, but it is gradually revolutionizing commercial salvage work in moderate depths. The heavy, inflated, deep water diving suit can be both a lifesaver or a killer depending on who is using it and what the situation happens to be. In the hands of any but the most competent man, the inflated suit seldom tends to fail safe, thereby turning a little accident into a big one. Blowing-up, squeeze, drowning through a rip in the suit, are some of the accidents that seldom or never happen with diving mask outfits. The only advantage of deep water gear, the ability to control bouyancy, is seldom required in mask rigs since they carry so few weights that the diver is never heavy on the bottom. Aside from commercial applications, the diving mask has other attractive features for the amateur and it will be shown in this chapter that in some cases the surface supplied mask can rival the self-contained 'lung' as regards versatility and portability.

AIR SUPPLY

As with all diving equipment, necessary air supply is an important consideration in mask diving. The helmet is essentially a large air cavity with air flushing through it at all times, but the mask, which fits tightly around the face, cannot be considered in the same manner. The volume enclosed between face and mask is so small and inflexible that no air can be taken from it by the lungs. Thus, while in the helmet there is available a large reservoir of air that can be tapped at any time, in the basic mask no such reservoir exists and all air that is breathed must come from the surface compressor. It is apparent that no CO_2 problem exists with the simple mask and the amount of air delivered to the diver is regulated entirely by the total volume of air necessary to maintain respiration.

Entering Table IV (Chapter II) at the three mile-per-hour figure already used for average exertion, and looking under the column giving the total air volume respired per minute we get a figure of 25/28ths of a cubic foot at sea level or very close to one cubic foot. Roughly half the time during breathing is spent exhaling so that one cubic foot must be received in half a minute of life. Since the air pump or compressor is operating all the time, half its air is wasted and

(51)

two cubic feet a minute must be delivered to the mask diver. Compare this figure with the three-quarters of a cubic foot figure for the helmet and the helmet advantage in air supply is readily apparent.

It is possible, however, to improve this situation by using a breathing bag to collect the air pumped down during the diver's exhalation and store it until the diver prepares to inhale. This principle is used by Desco with a small bag worn around the diver's neck and it permits a considerable reduction in air supply. The Desco bag is of small

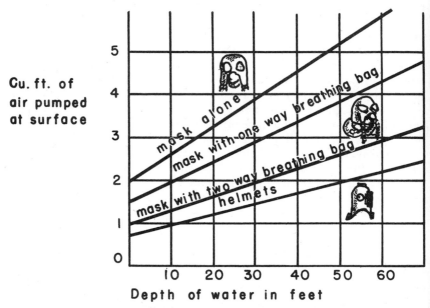

Figure 16. Minimum cubic feet of air per minute necessary with various types of shallow diving equipment. This graph is based on Haldanes 3 mph figure for air consumption and CO_2 production.

capacity and cannot cut the necessary air in half, but it will permit a reduction in delivered air to around one and a quarter cubic feet a minute delivered to the diver. The connection in the mask between bag and breather contains a one-way valve of soft rubber that prevents any expired air from returning to the bag. If this valve is removed, the bag acts as a two-way reservoir and we are approaching the helmet principle since CO_2 is now present in the system at all times. The second type of regulatory mechanism for air supply can be called the 'mask principle' and this is characterized by a lack of CO_2 in the system and a generally larger necessary air supply. The mask principle is in operation with no bag and with a one-way bag, while the helmet principle is in operation with a two-way bag and with a helmet. The closer we approach the full helmet principle, the smaller the necessary air supply becomes.

Even with a two-way Desco bag, it is still not generally possible to cut the air supply to that possible with helmets, for the bag is too small to supply a deep breath. When the air supply reaches the helmet minimum, the CO_2 has risen to large values (on the order of four to five percent) and breaths are deep, necessitating a large air reserve. In the helmet this air reserve is the total volume of the headpiece, which is sufficient to supply easily the most high volume lungs, but the bag will be empty about half way through the inspiration and the surface must rapidly supply the rest. With the Desco bag used in the two-way manner, one cubic foot per minute appears to be about minimum.

In order to operate a mask with the same air supply as a helmet, it is necessary to have a bag of at least one-ninth cubic foot capacity which is the total capacity of the deepest possible breath. There is at this time no neck-breathing-bag of this capacity manufactured commercially, so such a rig would have to be built at home or by a rubber goods supplier. The construction of such bags is fully considered in Chapter IV and the reader who is interested in such a project will find information on materials and methods of fabrication there. It should be noted that a one-ninth cubic foot bag will require over six pounds of weights on the diver.

The following table gives minimum air supplies at the surface for gear discussed so far. These minimums are not mathematical assumptions, but proven values investigated by hours of experimentation.

Mask with no breathing bag. . . . . :. . . . 2 cu. ft./min.
Mask with one-way breathing bag (no CO_2 in system)
1 to 1.5 cu. ft./min.
Mask with Desco breathing bag used in two-way manner. 1 cu. ft./min.
Helmet or mask with bag of greater capacity than lung. . .75 cu. ft./min.

HOME BUILT MASKS

Although the commercially available masks are fairly priced, the beginner may wish to make one from a surplus gas mask. The only objection to a gas mask diving outfit is that the slanted eye windows produce some distortion and may make distance judgement difficult. This is not too troublesome once familiarity with the equipment is established.

A sturdy, easily obtainable gas mask is the Navy Mark III mask manufactured by Mine Safety Appliance Company. This is probably

the best of the gas mask crop since it is made of thick rubber and
sturdy metal instead of fragile plastic and thin sheeting. There are
other masks of stiff fabric material that should prove satisfactory,
however, if this one is unobtainable. To convert this and most other
masks for diving use, one need only replace the thin plastic diaphragm
in the nose of the mask by a circle of thin brass or tough rubber and
connect the two hoses to a simple manifold. Since the hose may be
too long for individual needs, it can be cut to the desired length before
the manifold is attached. A breathing bag may be attached to the
flap exhaust valve at the bottom of the mask, but this is generally
too small an opening to be suitable and is, in any case, too low on
the mask and may collect water. Much better to cut a hole at cheek

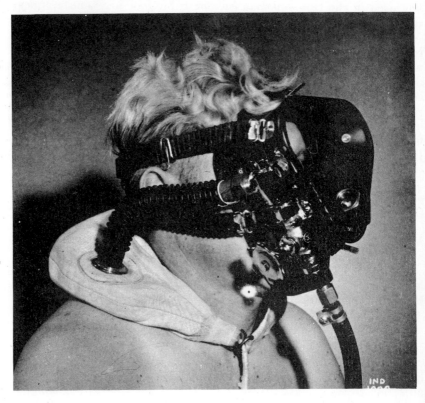

Figure 17. The Desco mask and breathing bag. The small handle on top of the right
hand plumbing switches the bag on or off. Beneath it is the air control valve and fitting for attachment of air hose. Visible through face glass is the air exhaust valve at
the left side of face. The small projections on each strap buckle permit instant release of straps for quick removal of the mask. A very fine unit. (Courtesy Desco)

level and fit the bag there. The accompanying photo (Figure 23) shows that a converted gas mask is entirely suitable for diving, since the Navy does not permit unsafe practices underwater. The two divers are wearing long underwear for warmth and have arranged the Mine Safety masks so that the tubes go behind the head and are affixed through a manifold to an air control valve at the belt. This gets the tubes out of the way, although the beginner may prefer to have everything in front where he can keep an eye on it.

COMMERCIAL EQUIPMENT

Thompson Engineering Company (Teco) makes an all rubber mask with large eye holes and twin lengths of flexible tubing leading from the cheeks to a simple metal manifold. The air escapes from around the corners of the mask, or, in a more expensive model, through a one-way escape valve. The mask is simple, and reasonably priced. The large, parallel eye windows give no distortion.

Diving Equipment and Supply Company, (Desco) make a mask of somewhat different design. It has a triangular face piece with an attached air control valve on the right hand side and an exhaust valve on the left. There is also a fitting on the air-control valve which permits the attachment of a Desco breathing bag with a lever that allows for the bag to be shut off when it is not desired.

The Desco mask now comes in three basic configurations. The least expensive is the basic mask without a manual control valve or breathing bag attachment, and is suitable for use in pools where the air supply is sufficient to supply two cubic feet a minute at very moderate depths. The so-called U.S. Navy outfit is the same mask with plumbing as outlined above and is necessary for use in the open sea with small compressors where the bag will be needed or where more than one diver is descending and each must control his air supply. For heavy duty commercial work and professional applications, the mask comes fully attached to the Desco back-entry dress (discussed in a later section) and with a hinged face piece that may be raised when the diver is in the boat. This mask may be obtained with full telephone equipment if desired. The full Desco mask-suit combination can put a diver on the bottom with the same negative bouyancy as a standard deep water diver, but while the deep water man's equipment weighs 200 pounds in air, the Desco will weigh only 60, a most worthwhile decrease. The full suit has been tested in a pressure tank to a simulated depth of 550 feet of water. It might be noted that the plain mask can be and is used with the Desco back entry dress. The casual diver who desires this unit will be much better off having the detached mask and suit since he can then use the mask alone in warm waters.

Figure 18. The full Desco Lightweight Suit, including weighted vest, telephone equipped mask and headdress, breathing bag (deflated), and emergency air bottle on right leg. The suit is equipped with fingerless mittens, but standard gloves having the first finger detached are better. (Courtesy Desco)

This is all very excellent equipment and it will certainly replace much of the deep water gear currently in use today. The amateur who can afford the Desco mask will find diving an easy matter, providing he goes slowly and with a full understanding of the principles involved.

The armed services used a mask, known as the Borga, which was equipped with a demand valve on the front of the mask. This device operated when there was a back pressure in the line so that when the diver sucked in, the mechanism was actuated and a gush of air rushed into the mask. Actually, what this gadget does is to substitute the surface volume tank for the breathing bag. That is, the surface tank collects air until the diver is ready to breathe it. The disadvantages of such a rig are numerous. If the air is supplied by hand, the pumper must maintain a back pressure in the surface tank and then work against it. The demand valve is the weakest link, so to speak, in the chain of equipment and may become clogged and inoperative at any time. The only place where the valve could be of service, and probably where it is most often used, is when the diver is being supplied with 400 psi (or higher) air from flasks in the diving boat. These are comconly used by the Navy, but seldom by amateur divers due to recharging difficulties. For normal use, the demand valve must be removed.

PUMPS AND COMPRESSORS

As already discussed, the plain mask requires a great deal of air and cannot possibly be supplied by the normal two cylinder hand pump. Even the mask with a two-way Desco bag is stretching the average hand pump (such as the Miller-Dunn) quite a bit. Therefore, hand pumps should be used with masks only if the diver is equipped with a large breathing bag of one-ninth cubic foot or more, attached in such a manner that breathing is easy. The authors recommend that, if possible, a gasoline driven compressor be used for any mask in preference to a hand pump. The Navy concurs with this opinion to the extent that it has given up equipping any of its shallow water diving sets with hand pumps.

With a hand pump, a minimum of three men are needed, one diver, one tender and one pumper, and often another pumper must be added. This cuts the individuals diving time to a minimum, whereas with a compressor, only the tender need be on the surface. The Morse #17 is a heavy duty hand pump that is considered suitable for deep water rigs in shallow depths. This pump would probably be best for general mask diving if a compresser is not desired.

Compressors are used for a great many things other than diving, and some care must be taken in selecting a satisfactory one. Those used by gas stations are usually designed to give high pressures (150 psi) and moderate amounts of air (1 to 3 cu. ft./min.). An ideal shallow water diving compressor should give low pressures (40 psi maximum) and high capacity (10 cu. ft./min.). Thus the diving compressor design should be a large piston working in a light weight head. Such a design would give large volumes of air with none of the bulk and expense associated with heavy castings. The nearest thing to these needs is found in high capacity paint spraying rigs.

Figure 19. A 45 pound twin cylinder diaphragm compressor by Desco. This is a portable unit furnishing somewhat over 3 cubic feet a minute at 40 psi. (Courtesy Desco)

Compressors designed specifically for diving are manufactured by most of the major companies. The smallest Morse compressor is still quite big and very expensive. Desco sells a series of small motor-compressor outfits that are portable and deliver around three cubic feet of air at moderate pressures, suitable for one diver to 40 feet if the breathing bag is used. Probably the best approach to the problem is the unit offered by Teco. Instead of a piston compressor, this company has used a vane pump principle to supply air. The vane pump is useless for high pressure applications, but perfect for diving since it delivers large volumes of low pressure air from a light, compact unit. The air is supplied continually, and there is no need to worry about oil vapor in the line. There are still a number of war surplus compressors on the market. The Dapco, which is similar to Desco equipment, is a lightweight diaphragm compressor and is standard with Army diving units.

Ready made compressor units are not too costly, but the beginner may have available a motor or compressor, or require more air than the least expensive ready-made sets, and so prefer to assemble his own air supply. The compressor is the first item to procure. Here are some hints for the potential purchaser:

3 cu. ft./min. must be considered as the minimum capacity at rated speed. 6 or 8 cu. ft./min. is better.

No ordinary piston compressor should run over 800 revolutions per minute. When run faster than this, the compressor will tend to throw oil down the air line, a very serious condition. There may be surplus military compressors designed for greater speeds, but these should be regarded with caution since they are seldom designed for more than intermittant use at 1200 RPM or higher.

Two small cylinders give smoother operation than one big one. This is especially desirable if the unit is mounted on a light base in a small boat where vibration can be unpleasant.

Rubber diaphragm compressors, used in spray painting, cannot be used too long at a time, but they are light and easy to maintain and should prove suitable for casual diving needs.

Two stage compressors are designed for high pressure use, are heavy and expensive. Don't bother with them.

If purchasing a used compressor, it is important to determine if the piston rings are sound. To do this, run the compressor at rated speed and hold a clean handkerchief over the air outlet. If the cloth becomes discolored, the compressor is throwing oil and must be fixed before being used in diving.

MOTORS AND MOUNTINGS

Electric motors are seldom used near salt water and have limited use for diving in any case. If one is desired (for use in a pool perhaps) a third to a half horsepower will take care of most needs.

Some four cycle gas engines manufactured by Briggs & Stratton, Lausen, Clinton, etc. make fine power units for portable compressor outfits. Usually for five to eight cubic feet per minute a one and a half to two horsepower engine will do the job. It is much better to overpower than under since breakdowns are much less frequent. Most small engines have little automatic governors that work from the fan breeze. Once they are set, the motor theoretically maintains constant RPMs regardless of load. These are indispensible for diving use since there may be large, rapid load changes as the diver increases depth or throttles down his air, and the motor may stall at an inopportune moment if the speed is not governed. Two cycle engines are not dependable enough for diving use. Naturally, proper upkeep, oiling, alignment, etc. of all powered diving equipment cannot be overstressed.

The best stationary mounts for motor and compressor are those sold by compressor companies, made out of cast iron with adjustable fasteners to accommodate different sized units. Often it is desirable to have the outfit very light and portable and, in this case, a good mounting is easily built of two lengths of two-by-four lumber with the machines lag screwed to the wood or fastened by bolts through heavy flat plywood on top and bottom. One of the two units should be mounted so that it is moveable. Proper belt tension can thus be maintained. The belt is usually just tight enough so that there is less than an inch of play when the machines are running at rated speeds. Selection of pulleys is best taken up with the dealers who sell the equipment.

The authors have used for some years a two horse Briggs & Stratton running a Quincy compressor rated at 8 cu. ft./min. at 800 RPM. This particular compressor has given excellent service and its reasonable new purchase price of under sixty dollars make it an attractive buy. In over 400 hours of diving the outfit has never failed.

SUBSIDIARY EQUIPMENT

Since even the best kept equipment can fail, it is necessary to consider the diver's plight if and when the air stops. Of primary importance is to keep air in the mask, for if this should escape, the diver's face may be badly squeezed. A two way breathing bag will give about half a minute before the CO_2 builds up to uncomfortable values. The one-way valve at air entrance on the mask or weighted belt is thus a very vital piece of equipment. In the Desco mask the inlet plumbing at the mask has an integral one-way valve, but the Teco, or converted gas masks must have a one-way valve affixed to the weighted belt and a whip of hose run from this to the mask air inlet. *Never use a diving mask without a non-return valve at the diver.*

A second necessary safety device is a volume tank on the surface. Commercial tanks of one-half cubic foot capacity are available at moderate cost, or a 400 psi surplus oxygen cylinder may be substituted. The commercial tanks will safely hold 100 psi and have inlet, outlet, and gage holes. The pressure tank evens out the air supply pulsations and acts as an air reservoir in case the compressor should stop. It will not serve in this latter role unless a check (one-way) valve is placed between the tank inlet and the compressor so that air will not leak back through the head and by the pistons, if the air stops.

Other accessories for mask diving are, air regulators, weighted belts, and the Desco suit.

Figure 20. An 8 cubic foot a minute Quincy Compressor, 2 H.P. Briggs and Stratton, surface volume tank with pop valve and three diver manifold, and two fifty foot lengths of shallow water hose. Notice the body rope attached to the left hand hose. This is put around the chest to affix the hose to the body when swimming in the mask without a lifeline. The hose between compressor and tank is metal coated since this whip of hose must withstand hot air from the compression process.

Regulators: The Desco mask may be purchased with a manual air valve at the face, while Teco manufactures both manual and automatic regulators which are affixed to the belt. For diving with a hand pump, these valves are not only useless, but represent a constriction in the line to make the pumper's job all the harder. When more than enough air is coming down, however, valving down has the advantage that it raises the pressure in the surface volume tank and builds up a large air reserve in case of emergencies. The manual valve also permits throttling down too noisy air and stopping the air entirely for short periods when a fish is to be approached. Remember that as the compressor pumps into a high pressure region, it does not give as much air, so that some compromise as to the volume tank pressure will be required for all diving conditions. However, never use a standard surface volume tank and a manual valve together unless the tank is equipped with a pop or safety valve, set to bleed air out of the tank at 60 or 70 psi. Otherwise, an indiscriminant pressure rise may rupture the tank and injure the tender. In big operations where the diver is fed from 150 psi air banks, the valve becomes necessary to prevent the mask from being blown from the face, but for most shallow diving they are not vitally needed unless two divers are supplied from one compressor.

The Desco Suit: One of the greatest contributions to shallow diving has been the development and manufacture by the Desco people of the back entry diving dress. This non-inflated diving suit permits the diver to remain underwater for long periods of time in the coldest water, providing he wears warm clothing under his suit. The dress is made of rubberized canvas, somewhat lighter than deep water suit material. The diver enters through the back, which is then folded in pleats and locked in a brass clamp. A rubber seat around the face is designed to fit against the Desco mask, although other masks can be used. Some masks do not fit as snugly as the Desco, and when minimum air is being supplied, the diver may find water leaking in around the edges of the mask on the inhale. The reason for this is that tightening the straps of some masks pulls the sides back over the head, but not against the seal of the suit. About the only way to alleviate this condition is to supply more air to the diver. The Desco suit is primarily useful in keeping the diver warm and is not usually inflated. This could be done, but almost every task on the muddiest bottoms can be accomplished without inflation. While it is convenient to be able to regulate one's bouyancy, many new dangers come into being when there is air in the dress. Blowing up, the squeeze, losing helmet air through a suit rip are some. It is perfectly possible to drop 20 feet as rapidly as possible in the Desco suit with no squeeze discomfort. Such a trick would be very dangerous with a low capacity air supply if the suit were inflated. When working in a prone position, it is possible to blow up in a non-inflated suit, if the mask does not seat firmly on the suit seal. Although ample warning is given by gradual bouyancy in the legs, the novice diver should deliberately attempt this in shallow water to get the feel of it.

As already noted, the most advanced Desco suit has the mask permanently affixed to the face seal. This arrangement should not be used unless the divers have a good sized boat with adequate tending, emergency air equipment, and are securely anchored. When the suit and detachable mask are used, the diver can always quickly remove the mask at the surface, dump his weighted belt, and easily float until pulled into the diving boat. But with the mask on for good, it is easy to get panicky before the hinged faceplate can be raised, should any emergency occur.

Emergency Air Reserve: There may come a time when entering a wreck underwater may be necessary. Special precautions should be taken. The aforementioned volume tank holds sufficient air in case of compressor failure, to get the diver safely to the surface from moderate depths, but if it will require some minutes for the diver to clear himself, an emergency air supply tank should be placed in the air line. A large surplus oxygen flask holding 30 cubic feet at 400 psi can be easily obtained at slight cost. The tank can be conveniently charged from a 150 psi tire air supply at a gas station through an inner tube valve welded into the tank. The tank outlet should have a needle valve, marked for proper adjustment if the air is suddenly needed. This can enter the diver's line through a T connector between the regular volume tank and diver's line. A check valve should be placed so as to isolate the diver and emergency tank from the rest of the system. This tank, if properly charged and used will give five minutes of breathing at 33 feet.

Belts and Weights: Weighted belts are necessary to sink the diver and may be purchased new, surplus, or made at home. They are most easily made by buying a large cartridge belt and placing lead bricks in the pockets, or by buying thick canvas and screwing the bricks to the sides. Whenever the belt is obtained, it should be simple and quick to release underwater in case of emergencies. For walking and working on the bottom, 15 pounds is a good weight for mask and bathing suited diver; for swimming, zero to five pounds; while 30 or more pounds are needed if the Desco suit is worn. Add two to three pounds if the breathing bag is used. After the weights are suitably placed on the belt, the one-way valve is firmly affixed so that any pull on the hose line will come at the belt and not at the mask. With the Desco mask, where all air valving is at the head, the hose can be tied to the belt with heavy cord with slack hose leading to the mask. The safety line fits loosely around the chest and is affixed to the hose in the manner described in the previous chapter.

Repair and Maintenance

If, at any time following a dive the diver coughs up phlegm that is yellowish and discolored, it is possible that the compressor is throwing oil, although this condition can also result from clogged sinuses as noted in Chapter I. Under no circumstances should diving continue until the oil loss is corrected. Oil vapor entering the lungs can coat the

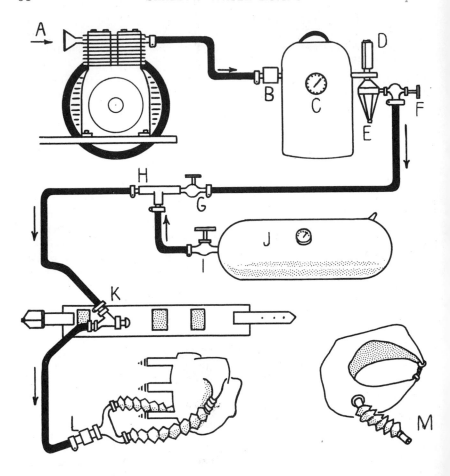

Figure 21. The complete air circuit for a one-diver mask outfit. Air enters through the compressor air cleaner (a), is sent through a one-way valve (b), into the surface volume tank (c), and comes out through an oil filter (e), and the gate valve (f). Pop valve (d) is set for 60 psi blow-off. Gate valve (g) is normally full open unless the emergency air supply tank (j) is required, when it is closed to isolate the system (h, i, j, k, l) from the compressor and volume tank. (h) is a T connection and (i) is a needle valve that is normally closed. It is marked for the desired air flow when the emergency tank is needed. (k) is the diver's air control valve and (1) is the one-way valve at the mask itself. If the Teco #402 or #403 valves are placed on the belt, the one-way valve is omitted at (1) since these valves have an integral one-way feature. If a hand pump is used in place of the compressor (b,d,e, and k) can be omitted, since they represent constructions and fulfill no useful purpose. If the emergency air supply is not required, omit (g, h, i, and j). The breathing bag (m) is attached to the mask when needed. For more than one diver, place a manifold at (e) and add more gate valves (f) to the manifold.

small air capillaries and lower the ability of these organs to supply the body with fuel. Infection can result from continual exposure to this oil vapor under pressure. Oil in the air usually comes from one of two causes. Either the compressor is running too fast or the piston rings have become worn and must be replaced. If there is any doubt on this score, an oil filter can be obtained and placed in the line between volume tank and diver. Such filters are usually obtained from compressor companies. Under no circumstances should oil be allowed near the rubber parts of a diving outfit, since it will rot and otherwise weaken them.

All equipment used near salt water should be washed often in fresh water and kept painted. White (unleaded) gasoline used in small, four cycle engines will lengthen their lives considerably, and equipment oil levels should be periodically checked.

The care of the Desco suit is an important consideration, since these suits are not cheap, even at surplus prices. Experience has shown that the Desco suit is most liable to wear out at the point on the feet where the black rubber soles meet the rubberized canvas. To protect the suit, a set of deep water diving shoes, which look somewhat like a pair of large ski boots, can be purchased. These shoes have the advantage of adding as much weight to the suit at the feet as the diver wishes to bolt on the shoes. They grip the bottom nicely and enable the diver to move about very rapidly. Never use such weighted shoes if there is any doubt about getting the diver rapidly up in the event of air failure, for a belt can be dropped while the shoes cannot in an emergency. If such shoes are too expensive, a pair of heavy rubber overshoes will do nicely in protecting the feet of the suit. If considerable work is to be done around rocks and other sharp obstructions, a set of chafing pants will go a long way in guarding the lower portions of the Desco suit.

If the diving dress shows signs of wearing through, it should be patched. This is accomplished in the following manner: Wash the suit free of salt, dry it, and clean the portion to be patched with carbon tetrachloride. Then rough up the surface with sand paper and apply three separate coats of Morse #4 patching cement; allow each coat to dry 30 minutes. Put a thin coat on the patch and allow it to become tacky, then put the patch on the exposed surface and work it down with the fingers to remove the wrinkles. A hand roller will aid in doing a neat job. Patching cement and patch material can be obtained from the Morse Diving Equipment Company.

MASK DIVING METHODS

In contrast to the helmet, getting into the water with a mask is extremely easy. The mask is put on in the boat after the compressor is running properly, and the diver goes over and down the descending line. Generally, if work or photography is to be done, the diver will require a negative bouyancy of 10 pounds or more, and a descending line will be necessary. The descent is made slowly, equalizing the ears in the manner already discussed and the tender takes care that the line is paid out easily, but if the diver should lose the descending line, the tender should hold fast to prevent a too rapid drop to higher pressures. Once on the bottom, the mask diver can go where he pleases and assume any position since the mask will operate with any diver orientation. Deep water suit divers are always amazed at the ease and naturalness of mask diving. Aside from the weights, there is practically no bulk at all to the equipment and one feels completely at home in the sea.

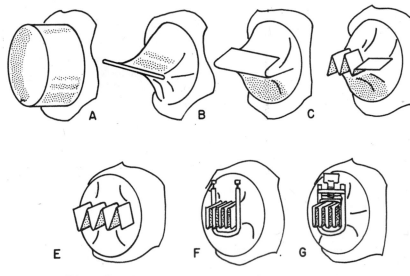

Figure 22. Illustrating the method used to seal the back of the Desco Back-Entry Suit. After the diver gets in through the tube of material, it is flattened (b), folded over once (c), pleated (d, e), and a clamp, supplied with the suit, is put over the pleats (f). Then the top of the clamp is screwed on as tightly as possible, using the fingers. If done properly, the suit is watertight to any depth.

When diving from a compressor supplying more than enough air, it is best to use the air control valve on the mask or belt to allow only just enough to enter the mask, thereby raising the surface volume tank pressure to 60 or 70 psi. A total pressure of 60 psi in the volume tank (four atmospheres) will provide 2 cubic feet of free air from a one-half cubic foot tank. This is sufficient to get the diver from 33 feet to the surface at a moderate rate with air to spare should the compressor suddenly stop. If this happens, both tender and diver will immediately be aware of it by the change in noise level in the boat and underwater. The tender immediately signals two jerks on the lines and begins pulling the diver up. Always signal first so that the diver will be prepared for the ascent that follows. The diver in turn jumps off the bottom gripping his lines with both hands and leaving any tools or equipment behind. He swims directly upward to assist the tender and on breaking surface grips his mask under the chin and lifts it bodily off so that his mouth is clear. This is not a real emergency and can be done at any time with no danger, providing the diver and tender have arranged the equipment in the manner specified in this chapter. Once the diver has reached the surface the tender must be sure to pull him to the boat rapidly so that his suit does not fill with water and force him under. With a suit and weights the diver cannot tread water and stay on the surface so if he surfaces far from the boat he may be in trouble unless he jettisons his weights. The best and safest device is a small emergency life preserver called Res-Q-Pac which inflates to a pair of water wings at a squeeze of the hand. Suit divers should always carry this unit clipped to their belt.

When using the suit the diver is very cumbersome compared to a swimmer. Should the diver lose his mask and allow water to flood into the suit he would be in a most dangerous condition.

When the diver first goes into the water he will be very boyaunt due to the air trapped in the suit, but by pushing upward on the boat and forcing himself underwater he will soon force most of the air out the escape valve and begin to sink, gripping, of course, the descending line. Suits have tight cuffs that must be pulled over the wrists very tightly. Should the diver find water seeping in at this point he may require snap tubing to cover both wrists and cuffs to produce added waterproofing. The authors have found that in very cold water it is worthwhile to purchase diving gloves and attach them to the Desco suit with clamps which may be purchased with the gloves. This makes the suit completely watertight and permits diving in the coldest water. Water may also seep in around the mask unless the lacing on the back of the head is drawn up tightly, pulling the rubber mask seat smoothly over the cheeks and forehead. The only real objection to a non-inflated suit is that one which is too large creases due to water pressure in uncomfortable places, particularly at the insteps. This can be alleviated by wearing thick underwear and possibly by allowing a little air to enter the suit from the mask when at great depths.

With a low capacity air supply, it is often noticed that water seeps into the mask during the inhale, regardless of how tight the head straps may be. While this is annoying, it is not dangerous providing the diver does not ignore the condition until enough has entered to gag him. As soon as water is noted in the Desco mask, the head is cocked to the left, placing the exhaust valve at the lowest point and the diver exhales strongly. This forces the water from the mask. With the Teco and Mine Safety masks a finger may be inserted under the chin and a water exit created while exhaling. This is necessary since in non-valved masks the air escapes from the highest point, around the forehead, unless an appreciable opening is made at a lower point. If the diver's hands are occupied so that clearing the mask is impossible, it can always be voided of water in the following manner. Tilt

Figure 23. Two Navy divers about to go under using converted Mine Safety gas masks for diving. The double air tubes go down the back to a manifold which is connected to air control valve affixed to weighted cartridge belt. Valve handle appears under right arm where it is readily available. Underwear is for warmth. (Official U.S. Navy Photograph)

the head back so that the face is pointing directly toward the surface and exhale strongly. The water will be forced from the mask from all edges, though some water may get in the eyes when this is done. This method will always work. If speeding up the compressor and pulling the straps tight do not almost stop water from coming in, a breathing bag must be added or a more powerful compressor obtained.

The air saving abilities of the breathing bag have already been discussed, but it is important to realize that the bag cannot simply be placed around the neck, connected to the mask, and used. If carelessly placed, the bag will not fill and will be useless. In any diving equipment with exhaust air escaping, the air will tend to leave the equipment at a point of lowest pressure or shallowest depth which is generally the top of the mask if the diver is upright. The entering air has three alternate paths in a mask equipped with a breathing bag. It can enter the lungs, it can enter the bag, or it can escape from the mask and be wasted. Obviously, if the mask if placed loosely on the face, the air that is not immediately inhaled will not enter a bag at neck level, but will escape at the forehead. Thus the upper straps on a bag equipped mask must be pulled very tight so that air normally escapes at the bottom. This is simple in the Desco mask, with an exhaust valve at the bottom, but must be experimented with in other masks where the air normally leaves at the cheek-forehead level. Taking the one-way bag as an example, the sequence is this: air enters and is completely taken into the lungs on the inhale, as the diver is exhaling entering air fills the neck level bag, and when this is full the air begins to escape from the bottom. The bag is secured in the proper position with a connecting strap affixed to the weighted belt which allows the bag to float up to the proper position. Be sure to affixe the bag strap in such a manner that the weighted belt can be rapidly dropped.

Difficulties arise when the diver assumes some position other than the normal standing one. If he lies on his back, the bag will be beneath him, whereas the escape valve will be at face level. Generally, in such a case the bag will fail to fill. In a face down lying position, the bag will most certainly fill, since it is the highest point in the air system. The best thing to do when first using the equipment is to try different positions while feeling the bag with one hand. It can be easily noted at what positions the bag is always remaining collapsed.

When using the bag in a two-way manner, the situation is quite similar. In this case we wish not only to have the bag fill with surface air, but we wish to be able to breath back into it, rather than exhaling all air overboard. In the Desco mask this happens quite naturally, since the escape valve is lower in the water than the bag and exhaled air quite naturally flows into the bag. CO_2 is now in the system and the required air is decreased. In the case of the recommended large (one-ninth cubic foot) bag the arrangement might be this: Mount the bag at chest level, connected to the bag by accordian tubing. Pull all mask straps tight and jam any mask exhaust valves fully shut. Put a one-way escape valve at the bottom of the bag. Now the entire system is closed except for the single escape valve. Air travels from bag to lung and back again as pure flushing air continually enters and

Figure 24. The lightweight suit with deep water gloves attached by brass clamps.

maintains the proper CO_2 concentration. The pressure within the system can never rise above the local water pressure, since excess air is continually escaping from the exhaust valve. This system has the advantage of easy breathing since the chest and bag are at the same pressure.

If a sufficient air supply is available, it is perfectly possible to keep two divers on the bottom. Each should have his own tender and both men can be supplied from the same volume tank if a manifold is attached. All surface valves should be wide open, and, if each diver has the same length and size of hose, each will get the same amount of air, providing they are at the same depth. But if one diver is hauled up, the pressure decrease on his mask will permit more air to flow in his lines and the corresponding decrease will cause discomfort to the deeper man, particularly since he needs more air in the first place. In the case of two or more divers down at once, each must have a manual air control valve and each must control his own air at all times to keep it at a comfortable minimum. If two men are to work together underwater they will have to arrange some signals since talking together underwater is difficult for the reasons explained in Chapter I. This is particularly true when there is air escaping from two masks.

SWIMMING WITH THE MASK

In areas that are so warm that no suit is required, the full versatility of the mask can be utilized. Traditionally, all surface supplied diving equipment is connected to the diver by both hose and lifelines, either separate or seized together. This is perfectly necessary for deep water gear which is weighty and with helmets or mask-suit combinations that are bulky. But with the mask and a bathing suit only, the use of a double link to the surface is not necessary for safety. To use this new method of diving, which the authors believe to be the most versatile available for all warm water diving situations, the diver must obtain floating shallow water diving hose (note that floating hose is a *type* of hose and is bought and specified as such). This hose will float with all its associated fittings so that when a coil is thrown into the water it lies out on the surface. The hose is affixed to the mask and fastened again at a belt, where it is tightly seized so that no direct pull comes on any air fitting, but only on the rubber of the hose itself. If more than one length of hose is used, the junction of the two lengths must be tied together with cord so that no pull comes here on the fittings. Finally, the boat end of the air hose must be lashed to a rail with slack hose in the boat between the lashing and the compressor. Now the diver, usually wearing swimming fins to aid in underwater movement, throws all his hose into the water before leaving the boat.

He goes into the water, clears any tangles in the hose, and starts off wherever he wishes. The hose trails along behind, and when the diver descends he pulls hose down with him. Since the hose floats, it will form a curve behind the descending diver up to the surface and cannot get tangled in coral or other obstructions unless they are actually higher than the diver. If the hose has been firmly attached to the belt, the diver need not hold it, but may swim with hands and feet, ignoring his hose until he actually reaches bottom where he must watch to see that rocks or other projections do not foul his rising lines. The diver will need only enough weight to give him a negative

Figure 25. Diving from a rocky headland off Massachusetts. With deep water dress it would be impossible to clamber down a rocky jetty, but with a lightweight suit this is an easy matter.

bouyancy of perhaps two pounds, so that he can stay on the bottom without struggling, but can rise rapidly if something should happen. Tending is not necessary with such a set up. If the air stops, the diver will instantly know it by the cessation of compressed air noise in his mask. Instead he will note a steady hiss of air draining from the volume tank. At this point he swims for the surface, exhaling naturally, and on reaching air pushes up his mask and treads water while pulling himself to the boat by the hose. Staying on the surface without air in the mask is a simple matter with one or two pounds negative bouyancy, particularly if the diver rolls over on his back, kicks strongly, and hand lines himself to the boat at a good clip. The important thing to remember in the event of air failure is that the diver should not attempt to swim up to the boat, for this could mean an underwater swim of 100 feet or more. Forget the hose and swim directly upward until the surface is reached, then head for the boat.

This is an ideal form of diving in warm, tropic seas where the number of diving personnel is limited, since two or three divers can be underwater with one man on the surface. While actual tending is not necessary, one man should always remain in the boat to keep an eye on the gear and generally look for anyone in trouble. He keeps the compressor operating smoothly, hands gear from the boat to anyone who desires it, and keeps other boats away from the diving area. The tender should know at all times the position of the divers, and assist in keeping snarls out of the various hose lines.

The authors have put three men underwater using this system many times and have never had the slightest trouble with it. In clear water the diver can easily see all of his hose and has no trouble keeping it clear of other hoses around him. Once underwater, the hose in no way drags on the diver who is just as free as if he were using self-contained equipment, until he reaches the end of his lines, of course.

In some underwater jobs, notably photography, it may be necessary to have one man wear a heavy belt so that he can use the camera without undue wavering due to currents. In this case, the heavier man is tended from the surface and uses both a hose and lifeline, while the other divers (the camera subjects perhaps) swim free with slight weight and no tender. As with other gear it is wise to have a Res-Q-Pac lifesaver so that if any diver reaches the surface in an exhausted condition he does not have to tread water or swim to stay up.

Possibly older divers may consider this a somewhat radical use of diving equipment. Actually, it is very likely the safest form of diving now possible. Not only is the diver almost neutral in the water so that he can surface easily, but he has the added safety of a hose line that will withstand more than 125 pounds of pull connecting him to his boat. With a suitable compressor and volume tank he has emergency air reserve to let him get to the surface and with fins and Res-Q-Pac he can lay in the water until fully ready to reach the boat. By using a weighted belt with a quick release hitch (described in Chapter V) he can jettison all his gear (mask and belt) without fear of losing it, for it can be hauled up on the hose at any time. The entire system has, in the authors opinion, an extremely high safety factor making it attractive to inexperienced or older divers whose endurance may not be high. Naturally when a suit with its associated weight and bulk is used, full lifelines and tending is necessary.

Figure 26. The lightweight suit showing deep water diving shoes to protect the foot area of this suit. Weights may be bolted to the soles of the shoes.

A SUMMARY OF MASK DIVING SAFETY

To the Tender

In event of air failure be prepared to assist the diver in getting his mask off.
Learn to clamp the suit properly, adjust the breathing bag, etc.
If the diver should surface and appear to be in any trouble, instantly go into the water to assist him.
Thoroughly learn the operation of all powered equipment.

To the Diver

Carry Res-Q-Pac or similar lifebelt device.
Maintain air flow at lowest comfortable level with control valve.
When swimming in coral or around a wreck, keep track of hose.
Each time you submerge check the breathing bag to see that it is filling properly.
Both tenders and divers should also follow, in general, the summary of safety in the helmet chapter.

Chapter IV

SELF-CONTAINED RECIRCULATING DIVING EQUIPMENT

One of the important and currently popular types of diving equipment is the so-called self contained type, in which the diver carries his own air supply on his person and is therefore completely independent of the surface, able to come and go freely without air hose, surface compressors or other connections. For many purposes this is a great advantage in that the diver becomes more a part of the underwater world he is entering, able to move freely through passages and around obstructing bottom formations without the encumbrance of air hose and life line which are easily caught and snagged. With such equipment a diver can descend to a wreck, enter through one opening and, leaving by another ascend to the surface, a feat obviously impossible with a trailing air hose. If the size of the necessary apparatus is small and the weight low, it is ideally suited to diving in waters where it would be difficult to use a boat and the associated compressor. Diving into a rolling sea off a rocky headland is usually simplest with self-contained equipment which can be carried to the water's edge and donned easily. In fact for all but heavy salvage work or for long periods of diving in a restricted area, the use of such equipment may be a decided advantage not only for the increased mobility, the lack of lines to the surface and the absence of compressors and tanks, but also as it frees all the people to dive; there are no line tenders.

The price which must be paid for these advantages varies with the design and utility of the equipment but in general the diver must face the added difficulties of recharging his unit, of assuming its complete infallibility and the increased dependence on his own resources, for in the event of any trouble he may have no help from above, no air reserve at the surface, no lifeline. With certain types of units using an atmosphere of pure oxygen, especially in deeper water, he has the hazard of oxygen poisoning in addition to the other diving diseases. In spite of all these factors the development of reliable commercial equipment has progressed to such an extent that their shortcomings are well known and, operated within their limitations are quite safe. It is the purpose of this and the next chapter to discuss these short-comings and evaluate the design of self-contained equipment so as to minimize the dangers and increase the reliability of such

Figure 27. The Mine Safety Appliance recirculator. This unit includes an oxygen valve, needle valve for flow adjustment, and air circulation governed by valves in the tee shaped mouthpiece. (Courtesy M.S.A.)

experimental units as the reader may build, and to suggest modifications of commercially available units to improve their practicality or safety.

RECIRCULATING PRINCIPLES

There are two basicly different principles which are in general use in self-contained diving. One involves the recirculation of a relatively small quantity of respirable atmosphere in a closed system (i.e. no exhaust), the waste products from the diver's exertions (CO_2) being continually absorbed by chemicals and replaced by pure oxygen supplied at the proper rate from a small high pressure oxygen flask. Such units are properly called *diving lungs* or counter-lungs, for they have a fabric or rubber gas reservoir, in and out of which the diver breathes (the gases passing through a chemical cannister on the way), which is in effect an artificial 'lung'. The other principle is simpler, the diver merely carries compressed air in large cylinders usually on his back, and breathing-air at a comfortable pressure is supplied by a valve, the expired air being exhausted or 'thrown away' into the surrounding water out of the diver's way.

Both these types have their own peculiar merits and disadvantages and there is no clearcut answer as to which is best. There are authorities who speak for each type. The Italian and British navies prefer the recirculating lungs because for demolition work they leave no betraying wake of bubbles at the surface; the French and to some extent the American navies use the throw-away compressed air units as there are no depth limitations imposed by oxygen poisoning.

Let us consider the recirculating lungs. These use chemicals to purify the exhaled atmosphere, which is breathed into an air reservoir and rebreathed after the lost oxygen is replenished. It is worth noting that only the oxygen which is actually taken up by the diver's lungs and burned in the body must be replaced; this is not the quantity of air breathed per minute, indeed it is many times smaller (see Table IV column (1)), and herein is one of the principle advantages of the lung. The rate at which oxygen is consumed by the body, the metabolic uptake, is governed by the activity of the diver, and may vary over a factor of six to one, depending on whether the diver is lying quietly on a sofa testing his equipment, or digging an anchor out of heavy mud in 20 feet of water. A unit which was designed to last for one hour under heavy working conditions might last up to six hours under conditions of no work. The amount of oxygen burned is, however, independent of the pressure. That is to say, for an equivalent activity on the diver's part a certain quantity of oxygen will last as long at the surface as in 25 feet of water. From Table IV in Chapter II we see that 1/28 cu. ft. per minute is a fair average. This compares with one and one half cu. ft. of air which might be breathed in an equal time using a surface supplied mask.

A person at sea level breathes between .7 and 1.5 cu. ft. per minute. This air, assuming that it is fresh, contains about 20 per cent oxygen and 79 per cent nitrogen. The lungs extract about one fifth of the available oxygen (or one-twenty-fifth of the volume of air), replacing it with an approximately equal volume of carbon dioxide. The exhaled air is thus about 16 per cent oxygen, 4 per cent carbon dioxide and 79 per cent nitrogen. If pure oxygen were breathed, the exhaled air would contain about 96 percent oxygen and 4 percent carbon dioxide. If then, we can absorb this 4 percent CO_2 chemically from a full breath of two or three liters (i.e. two or three quarts), and replace it with pure oxygen to keep the volume constant, we could breathe it indefinitely, as its composition would not change. This is the basis of operation of recirculating diving apparatus.

The absorption of carbon dioxide is accomplished by passage through a cannister of soda lime or other absorbant. This chemical is largely slaked lime, or calcium hydroxide, with a small percentage of sodium hydroxide, and is formed into small granules with an inert filler which will not disintegrate when wet. For diving purposes a high moisture content type, about 20 percent should be specified as gas absorption is more rapid. If the material becomes very wet its large surface area is cut down, greatly lowering the speed of absorption of gas, and the small content of sodium hydroxide is dissolved out giving a highly caustic alkaline solution. This can be dangerous should it get into the breathing lines, and particular care must always be taken to see that no water reaches the chemical canister in units of this type. It is not difficult to design units which prevent such liquids from getting into the diver's mouth, but such a possibility should be considered both in design and purchase of commercial units. If the recirculating lung user is not too concerned with expense, it is recommended that he obtain the absorbant Beralyme which has two major advantages over soda lime. In the first place it is much less caustic, and a self-designed unit which leaks will be much less liable to spew a strong basic solution into the user's mouth if Beralyme is used. Secondly, Beralyme is an indicator and tells whether it is still capable of absorbing carbon dioxide. When in proper condition it is pink, turning to blue as its absorption power is exhausted. Soda lime and Beralyme are obtainable from Desco, and soda lime, under the trade name Cardoxide, is also obtainable from the Mine Safety Appliance Company. Beralyme is about twice as expensive as soda lime.

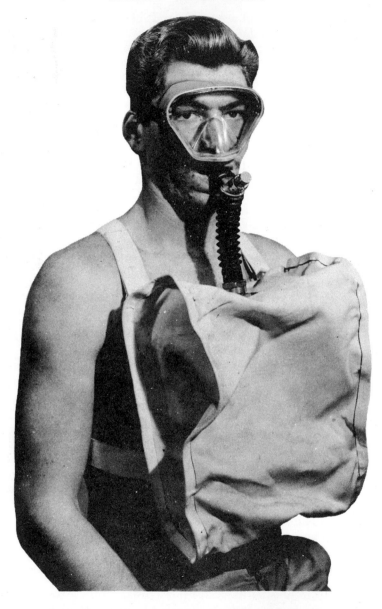

Figure 28. The Desco Model A recirculator. Oxygen bottles and absorbant cannister is inside the large breathing bag and the oxygen bottle valves are actuated through the bag. Notice the excess pressure relief valve at the mouthpiece. (Courtesy Desco)

The rate of depletion of the soda lime depends like the oxygen consumption on the activity of the diver, but for moderate work a pound of chemical will last up to one hour, during which time the diver will have burned about two cu. ft. of pure oxygen. Unlike Beralyme, there is no simple way to tell whether or not soda lime is exhausted; there is no change of color or consistency, and only a chemical analysis could be depended on. Therefore it is necessary to keep careful check on the degree of exhaustion, both by noting the total diving time on a charge, and the amount of oxygen used. Fortunately the exhaustion is gradual and the diver notes more labored breathing, with panting and discomfort, a seeming shortness of breath, signs

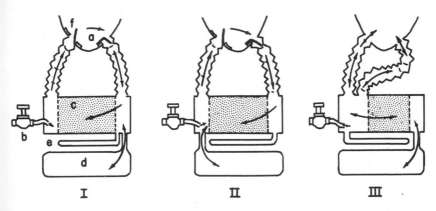

Figure 29. Three basic recirculating arrangements: a: mask or mouthpiece, b: oxygen needle valve, c: soda lime or Beralyme, d: breathing bag, e: water trap, f: rubber valves to control flow direction (should be placed in mask or at mouthpiece). Note absence of any valves in III.

which increase slowly over 10 or 15 minutes of light work, signs which should not be ignored.

Should the oxygen supply fail during a dive, there is a period of several minutes before the atmosphere in the breathing bag is gone. In 33 feet of water a four liter breathing bag containing pure oxygen would contain eight liters of oxygen (measured at sea level pressure) sufficient for more than five minutes, surely adequate time to reach the surface. As the diver rises from the bottom the gas in the system expands, and it is not difficult to adjust the rate of ascent so the system is full at all times; such a rate is much slower than is generally used in ascending, so that oxygen failure is really not a great hazard provided the diver is able to start ascending at once. Obviously from the interior of a wreck, for example, this might not always be possible. Although there is some safety factor, such situations should be avoided.

The principal advantages of the recirculating rig are: a) small size for a given diving time, b) ease of recharging (as pure oxygen is widely available and chemicals are relatively inexpensive), c) low rate of oxygen consumption, and d) silent operation. This latter point is important to underwater spear fishermen who have found the noisy blast of air escaping from conventional equipment or throw-away gear may scare wary fish.

CONSTRUCTION OF A RECIRCULATING UNIT

The main components in a rebreather lung are:

A flexible air reservoir to accommodate the air exhaled from the lungs. This bag should be of strong flexible material that is rupture proof and puncture resistant.

A high pressure oxygen flask with a needle valve to control the small amounts of oxygen.

A soda-lime cannister capable of holding one to two pounds of chemical.

A mask or mouthpiece.

A suitable mounting arrangement with air tubing, valves, etc.

Oxygen is most conveniently carried in a small high pressure flask of the type used widely in laboratories, operating rooms, and in industry, charged to 2200 psi. A four cu. ft. diver's emergency air flask is very suitable. Oxygen at this pressure is widely available from welding supply houses and is of sufficient purity to be entirely safe. There is little gain in the use of lower pressure cylinders as they become too large to contain the required amounts of gas. The valving of the high pressure gas must also be considered. Unlike the throw-away units the flow of oxygen is small and is relatively constant. It is therefore satisfactory to use needle valves of the high pressure type which are available from large scientific companies. In use it will be found that readjustments of the valve are infrequently necessary and so are no great inconvenience. Commercial units of more advanced design may use either an automatic metering unit or a demand type regulator to free the diver from any necessity to control the gas flow but these are refinements which are expensive and if not carefully constructed may be hazardous. In special cases the added complexity may be worthwhile, in general not.

The refilling of oxygen flasks is of little difficulty provided a fitting is available to connect the diving flask to a large welding cylinder. (see Figure 34). Perhaps the easiest method is to make a fitting by taking a four inch length of hexagonal brass stock, drilling a small hole lengthwise through it, tapping each end of the hole with some convenient thread (¼ inch pipe thread will do), and mounting a flask fitting at each end. The bottles may then be directly connected to a cylinder of welding oxygen and the pressure in the system allowed to equilize *slowly*. Naturally the diving bottles will not receive full pressure, the equalized pressure becoming lower and lower as the welding cylinder empties.

Figure 30. The Momsen submarine escape recirculator. The small bag with attached mouthpiece is the entire unit. The round plug in the center of the bag is unscrewed to fill a small cannister with absorbant. There is no oxygen bottle. (Official U.S. Navy Photograph)

There are three ways the apparatus may be arranged. (see Figure 29). The air on exhalation may be breathed into the reservoir and on inhalation pass through the chemical canister before reaching the lungs, or it can pass through the chemical on the exhale before reaching the breathing bag. The circulation in both cases must be governed by properly placed nonreturn valves. Mr. D. F. Comstock has shown us a unit in which the exhaled gas passes through the canister into the reservoir and again during the inhale. This design is extremely simple, there being no one-way valves. This is essentially the principle of the well known Momsen Lung, used so successfully in submarine escape.

An overlarge air-bag coupled to a mouthpiece through a small chemical canister comprises the entire unit. The bag is initially filled with oxygen or air if necessary, and the ascent from deep water is made using the oxygen available in the oversize bag. No high pressure flask of oxygen is included as sufficient oxygen is contained in the bag to allow the submariners to reach the surface. All of the three types are satisfactory, although the circulating ones, more difficult to build, restrict the air flow less and make breathing easier. In all cases the air lines should be kept large ($\frac{1}{2}$ inch diameter or more) and as short as possible.

The contemplated duration of dives with one charging of the unit largely governs the sizes of the oxygen flask and soda-lime canister. It should be remembered that any leakage of oxygen from the system must be made good from the high pressure flask. Furthermore, during a descent from the surface, oxygen must be valved in to keep the volume of gas in the system constant. This is due to the Boyle's Law effect of the water pressure on the gas. At 33 feet the breathing bag contains twice the amount of gas it did at the surface, and if the diver ascends this gas will expand and escape from the system. This represents additional oxygen loss beyond the one liter a minute demanded by metabolism. It is well to have a generous over-supply of oxygen to allow for these needs. There are other reasons why excess oxygen is important. Should the soda lime become exhausted, and breathing become more difficult, extra oxygen may be admitted and the unit operated as a throw-away unit until the diver reaches shore or a boat. In case the breathing bag should be punctured or ripped, or a large leak appear in the system, enough oxygen could be admitted to offset the leak until safety could be gained. For a rig whose calculated length of dive is one hour, the total metabolic uptake for moderate exertion would be two cu. ft. A high pressure flask, thirteen inches long by four inches in diameter filled with oxygen at 2200 psi holds four cu. ft., is conveniently small, and contains an adequate reserve. Bottles of this size are obtainable surplus from medical supply houses, or from manufacturers of mine safety apparatus.

The design of a chemical canister is important since, aside from being large enough to hold the desired amount of soda lime, it must be of the proper shape to insure efficient absorption of CO_2 yet not be too great a breathing block. It must also have a trap of some sort for any water which may collect in the system. One pound of soda lime will absorb sufficient CO_2 to sustain a diver for at least an hour doing moderate work. This figure allows some safety factor, since it is possible to stretch a pound further, but since the soda lime may not work with 100% efficiency due to bad designing of the canister, one pound an hour is a good estimate. Should sufficient water reach the chemical to wet it down thoroughly and extract the water soluble soda, not only will a very caustic solution result, but also the chemical will become very much less effective. For this reason, some space should be allowed in the canister into which small amounts of water may drain. This space should not be such that air can bypass through it around the chemical. A cylindrical canister is the best since it holds the most for a given surface area, but other shapes might be adapted. Seamless copper pipe is available from plumbers, and the two and one half or three inch size makes a fine container. A cylinder two and one half inches in diameter and nine inches long holds about one and one half pounds of soda lime when

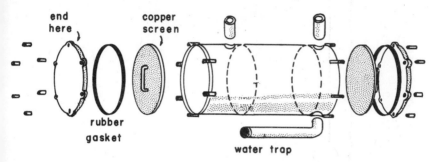

Figure 31. A typical absorbant cannister design. The screening fits into the dotted lines and the gasket and end pieces are bolted on each end. The breathing bag can exit at either end depending on the choice of flow arrangement, but its tube should be on top of the cannister. The oxygen can enter at any point. With this type of simple water trap, inverted swimming will not be safe unless the diver is sure no water has entered the unit. For arrangement III Fig. 29, the gas enters at one end; the bag hose is affixed at the other. Then gas flows in both directions.

full. The length of chemical portion of the cannister should be at least twice the diameter so that the air can traverse sufficient chemical to absorb completely the CO_2. There should be no chemical through which the air does not pass, no pockets or traps where the soda lime may accumulate and not be subject to air. Copper screening should be used at each end of the canister to prevent the pellets or granules of soda lime from being sucked into an air line. Window screening or any fine mesh which will contain the chemical is all right, except that iron screening may rust, and if used should be inspected frequently. Cotton batting is unsatisfactory since it will not pass air easily when wet.

The breathing bag operates as the reservoir for the air after it has been exhaled from the lungs. The bag may contain purified air which has been passed through the chemicals, or air which will be purified before it returns to the lungs. This depends on individual design.

Figure 32. Recirculator built by the authors. Mouthpiece has a shut off valve which has proved to be very useful. The excess pressure vent is simply a short length of tubing with a fine slit which passes oxygen into the water only when there is an excess in the system. The air circuit has no valves.

Obviously the bag should be made of some flexible material which will collapse readily as the air is removed from it by the diver. The volume, when distended, should be larger than the volume of air in a deep breath, two quarts or greater usually being sufficient. Some persons may require a somewhat larger bag, and a larger bag tends to offset the volume changes due to change in depth or small excesses in gas when the needle valve has been improperly set. Mounting problems become more difficult as the bag size is increased, and some compromise must be made after the shape of the bag has been decided upon. The aforementioned Desco breathing bag is not large enough for this use, although two might serve. The choice of material for the reservoir depends largely on what is available. Light diving suit material is best, but poncho material or fairly heavy rubber sheeting may be satisfactory. Some air pillows, if they are rugged, make good reservoirs. The material should be tough and waterproof.

The authors have found that a good grade of convertible top covering material is very satisfactory for breathing bags. It is very similar to diving dress material in construction; it is composed of two sheets of light canvas bonded together with a layer of gum rubber; it is completely waterproof and tears with great difficulty. It may be cemented and joined with diving suit patching material, using neoprene bonding cement, and then stitched by machine for greater strength.

The authors have seen a breathing bag made by Robert Edgerton from an inner tuber of the motor-scooter variety. It was worn about the neck like a collar, and was satisfactory for light duty. Should the reader have trouble with the breathing bag, he can obtain a finished bag of the correct capacity (about four quarts) from a surplus Mine Safety breathing unit, or purchased from the company as a spare part.

The bag should be mounted at upper chest level. Any other position will make either the exhale or the inhale difficult and tire the diver.

The oxygen can enter from the needle valve at any point in the system that is convenient, since the oxygen will mix with the air anywhere. Some provisions must be made to recharge the oxygen cylinder. Most small oxygen cylinders, especially of the surplus aviation type, have an outlet that requires a medical fitting. This is identical to the fitting used with welding oxygen cylinders except that it fits against a flat seat and requires a flat ended nipple. Since the welding cylinders use a round ended nipple, a charging fitting can be made from one of these, merely by facing it off in a lathe. The nuts are identical. Other cylinders, particularly the standard bail-out bottle, require a yoke clamping over part of the valve mechanism. This yoke is used in medicine for anaesthesia administration, and is best bought from a medical supply house as it is difficult to find anywhere ease. Recharging is done in the same manner as with the large bottles used in the throw-away outfits. Even though the large welding cylinder is brought down to 1000 psi, the diver will still be able to make dives of adequate length. Any fittings carrying oxygen pressures of 2200 psi should be completely clean of grease, water, or dirt of any kind. The grease or oil would flash or explode and cause

Figure 33. Some representative surplus 2200 psi oxygen flasks. From right to left; 15 cubic foot, 6 cubic foot, 4 cubic foot, and 1 cubic foot bail-out bottle. The 15 and 6 foot bottles have on-off valves which are not suitable for air metering. The bail-out bottle has a non-waterproofed gauge and a needle valve. It is suitable for an emergency air supply.

serious damage. It is for this reason that guages used with high pressure oxygen always read, "Use No Oil." Sea water in the flask is also to be avoided with great care, since the pure oxygen in great concentration speeds up rusting many times and can quickly weaken an air bottle to the point where it might explode while charging is taking place. To prevent this from happening, a flask should always have a few pounds pressure in it to keep contamination from getting in. Dirt in the needle valve can stop the air at a bad moment.

The mask or mouthpiece is a device that may give some trouble if the requirements are not thoroughly understood. The main difficulty here is that positive pressure exists in the mask and the tendency is for the air to escape around the corners of the mask. Converted gas masks, such as the Mine Safety Mark III are generally unsatisfactory since they are designed to seal against the face only when a slight vacuum exists within. Of the masks described in this book, the Desco seems to have the most desirable characteristics for use with a recirculating outfit. This opinion is substantiated by the fact that Desco sells a recirculating outfit using their mask with an oxygen flask and a container with Baralyme. The reason that the Desco is superior for this use lies in the fact that the Desco was designed to seal on a suit, and tightening the straps on this mask forces it against the face, rather than back over the head. If another mask is to be used, it must be modified to make it suitable. This modification consists of placing rubber sheeting all around the inside, glued to the mask at the outer edge. If this is done properly, the positive pressure in the mask will hold this flap against the face, and no gas will escape. It is very important that nothing escapes from the mask, because the loss represents a drain on the small gas supply carried. Probably the most satisfactory solution to the mask problem, and also a simple one is not to use a mask at all, but a mouthpiece. A mouthpiece is perfect for a recirculating outfit because there is no way for water to get into the system around the face, or for air to get out. Excess volume of gas in the system is easily blown out past the mouthpiece or exhaled through the nose into the mask.

A very useful addition also is the use of a shut-off valve at the mouthpiece. The British, who pioneered the development of soda-lime equipment use such a valve on much of their equipment, e.g. the "Salvus" manufactured by Siebe, Gorman. It is very convenient while swimming along the surface to be able to shut off the equipment and breathe surface air, thus conserving oxygen, and allowing normal conversation. The unit can be kept ready to go, with the breathing bag inflated, and put into operation merely by a quarter turn of the mouthpiece valve. A small self-contained unit can be worn as a safety measure in addition to the other diving equipment, and be kept ready to go at any depth with a mouthpiece shut-off. Such a valve also prevents water from getting into the interior of the equipment, always a potential source of trouble.

The connecting air lines in the apparatus should be of large internal diameter, $\frac{1}{2}$ inch and up. They should also be as short as possible. Accordion tubing from gas masks is the best. If this cannot be obtained cheaply from surplus outlets, it can be obtained from medical supply houses where it is sold to users of pulmotor and anaesthesia equipment. This tubing is used to connect the mask with the canister, and to bleed air from the needle valve into the system.

Mounting the components is important, since compactness is a measure of utility. All controls should be easily available, and no normal body motions impeded. One simple arrangement is to mount the cylinder of oxygen, chemical canister, and the breathing bag on a sheet of aluminum or copper with the mask or mouthpiece attached by accordion tubing. This may be strapped on the chest by wide

Figure 34. Charging fitting connecting a large oxygen storage cylinder with the recirculator bottle. The left hand fitting on the connector should fit a standard welding oxygen fitting so that these bottles can be rented and used as oxygen supply. The bottle on the right is a divers emergency supply bottle with a needle valve (projection on farthest right).

bands over the shoulders and around the waist. A Mae West life preserver makes a good mount with the securing straps sewed directly to it. If the system is a circulating one, small rubber flap valves must be placed in the mask or mouthpiece to keep the air going in the right direction. These valves are easily cut from thin inner tubes and mounted so that they blow open when the air flows in the desired direction, but seat firmly to close the line when the flow is in the opposite direction.

The unit when completed should be tested thoroughly in the air before any attempt is made to dive with it. Preliminary testing includes checking the reservoir and canister for leaks, and the mask air lines, and reservoir for constrictions and proper valve operation. When the canister is fully charged with soda lime, it should be possible to take a deep breath and breathe comfortably for several minutes until the volume of air in the reservoir has grown noticeably less. When this happens, more oxygen is valved in to fill the bag again. The needle valve may be left slightly open so that oxygen is added as used, and with practice, it can be left alone for five or six minutes before resetting is necessary. If all this can be accomplished on land, the diver is ready for underwater testing in shallow water, and finally for the full scale diving. When testing this apparatus underwater for the first time, it is convenient to have another diver, or at least a man in swimming goggles watching the operation from underwater. There should be *no bubbles escaping* from this apparatus if it is working properly.

OXYGEN POISONING

Even before 1900 experiments were conducted to determine the effect of breathing pure oxygen both at atmospheric and at higher pressures. Although it was noted during these experiments that damage to lung tissue occurred in test animals at high pressures (up to 300 psi) it was not until the 1930's that carefully controlled experiments for humans were conducted. A complete account of these is given by R. H. Davies in *Deep Diving and Submarine Operations;* we will quote only the conclusions reached by Behnke in 1936. He found that under quiesent conditions men could breathe pure oxygen at an equivalent pressure of 66 feet of water for three hours, at 99 feet for only one half hour. Continuance of the experiments beyond these periods however, resulted in the symptoms of oxygen poisoning.

During World War II these conclusions had to be modified in the case of divers and frog-men using self-contained apparatus with pure oxygen. Experiments by groups in England and Germany have been published since the war which show that men who must exert themselves in the depths are much more prone to oxygen poisoning than men who are only moderately exercising. It was noted that different persons exhibited varying susceptibility to undiluted oxygen, and that it was generally unsafe to exceed a depth of 35 feet. It appears that in shallower water, unlimited diving on oxygen has no adverse effects. Although many people can successfully reach greater depths (up to 90 feet for short periods) without harm, no general rule giving the maximum safe depth will encompass such varying factors as water

temperature, activity of the diver, and the diver's natural susceptibility. Small amounts of CO_2 in the diving apparatus due perhaps
to incomplete absorption by the soda-lime or too much dead air
space may also increase a person's sensitivity. For this reason any
recirculating apparatus must have short lines and minimum spaces
for exhaled air to collect and not pass through the absorbant. The
designer of a system using the gas flow circuit III in Figure 29 must
thus be careful that he does not have a large volume of tubing in which

Figure 35. An interesting home made recirculator by Mr. Robert Keagle of Minne-
apolis. The unit uses two large bottles and a single Desco breathing bag as an air
reservoir. As noted in the text, this air bag is not quite large enough, but with the
great available air supply in this unit would probably serve. Mr. Keagel uses the
equipment to spear carp in Minnesota waters and one is shown on the spear. (Travis
Photo)

CO_2 can collect, since this will bring on oxygen poisoning all the faster. In the case of gas circuits I and II in the same figure, note that valves are at the mask rather than somewhere else in the system. If this is done, only the mask or mouthpiece, having insignificant volume, will contain gas which is not continually driven through the absorbant. The British frogmen were limited to 35 feet, and apparently had little trouble save for the few times the hazards of war forced them to descend to greater depths.

The onset of oxygen poisoning, resulting from a disregard of the safe depth, is characterized by twitching of the lips, followed by dizziness and nausea. These symptoms should not be ignored, for convulsions follow, which underwater would probably prove fatal, as a result of the diver's inability to retain the mouthpiece. Recovery from the initial symptoms is usually complete a few minutes after return to surface air. If exposure to hazardous pressure conditions is prolonged however, there is no guarantee that permanent damage will not occur. A diver who notices muscle twitching, especially about the lips should therefore surface immediately, and cease using the oxygen apparatus. No difficulties will be experienced if such action is taken at once.

For the reader who has become discourged by such a list of hazards, let us say that in water shallower than 35 feet, the use of pure oxygen is entirely safe. The above exposition was for the purpose of aquainting divers with the effects expected at depths greater than this, and was not intended to frighten those who might use such equipment in less than 35 feet of water.

There have been many attempts to design closed circuit diving equipment which will in some manner avoid the poisoning due to pure oxygen, yet preserve the main advantages of the soda-lime design, mainly: low consumption of gas, silent operation, and little or no exhaust gas. The German Draeger Works designed a unit with flasks of both nitrogen-oxygen mixture, and air-oxygen mixture; the gases escaped from a small nozzle into a venturi. These entering gases circulated helmet atmosphere through a carbon dioxide absorbant, some excess of gas being exhausted overboard. Three point six liters per minute of this gas mixture flowed from high pressure flasks; this amount was sufficient to circulate over 90 liters per minute of the helmet atmosphere through the absorbant. A small amount of exhaust gas escaped constantly from a valve in the helmet, and the helmet atmosphere always contained nitrogen in addition to oxygen. The entire equipment, using a deep-water type helmet with 40 cu. ft. of gas compressed into cylinders carried on the back was suitable for depths to 120 feet, and at such a depth, would allow a dive of one and one-half hours.

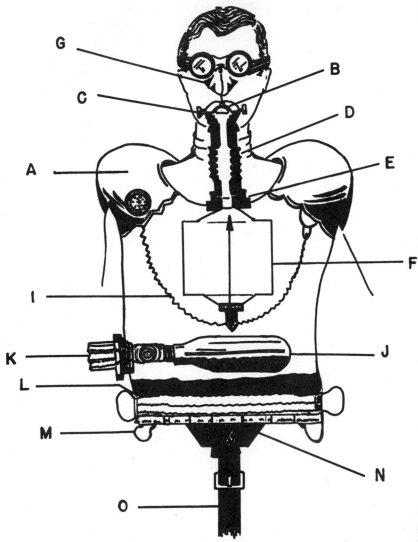

Figure 36. A self-contained recirculator of German Draeger design, redrawn from a captured enemy document. This is similar in gas circuit to the Desco Model A. The lettering applies as follows: a: breathing bag, b: mouthpiece, c: mouthpiece stopcock, d: accordian tubing, e: fitting for filling cannister, f: absorbant cannister, g: noseclamp, i: wire spring to support cannister inside bag, j: oxygen flask, k: hand wheel for gas flow regulation, l: buckles, m: spring clamp so that bag can be opened and closed, n, o: girth straps. The goggles are pressure relieved by a tiny tube running from the mouthpiece, but this is sloppy design. With a mask, the unit should be satisfactory.

Other somewhat different techniques have been developed by the British to circumvent the 35 foot limitations imposed by pure oxygen. In most cases the designs have depended either on forced flow of helmet atmosphere using a venturi (as in the Draeger unit) or on a gas metering system which operates at a pre-set rate independent of the diver's depth or depletion of the gas reserve. All this equipment must be highly engineered to operate successfully, for as we shall see presently, too little oxygen can be as dangerous as too much, and the metering mechanisms must preserve just the right balance of nitrogen to oxygen despite all changes in environment. Such complex equipment requires careful computations in addition to foolproof design, beyond the capabilities of most amateurs.

With the exception of highly specialized commercial equipment which uses oxygen-nitrogen mixtures, it is unsafe to use any gas *but* pure oxygen in closed-circuit rebreather lungs. The reason for this is not generally known, but has been well established. Consider a rebreathing unit whose breathing bag is initially charged with *air*. As the oxygen is taken up by the diver, the concentration of nitrogen in the lung increases progressively until, if the diver were not to release fresh oxygen, the atmosphere would be pure nitrogen. There would be no oxygen remaining to support life, and the diver would asphyxiate. The great hazard here is: *There Is No Warning.* The diving lung still is 80 percent full of gas (at sea level pressure) and the usual warning of depleted oxygen, increasing carbon dioxide (which makes breathing difficult) is entirely absent. In a submarine forced to submerge for too long a period, the exhaustion of the oxygen is noticed only because of the ever increasing CO_2 concentration which gives adequate warning of impending danger. In a diving lung we remove the CO_2 chemically, and there is no discomfort, even to the point of actual damage to brain tissue from gradual depletion of the oxygen. For this reason rebreathing units should only be charged with pure oxygen, and no trace of air should remain in the breathing bag or in the diver's lungs before submerging. To purge a system of air before diving, put the unit on, and fill the lung with oxygen. Inhale deeply from the breathing bag and exhale (through the nose for example) into the air. Refill the bag from the oxygen flask and repeat. After filling the lung from the flask take care to breathe only from the lungs thus avoiding the introduction of more air. In this manner, all complications arising from excess nitrogen may be avoided.

It is important to remember that the absorption of CO_2 should be as efficient as possible, as the use of pure oxygen seems to make the diver more sensitive to low concentrations of this waste gas. Incomplete CO_2 removal, coupled with extreme exertion on the diver's part may result in a severe headache after surfacing.

Figure 37. The Desco Model B recirculator. This unit is similar to the Mine Safety gear and has about the same features. The large valve on the bottle is an on-off device used in charging the flask. The small valve above the gauge is for fine control of oxygen flow. Cannister is on the back and the shoulder mounting is the breathing bag. (Courtesy Desco)

COMMERCIAL RECIRCULATING EQUIPMENT

There are currently two major companies producing recirculators of various types in the United States. One is Desco, which makes three units of differing complexity and price. The Desco model A lung is a simple unit operating on gas circuit III shown in Figure 29. The lung has a large breathing bag which contains two oxygen bottles, one for normal use and the other for reserve. The valves on the bottles are operated through the rubber fabric of the bag and are thus completely protected from the salt water, while at the same time, they are easily reached by the diver. It is difficult to imagine a recirculator of simpler design than this, and the unit would probably be best for the inexperienced and casual diver. The Desco model B is a more advanced unit at a higher price. It uses gas circuit II in Figure 29, and comes equipped with the Desco mask rather than a mouthpiece. The single cylinder contains eight cu. ft. of oxygen, and is equipped with a pressure guage to maintain check on the gas supply. The most complex recirculator on today's market is the Model C which uses gas circuit II plus many other refinements. The oxygen is metered through an orifice at one liter (1/28 cu. ft.) per minute. During times of exertion, the orifice can be bypassed permitting extra oxygen to enter the system. A bouyancy control lever is available to the diver which controls the degree of inflation of the breathing bag, permitting him to rise or sink at will. For deep water work an added cylinder will admit nitrogen or helium to do away with the oxygen poisoning difficulty, but this is nothing for the average diver to play with. The Model C is a most interesting piece of equipment, but probably not within the reach of the average amateur. In any case, its many controls would very likely confuse the inexperienced diver who will do well to stick to the Model A or B.

The Mine Safety Appliances Company, a very respected firm in the respiration field, also make an underwater recirculator similar to the Desco Model B. This unit has a large breathing bag as shown in the photograph, Figure 27, and forced circulating of air. It is apparently very similar to the Model B except for the different mask. Notice particularly the pressure release valve on the top of the mouthpiece which the amateur constructor would do well to include

Another recirculator that is gradually finding its way into the country is the Pirelli. This unit is very small and compact with a tiny absorbant chamber and small bottle. The oxygen bottle has a spring loaded valve that can be depressed with one finger, and closes automatically when released, a very neat feature. Another interesting aspect of this unit is the mask-snorkel combination to be worn on the head. The mask has a three-way valve which permits breathing from

Figure 38. The Desco Model C lung. This is a very complex and expensive unit. The absorbant cannister is at the top, breathing bag next, and two oxygen bottles with a regulator at the bottom. The standard Desco mask is used with a pressure excess relief valve under the chin. (Courtesy Desco)

the air, from the lung, or from the snorkel. The mask is, unfortunately, rather difficult to put on, and fits very tightly over the entire head. It might therefore be dangerous if something went wrong, since removing it would be a rather long job. Although the authors have not used this equipment, it appears that the headpiece should be replaced by a Desco type mask that is easily removed, before any serious diving is attempted.

The British have designed and built a large number of very involved recirculators for various military jobs, but for some reason they have had no interest in exporting any units to the United States. The previously mentioned Salvus is rather bulky and awkwardly designed, with the bottle at the diver's waist far from the other portions of the equipment.

The reader should be very cautious in purchasing surplus equipment that he does not attempt to use a regenerating unit such as the Mine Safety Chemox, for underwater work. This equipment uses one canister which contains a chemical to absorb the carbon dioxide and supply new oxygen simultaneously, an attractive idea. Unfortunately the reaction occurs due to the reaction of chemicals with moisture in the breath. Should a lot of water suddenly contact the chemicals, the unit might explode, and granules in the mouth of the user can burn the tissues. *Under no circumstances should such a unit be used for diving.*

One basic device the recirculating user must have is a depth guage. A very simple one is available at moderate cost utilizing a plastic tube in which surface air is trapped and compressed underwater. The guage reads depth very clearly and is entirely suitable for fixing the safe limits for oxygen poisoning prevention. It can be obtained from almost any supplier listed in Appendix B of this book.

Weighted belts are, of course, another necessity for the recirculator if it is to get underwater. A four quart breathing bag will require eight pounds of weights to sink it and the canister and associated air lines will take more. For swimming in the average recirculating outfit, 10 to 15 pounds of weights will be necessary.

USE AND MAINTENANCE OF RECIRCULATING DIVING EQUIPMENT

Once the principle of recirculating equipment is well understood there should be no difficulty with its proper operation. With new units, a 20 minute trial above water will aquaint the diver with the basic operation, and some time spent in shallow water will illustrate the effect that pressure and orientation have on ease of breathing. The breathing bag should be kept inflated to a comfortable level by careful setting of the needle valve. The diver has limited control of his underwater weight through this adjustment; in some cases the fully inflated breathing bag has sufficient bouyancy to act as a life preserver if the mouthpiece valve is shut. It is important that care be taken to avoid the entrance of water into the breathing system. This is accomplished by always having the mouthpiece valve shut save when the unit is in operation.

Manufacturers recommend that oxygen flasks never be emptied completely, but just before exhaustion be shut off and removed from service while still containing a few pounds pressure. In diving service this is particularly good advice, for salt water (or even fresh) has vastly increased rusting power under the influence of oxygen or air at high pressure; a weak, internally rested area in an air bottle would be undetectable yet a severe hazard.

After use in salt water all equipment should be washed in fresh water and stored in a dry place. Residual salt will rot fabric and rubber parts, and gradually corrode bronze or brass fittings. Needless to say, neither iron, steel, nor aluminum are practical materials for use around salt water, although anodized aluminum if kept painted will work well in fresh water.

Screws and nuts and semi-permanent joints in equipment can be disassembled more easily after use in salt water if they are coated with colloidal lead pipe compound before assembly. This compound prevents galling of threaded parts by forming a thin plating of lead, eliminating frozen screws, etc.

Once the recirculator user has tested his equipment thoroughly in waist deep water, or in a swimming pool, acquainted himself with the controls, and spent some time going up and down to shallow depths of not more than 10 or 15 feet, he is ready to put the unit to work in the open sea. The unit should fit comfortably on the body and be strapped so that the bouyancy of the breathing bag will not force the assembly out of place on the chest or back. In the water the re-circulator diver can hold onto the boat while purging the air from the system and then fill the bag with oxygen and submerge. A descending line is necessary at first since it may be necessary to fiddle with the valve while descending, and if he is not careful, the diver will be sinking as he is preoccupied with his equipment. Once the lung-user is well acquainted with his equipment, lines will no longer be necessary and the diver can swim freely about. It is most strongly recommended that no self-contained diving be done alone, and that the recirculator equipped diver always use the 'buddy system'. One mistake that amateur divers often make is to be bashful about rendering assistance to another diver on the grounds that it might embarrass the assisted one if he really didn't need help. This may result in one man floating around uselessly watching another desperately clawing for the surface, and then finally going over when the situation has gotten desperate. If there is ever the slightest doubt about the behavior of a 'buddy' in the water, get over to him at once, note what he is doing so as to diagnose the trouble, and then help without confusing the situation further. Alternatively, if you are in trouble, signal for help at once and go for the surface. Nobody is a 'sissy' because he can't get his air supply to operate, or gags on a mouthful of water.

Even the best designed unit will have a little moisture in it after use, simply because the humid air from the lungs is cooled and releases some of its water while traversing the air passages. The maximum amount per hour due to this cause is only one or two ounces, and will not create a serious hazard.

Chapter V

SELF-CONTAINED THROW-AWAY DIVING EQUIPMENT

The simpler type of self-contained diving equipment consists merely of one or more flasks of compressed air, carried by the diver plus a valve mechanism to meter the air into a mask, helmet, or mouthpiece. The tanks are usually carried on the back, supported with a canvas or web-strap mount with the regulator secured to the tank outlet. There is no basic difference between such units and conventional shallow water gear supplied by a surface pump. The air requirements are the same as for a mask diving outfit with a one-way breathing bag, for the air only flows from the tanks when the diver inhales and is conserved on the exhale. For this system Table IV in Chapter II gives an average air demand of one cu. ft./min. Unlike the diving mask, however, air must not be wasted since there is not an inexhaustable supply as when a compressor is pumping in the open air. Along with the basic tank and air regulator, some throw-away units are equipped with an extra or emergency air supply to prevent the diver from running out of air unaware in deep water.

Generally, the exhaled air is never trapped in the apparatus, but is exhausted or 'thrown away' into the water. There is thus no problem of CO_2 concentration, although this means a somewhat larger air demand. There is also no problem with oxygen poisoning, but the amount of compressed gas used is 28 times greater in the throw-away than in the recirculator and increases with increasing depth and increasing exertion. Unless the tanks are of high capacity, the diver finds his time submerged may be very limited before he is forced to the surface to replace or recharge the tanks. The throw-away principle (known in Europe as the *open circuit* principle) has the main advantages of simplicity and of supplying fresh air with the attendant absence of chemicals or hoses to the surface.

THE DEMAND REGULATOR

The air supply mechanism must supply large quantities of air during the inhale, but should not be discharging during the exhale. For this reason a needle valve, such as are commonly used to control oxygen flow in the recirculator, is not too satisfactory. There has been one unit on the diving market which utilized a constant flow needle valve and a breathing bag at the chest to catch the air while the diver exhaled.

(102)

Figure 39. View of the "Aqua-Lung." Notice the position of the regulator above the tank and the emergency air supply release handle extending down the side of the compressed air flask. Swimming fins and a mask complete the outfit.

On the exhale, air from the lungs went overboard as in the conventional throw-away. This is not a suitable diving rig for anything but the shallowest water and simplest task, for any change of depth or exertion will require a large change in air supplied and air must be wasted no matter how often the diver resets the needle valve handle. All other throw-away equipment uses the demand regulator. This is a valve mechanism which is actuated by the pressure (or lack of it) in the air line leading to the diver's mouth and only operates when the lungs are producing a reduced pressure in this region, i.e. on 'demand'. The slight pressure existing in the breathing tubes during exhale is sufficient to close the valve and stop the flow of air. Such a principle is not new with diving, being used in welding regulators for many years, and was put to work during the war to meter oxygen to aviators at great altitudes. Commercial diving equipment utilizing such a regulator is manufactured in England by Seibe Gorman & Company, in the United States under the name Scott Air Pack, by Desco, by the Sea Net Company, by Diver's Supply Company, and (under a French patent) by the U.S. Divers Company who distribute the Aqua-Lung. Of these various rigs, the Aqua-Lung is best known, having been developed in France by Jaques-Yves Cousteau and Emile Gagnan in 1942-43. All of these demand type units deliver air freely, without reference to the diver's depth, for the automatic valve operates on the basis of pressure differential created by lung suction.

In the Aqua-Lung, for the first time, the exhaled air was exhausted close to the diaphragm controlling the flow of air. In this manner no possible position of the diver can place the exhaust valve above the diaphragm, thereby preventing the water pressure from actuating the valve and venting air uselessly into the water. The regulator assembly is of the two stage type designed specifically for diving use. In the United States the tanks are of alloy steel containing 38 or 70 cubic feet of air at a pressure 10% over the rated pressure of 2200 psi (such an excess is tolerated since World War II). The Junior model uses a single 38 cubic foot tank, the standard one a 70 cubic foot tank, and the Navy double tank block uses two 70 cubic foot tanks. In Europe the tanks are of somewhat smaller internal volume, are made of duraluminum, and are pumped to 3000 psi, a pressure not allowed in this country. Many of the foreign units have an air reserve valve projecting from the bottom of the tank.

The regulator operates in the following manner (see Figure 40): The high pressure air from the reservoir goes through a filter screen into an intermediate pressure reducer which keeps the pressure in a small internal cavity at a constant value (around 60 psi) despite the gradual drop in the main flask pressure. The release of the intermediate pressure air is governed by a valve mechanism coupled to a flexible diaphragm which separates the low pressure chamber (connected to the breathing tube) from the water. When the diver inhales, the slight decrease in pressure in this chamber deflects the diaphragm inward and opens the air valve, releasing a supply of air. When the diver stops inhaling, sufficient air escapes to force the diaphragm outward and halt the flow. To make breathing easy, the diaphragm must respond easily and quickly to very small pressure differentials.

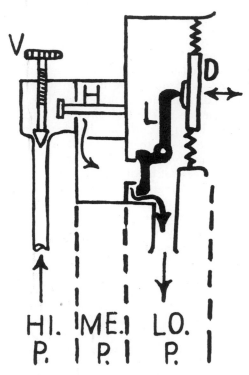

Figure 40. A schematic of the Aqua-Lung regulator. Air enters from the high pressure bottle, and is turned off by the valve (V) when the lung is not in use. The high pressure regulating valve (H) controls the flow into the medium pressure section (details not shown). When air is withdrawn from the low pressure exit tube, the diaphragm (D) moves inward actuating the lever (L) which opens the passage between the medium and low pressure sections. The air, after traversing the tubes and lungs, must exit close to (D) in the water.

It is this sensitivity which makes it necessary to have the air exhaust valve (a non-return type) mounted close to the diaphram, for otherwise small differences in water pressure between it and the diaphragm might force the rubber inward and actuate the air release continuously, thereby draining the tank rapidly.

The customary arrangement has rubber accordian type tubing connecting the regulator to the mouthpiece (newer designs use neoprene, a snythetic and vastly superior material). As the regulator is mounted at the top of the tank, which is carried on the back, the regulator is in back of the neck so the two tubes pass on each side of the head. This would appear to be a wise system since a single tube will drag unevenly on the mouth and tire the jaw muscles used in gripping the mouthpiece.

The regulator is coupled to the tank with a yoke mechanism very similar to the standard medical fitting, although the seat has a plastic gasket and is not a metal to metal contact. The standard tank has only a shut off valve, operated by a wrench, but a special air reserve device is available for those who may dive in deep water (over 30 feet) or under hazardous conditions such as in wrecks. This consists of a small spring loaded constriction in the high pressure air passage. While the tank pressure is high the air has no difficulty traversing the constriction, but when the pressure drops to roughly 300 psi ($\frac{1}{8}$ of the tank capacity) the air passes with difficulty and definite warning is given the diver by the decreased ease of breathing. This is an infallible signal that air is running short. The diver then opens the air reserve valve on the tank which releases the spring loaded constriction and allows the remaining air free access to the regulator. Sufficient diving time is made available in this way to allow the diver to reach the surface easily. This feature is commonly omitted, at the divers descretion, if no diving is attempted in greater than 30 to 40 feet of water. With a little practice it is possible (usually) to forecast half a minute or more before the tank empties. In 40 feet of water, however, if the air stops suddenly during the pursuit of a fish, the diver might experience difficulty in gaining the surface, and would run the risk of air embolism should he foolishly hold his breath in the rush upwards. If there is the slightest doubt on this score, the air reserve is a vital item, and can be obtained from the U.S. Divers Company. Mr. Bussoz of this company informs us the price is $25. Since the reader who may have a non-air reserve unit will have invested up to $150, this reserve valve can be considered as an insurance policy against having to dump the entire lung in a bad spot when the air runs out.

The exhaust valve is of the small rubber flap type, similar to those used in gas masks. It should be checked occasionally as salt, or small particles of debris may prevent its closing properly, resulting in water being drawn into the mouth on inhaling. The rubber may deteriorate with age and should be replaced if the region near the metal is cracked. It can be very serious to the user if the valve comes off or entirely fails.

A diving mask of the sort used in spear fishing is commonly worn, covering the nose and eyes. Goggles are not adaptable to Aqua-Lung diving as there is no means of introducing air into them as one descends. They are pressed onto the face with increasing pressure, soon becoming unbearable. In a descent wearing a mask one exhales slightly through the nose to offset the pressure. As with mask diving, the diving mask may be cleared of water by leaning the head back so that the face is pointed directly upward and exhaling vigorously through the nose.

Most of this previous discussion has dealt specifically with the Aqua-Lung since this is in such common useage, but much of it applies to other equipment of this general type. The Scott Air Pack is made mainly for rescues in smoke filled houses and is not too successful for diving since its exhaust is at the mouth and the regulator diaphragm is at the back of the head. The Desco model was not yet in production at time of writing and no information was available. The Sea Net lung known as a Frogman Breathing Unit is very similar to Aqua-Lung with two tubes and regulator on the top of the back tank. Most inexpensive of these throw-away units is the Sport Diver marketed on the West Coast. The diver who uses this gear is taking a chance since it is definitely not as safe as other somewhat more costly rigs. The regulator, which appears to be single stage only, is at the diver's mouth which keeps the diaphragm and exhaust at the same pressure, but this means high pressure hose must lead from the back to the mouth. The single tube would make gripping the mouthpiece hard while swimming due to the water drag. New devices will appear on the market after this book has gone to press, and it is important that the reader understand the fundamentals of good design in diving so that he can evaluate products as they occur. The mere appearance of a product on the market does not guarantee its safety. Ear plugs are sold by many companies for diving though they are obviously dangerous and undesirable. The consumer must be the final judge and reject any device which violates safety in any way.

ACCESSORIES

It is customary with the Aqua-Lung type of equipment to wear swim‧ fins, and only sufficient weight to balance the diver in the water. In this way the diver is free to swim about and rise or descend at will. Usually from two to six pounds of lead or iron is sufficient unless the diver wears a waterproof suit with underwear or sweaters underneath. In this case 12 to 15 pounds may be necessary. Suppliers of the Aqua-Lung furnish a web belt with one pound iron weights drilled with a slot so that they can be slipped on or off the belt at will to adjust one's bouyancy. The belt should always be knotted after the weights are on or weights will be lost during diving operations. It is imperative that the weights be instantly removable at any time in the water. D. Rebikoff suggests the quick release hitch shown in Figure 42 which accomplishes this action with a pull on the free strap. The authors urge that this method of fastening be adopted by all divers. This

Figure 41. The Fenjohn vest for supporting the Aqua-Lung. The vest is put on by a zipper up the front. The diver is shown holding a Fenjohn underwater camera. (Courtesy Fenjohn)

hitch is also useful with the Aqua-Lung straps, for it speeds the release of the tanks when required. Extremely heavy weights are not usually used, but in turbid water or strong currents a 30 or 40 pound belt might be an aid if it were desired to stay securely on the bottom. Remembering that the diver must be able to surface instantly at any time, it is obvious that a reliable quick release feature be used on such a belt. Probably a life line affixed to the belt would be necessary so that the belt could be recovered easily when dropped.

The air in a fully charged 70 cubic foot cylinder weighs 5.6 pounds and as it is exhausted, the tank becomes more and more bouyant. Sometimes the practice is to carry one or two pounds more weight than is necessary, so as to sink the diver more rapidly and with less effort. During the course of a dive the extra weight is offset as air is consumed and the diver regains a net positive bouyancy. When the air is exhausted he must be able to swim on the surface, possibly a fairly long distance and this must be possible with a minimum effort. It is a mistake to carry too much extra weight since then surface swimming is

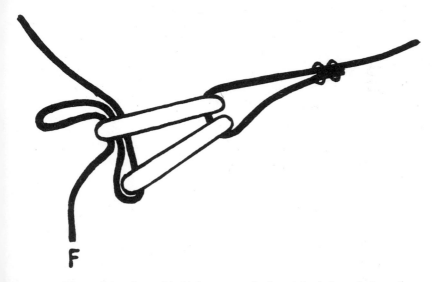

F

Figure 42. The quick release hitch for a standard weight belt and Aqua-Lung harness. This hitch must be used on any diving belt that has the double metal loop method of fastening since any other type of knot with these loops will jam. To release the hitch, pull on the free end (F) and the knot pulls out. Then the belt may be removed by allowing it to fall from the waist.

all the harder. If the diver is forced to surface and has trouble swimming due to weight and bulk of his equipment, he can obtain the most bouyancy from his equipment by swimming on his back with only his face above water. This is much easier than swimming on the stomach since each stroke does not lift a portion of the tank-regulator system out of water with the attendant decrease in bouyancy. Many users of this equipment· carry Res-Q-Pac, already described in previous chapters, and this now seems to be a mandatory safety measure.

Experience has shown conclusively that the most dangerous point of an Aqua-Lung or other throw-away unit dive is when the air runs out and the swim for boat or shore begins. In three cases known to the authors, novice divers got into serious trouble at this point. One was forced, in a choppy sea, to jettison his equipment including a tank, regulator, belt, etc. Another required rescue from onlookers on shore. It would be very foolish for any reader of this book to overlook the danger inherent in the dry tank situation. Let us summarize the safety solutions to this point in self-contained diving:

Fasten lung and belt to body by quick release hitch.

Carry operating Res-Q-Pac at all times.

Use air reserve device for deep water (35 feet or more) and when unit does not give warning of tank exhaustion.

Swim on back if possible when air is gone.

Unfasten belt then lung if swimming becomes too difficult.

In cold water the problem of warmth is important. There are many styles of waterproof, rubber suits on today's market which have been designed for free-swimming. Such suits are made of thin rubber, but allow the diver to wear dry underwear and sweaters. These suits are covered in some detail in the following chapter on underwater fishing. Three special diving dresses will be covered here since they lend themselves to self-contained diving, both with recirculators and throwaway, though one is specifically designed for Aqua-Lung.

The Desco Frog Man Dress: This is a non-elastic dress which is roomy enough to cover a man dressed normally in pants and sweater and is in two sections split at the waist. Once in the dress, the two halves are joined together by a double seal, making the dress essentially waterproof. The most interesting feature of this unit is an air pump made of a simple rubber bulb and affixed to the dress shoulder. The diver after donning the dress can expel as much air as he chooses from it by pumping the bulb and therefore enter the water ready to go under. Should he be going down fairly deep, he can retain air inside the dress and pull himself downward on a descending line until he is no longer bouyant and can sink normally. Care must be taken when free-swimming with some air left since above some level in the water the dress will be bouyant and hurriedly lift the diver to the surface, much to his surprise and perhaps consternation. This suit has an open-face and a seal around the cheeks and forehead like other suits of this type.

Elastic Frogman Suit (Desco): A skin tight suit similar to many described in the next chapter, this suit has back entry and two air escape valves on chest and head. What makes it of especial interest is the optional feature of dispensing with the back entry flap and substituting a double water-proof zipper. Unfortunately, even the manufacturer states that the zipper may leak a little so perhaps an underwater zipper is not yet a real success.

Cousteau Constant Volume Suit: This diving suit is not yet available in this country but should soon appear. It is designed specifically·for the Aqua-Lung and has a mouth fitting through which the mouthpiece goes into the head space. The suit is entered through the neck which has a super-stretchable rubber seal. It requires two men to get the diver through this opening. Once inside the main part of the suit, the headpiece is affixed at the neck by means of an aluminum ring. This hood is made of flexible waterproof material like the suit itself and once on, the mouthpièce is put in the mouth and the Aqua-Lung tubes connected outside the rubber. There are three air escape valves in this dress, one on top of the head and one on each ankle. The ankle valves are designed to vent air if the legs go up over the head, thus preventing the diver from blowing up. The theory of the constant volume aspect is that as a diver goes deeper the increased pressure squeezes the suit tightly and makes movement painful. To alleviate this difficulty, the diver snorts though his nose and adds air to the interior of the suit. On an ascent, the three valves release this excess air so that the· suit will not swell undully. Through this suit, Cousteau has attempted to design some of the advantages of deep water suit useage into a free swimming unit, but in so doing he has produced a fairly complex system for the average diver. Generally, the average rubber suit must be taken to 60 or 70 feet before any compression pain occurs due to pressure on the suit. Beyond this depth the Cousteau suit will be very useful, but in shallow water its complex entry system and full hood does not make it attractive for the casual diver. It should be remembered that when the air runs out the diver must get to the surface and stay there. Also all air must be gotten from the surface while the diver makes his way towards shore or boat. In this rig, this would mean disconnecting the lung tubes from the mouth and then trying to hold the head out of water. Should water enter the suit through this mouth hole, the situation would be very grave. In short, the average underwater swimmer requires a suit which can permit instant switch from diving unit to air breathing and have no possiblility of water filling, short of a suit rip. The Cousteau suit will be useful for professional workers in great depths, but does not seem to be highly safety-factored for the amateur, unless a safety line is used at all times.

CONSTRUCTION AND MODIFICATION OF THROW-AWAY EQUIPMENT

Shallow water helmets, either homemade or commercially constructed, may be adapted to self-contained use simply by mounting one or more compressed air bottles at the back. Such an adaptation is an exception to the general rule requiring demand regulators, for there is no lowering of pressure in a helmet due to inhaling and the demand valve will never operate. A needle valve is satisfactory and the diver can adjust air as needed. Swimming in such equipment is impossible and when the air supply is exhausted the diver must either discard the helmet or have a lifeline he can climb to the surface. Air supply requirements are the same as in usual helmet practice as described in Chapter II. A 30 cu. ft. air flask should give 40 minutes of diving, maximum, just under the surface.

To use a mask or mouthpiece, a demand regulator is required. These are complex pieces of apparatus and not at all suited to home construction. The Aqua-Lung regulator unit is available separately for those who wish to couple it to other than Aqua-Lung tanks. A few high pressure aviator breathing regulators are still available surplus and may sometimes be obtained new through aviation channels. These last are usually of aluminum construction with a pressure gauge and a rubber diaphragm. They are not too satisfactory around salt water but if kept clean and free from corrosion may operate reliably. They should be dissassembled and carefully painted inside and out with a water resistant paint, such as clear or pigmented glyptal laquer, taking care that the paint does not interfere with the operating parts. The pressure gauge must be removed and the fitting capped or plugged. The diaphragm should be replaced with a heavier grade of rubber, preferably synthetic neoprene. The plug-in oxygen mask fitting should be changed to a more foolproof coupling, possibly of the threaded type.

Any compressed air tanks should be of the type certified to carry 2200 psi, for the commonly available 400 psi tanks are too bulky for the amount of gas they contain. They can be equipped with a standard medical fitting, very similar to but not useable with the Aqua-Lung, or the Aqua-Lung tank valve assembly can be purchased. The proper type of yoke is then mounted on the regulator and the unit is ready to go.

Recharging air bottles is apt to be somewhat of a nuisance, particularly in a region away from diving air sources. Many of the large compressed gas or liquid air companies will refill tanks as will some fire departments. In active diving areas such as California and Florida a great many sports stores now can charge tanks. One or two of the large 220 cu. ft. oxygen cylinders might be purchased or rented and used as an air reservoir, but even these are not too satisfactory as the pressure drops too fast in the big bottle. The German Navy used such an arrangement to fill small diving cylinders but had a special type of handpump to finish filling the flasks to rated pressure. These pumps are not available in this country and, in addition, the labor of pumping

Figure 43. The Desco 'Frog Man' suit. A typical thin rubber suit for free swimming and self-contained diving. The rubber gloves would be useful for lobstering. (Courtesy Desco)

two 70 cu. ft. flasks to 2200 psi or even from a fully charged 220 cu. ft. cylinder would be great.

For the serious and active diver, there remains the possibility of obtaining a small high pressure compressor from the Cornelius Company which, with some modification, can be coupled to a gasoline engine of the Briggs and Stratton type. Cornelius makes two models at the present time, the larger having a capacity of two cu. ft./min. at a maximum pressure of 3000 psi, and the smaller a rating of .4 cu. ft./min. at 1500 psi. Unfortunately, both are connected to a 28 volt motor for aircraft use and the shaft is integral in both units so that attaching a gasoline engine would be difficult. The reader could obtain a transformer to operate these units off a 110 volt A.C. line except that the compressor motor is rated as D.C. and might not operate on A.C. In any case the amperage requirements, 60 and 20 amps respectively, would be difficult and represent a considerable drain on a normal lighting circuit. Possibly in the future these items will be made available without the electric motor.

Pure oxygen can be used in the Aqua-Lung or similar equipment provided the cylinders and valves are oil free. When used, the depth limitations discussed under recirculating equipment immediately apply. Unfortunately, oil lubricated pumps are customarily used to supply air and will leave a thin film of oil in tanks. Oxygen pumps on the other hand are lubricated with a glycerine-water mixture or other non-inflammible substance, as oil and oxygen under pressures greater than 800 psi may ignite spontaneously. Therefore, once a tank has been filled from an air pump, it is unwise to use oxygen until the tank has been completely cleaned. Also, the complete exhaustion of tanks may allow a little sea water to enter and then oxygen added will erode and rust through the walls in no time at all. Since compressed air is usually available, it would be foolish to use oxygen in such large tanks with the attendant dangers outlined above.

One of the recuring difficulties met during operation of Aqua-Lung and similar equipment is entrance of water into the breathing tubes. Means of dealing with this circumstance while underwater will be discussed later, but it suggests a useful modification of existing equipment. The use of a mouthpiece valve has been mentioned in connection with recirculating apparatus, but is also very useful here as well. These are made from telescoping tubing or similar stock and arranged so they can be shut off by a quarter turn of a short handle. No single design is suitable for all the different varieties of mouthpieces now in use and the exact design depends upon the user's preferences. A valve allows the diver to swim freely on the surface without having to prop the mouthpiece on his head or keep it in his mouth and waste air. During maneuvering into and out of the water there is no possibility for water to enter the system and the unit is quickly put into operation with assurance that the first breath will not be a mixture of air and water. Even more useful would be a three-way valve with a snorkel tube added to the mouthpiece. Then the air could be shut off and the diver could cruise just under the surface breathing from the surface through the snorkel. The third position would shut both compressed air and snorkel off and would be used when the lung is not in use or when the diver is getting into the water. It would be a simple matter to look for fish from the surface, quickly flick the valve to compressed

Figure 44. Several Aqua-Lung swimmers underwater. The bubbles from the lung exhaust at the back of the neck and do not interfere with vision. (Canadian Liquid Air Co.)

air position and make the dive. The saving in air from the tanks would pay for such a modification in one or two days of diving.

Many British self-contained units have the mouthpiece furnished with a rubber strap which encircles the head and holds the mouthpiece firmly in place. It is not uncomfortable and takes the strain off the mouth and lips, which ordinarily must support the mouthpiece and tubes during a long dive. A strap of this kind also prevents any sudden

Figure 45. The Costeau Constant Volume suit (on right) and an American short rubber suit. Captain Costeau is wearing his own invention. Notice the neck ring which is the seal between he'adpiece and the remainder of the suit. The air escape valves are clearly visible on head and ankle. The Aqua-Lung mouthpiece fits through a sealed hole in the suit. (Courtesy U.S. Divers Co.)

dislocation of the equipment from removing the mouthpiece from the mouth. Any such strap should not be so tight or complex that it prevents the diver from instantly getting his mouth clear when he surfaces as the air runs out.

OPERATION OF THROW-AWAY EQUIPMENT

The Aqua-Lung will be considered here as it is representative of this type of gear and is in widest use.

Initial operation of the Lung is very simple. The cylinder pressure is checked with a gauge and the gauge is then replaced by the regulator assembly. This should be tightened firmly into place, though care should be taken not to overtighten, a common error. The soft teflon gasket will seal well with moderate pressure and overtightening will cut into and deform it. The compressed air is now turned on and the operation of the regulator checked by drawing one or two breaths of air from the mouthpiece. If used, the air reserve valve is in the off position. After swim fins and weighted belt are in place, the tank may be placed on the back and the shoulder harness and buckle secured. When the diver has a sunburn these straps will cut painfully and underwater the tank often gets misplaced on the back. One solution to this is purchase of the Fenjohn Vest, an accessory designed for the Aqua-Lung. This vest fits over the shoulders and around the trunk and is closed by a zipper. The tank is supported from the back of the vest in the usual manner, but since the vest fits closely the tanks cannot skew around.

The diver enters the water carefully so as not to ram the tank against the back of his head, and swimming slowly or lowering himself on a rope he soon becomes accustomed to the apparatus. The dive may be continued until the air reserve device functions or, in a lung not equipped with air reserve, the first signs of increased breathing difficulty manifest themselves. At this point an immediate return to the surface occurs, but not a frantic scramble. Stay calm and don't hold your breath on the way up. It is always a good idea to ascend liesurely except in the most dire emergency, 25 feet per minute being the accepted figure. In depths over 36 feet (using air, not oxygen) decompression may be necessary depending on the duration of the dive. Appendix A gives decompression tables to 150 feet which may be used under all diving circumstances, but since Aqua-Lung is so widely used, the authors have prepared a short-cut decompression table based on a series of calculations illustrated in figure 47. Briefly, these tables are constructed as follows: The average air demand of a diver is taken to be one cu. ft./min. at the surface and an increasing amount in proportion to increasi g depth (Boyles Law). Then three curves of time versus depth were drawn indicating the maximum possible time a diver can spend at any depth with 35, 70, and 140 cubic feet of air corresponding to the three types of Aqua-Lung units. Superimposed on the graph are three decompression curves for the case of immediate ascent, rapid ascent with a six minute stop at 10 feet depth, and rapid ascent with

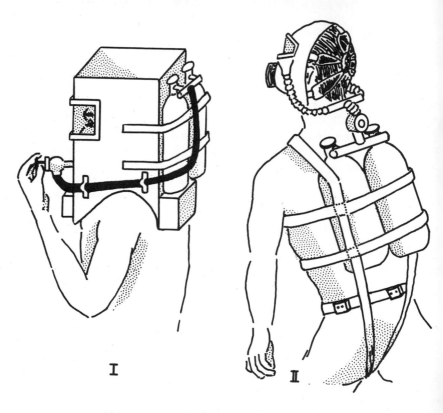

I

II

Figure 46. Suggestions for a home built throw away unit. It is a wooden helmet with air bottles strapped on the back and a needle valve to control the gas flow. It should always be used with a safety line and should have a warning gauge so that the diver can surface in plenty of time. II is a gas mask unit with a standard surplus demand regulator. Two 15 or 30 cubic foot bottles are mounted in a sling on the back. The regulator must be mounted at the back of head.

a 13 minute stop at 10 feet depth. The zero stop curve is from U.S. Divers Company who first represented decompression data in this useful way. Now using the graph to prepare a table we see where each tank capacity curve intersects each decompression curve and note accordingly. The results are shown in Table VI.

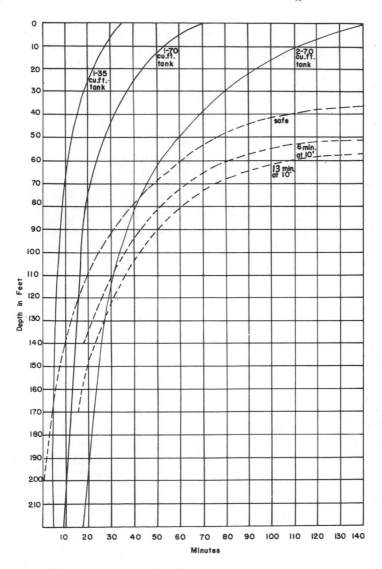

Figure 47. Decompression and duration data for three different bottle capacities. The solid lines are duration lines. That is, they give the time one can spend at any depth with the given bottle capacities. The dotted lines give decompression data. Where the 'safe' line intersects each solid line we know that is the maximum depth possible with the given bottle size without decompression. Exceeding this depth requires the use of one of the other two curves, which are labeled with decompression instructions. (safe curve, courtesy U.S. Divers Co.)

TABLE VI

Tank capacity	Safe depth range	Range for 6 minute stop at ten feet	Range for 13 minute stop at ten feet
38 cubic feet	0 to 168 feet		
70 cubic feet	0 to 130 feet	130 to 150 feet	
140 cubic feet	0 to 73 feet	73 to 98 feet	98 to 119 feet

To use the table one must have a depth gauge and a water proof watch (the watch is only necessary if outside the safe depth range). The diver notices in his gauge the deepest water into which he swims and attempts to stay within the safe depth range listed above. For instance, using the double tank 140 cubic foot lung, stay within 73 feet of the surface and no decompression troubles will result. The other entries in the table are for dives which may have to be somewhat in excess of the safe limit. In the case of a 70 cubic foot tank, the diver will have some eight minutes of diving when the air reserve device functions. He can then go to 10 feet, stay there until his air is gone, and be properly decompressed for the six minute range of the table. Thus in the 130 to 150 foot range with one large tank and the 73 to 98 foot range for two large tanks, no watch will be needed as the reserve device will function as a timer. Naturally, no dives to these depths are made without air reserve warning. The authors suggest that all but the most experienced stay within the safe limit.

Below 150 feet the problem of nitrogen narcosis appears and no dives in excess of this depth should be made with air. The Aqua-Lung makers recommend 130 feet as the maximum depth and this would appear to be a good idea. The water is dark at this depth, the bottom very shadowy and a man in trouble has to be good to get out of it down so far. Captain Cousteau has said, ". . . one truth is abundantly evident: the Aqua-Lung provides no absolute guarantee of immunity below." This is true not only for Aqua-Lung but for all diving equipment. Safety depends as much on the training and experience of the diver as on the proper operation of the apparatus.

In extreme depths even the air reserve device is insufficient protection against running out of air, for if there is enough reserve to reach the surface, there surely is not enough for adequate decompression.

At any depth getting water in the breathing tubes can vary from an annoyance to a real hazard. Should the exhaust valve leak, or the mouthpiece be dropped momentarily, the diver finds his breathful of air contains mostly water. Small amounts of water can be swallowed, but if the diver is fighting for air, as sometimes happens, the water may gag and induce panic. Other means of ridding the tubes of water are needed.

One method of ridding the tubes of water is to tip the head to the side so the exhaust tube is lowered, and the inlet tube drains into it. A breath is taken and sharply expelled along with most of the water. As it is difficult to determine which is the exhaust line in times of

Figure 48. A busy scene in the water. The constant volume suit is in the left rear. The diver in the right rear has propped his Aqua-Lung mouthpiece on his mask to prevent water from entering it. A shut-off valve makes this unnecessary. Notice the short, front entry suit on the man climbing the ladder. (Courtesy U.S. Divers Co.)

stress, the authors recommend a band of paint around the exhaust tube, an inch or so from the mouthpiece. This will serve to identify the tube to be lowered so as to drain water towards the exhaust.

A more drastic method but also a more dependable one is taught by the Navy to UDT divers (frogmen). This is to take the mouthpiece from the mouth and hold it above the regulator. Since the pressure at the mouthpiece will then be lower than the pressure at the regulator (since it is not as deep) the valve will operate and blow air through the inlet tube clearing it of water. If the head is thrown back, the mouthpiece can be placed in the mouth while still discharging air, and a full breath taken. The other tube is then emptied as this breath is exhausted. The Navy taught this method to the extent of making a diver swim down in the water, put on the lung, and expel the water from the tubes. This rather dangerous exercise resulted in (unofficially reported) casualties and has apparently been discontinued. The water clearing is sound, however, and particularly good because it can be done with empty lungs.

In summing up the previous two chapters it may be worth while to note the differences and similarites in operation of the two basic self-contained units. Actually, the recirculator should be used in exactly the opposite way as the throw-away if optimum submersion times and operational ease are considered. The throw-away is penalized on air consumption by Boyles Law so that the deeper the diver goes, the more air he uses, and the sooner he must come up. Therefore the optimum method with a throw-away is to stay as close to the surface as possible and dive into high pressure regions only when necessary. European divers conserve air by counting three seconds between breaths and relaxing as much as possible in the water. In this manner, the sea level air consumption can be reduced to .75 cu. ft./min., or less. The recirculator, on the other hand, is not penalized in air consumption by depth, since the oxygen flow depends only on metabolic requirements of the breather. But if the recirculator user were to rise and sink often as the throw-away diver does, he would not last long before running out of oxygen, for with each descent he must valve in gas to fill the breathing bag, and then throw it away on the ascent. The recirculator is thus best used at a constant depth with few changes. The throw-away is fundamentally a simpler unit, but suffers from recharging difficulties. This will be covered more fully in Chapters VI and X.

Chapter VI

SPEARFISHING

There is no doubt but that hunting fish under the sea has become a sport of first rank. During the past several years more and more swimmers are finding that the curoius inhabitants of the undersea jungle make sporting and interesting adversaries. The sense of adventure, the strangeness of the sea scape, and the slow, dreamlike motion of the underwater world combine to attract all kinds of people beneath the surface.

It is difficult to put into words the attraction of the undersea, although many have tried. To the diver who first dives in cold, somewhat murky waters, diving is perhaps an interesting but somewhat uncomfortable pastime. The freedom of the body, the pressure on the ears, and the smell and taste of the apparatus are conflicting sensations which confuse and disturb the beginner. Far better to begin underwater work in Florida or Mexico, where the warm, clear water feels close to body temperature, and the novice can lie on top of the water and stare unbelievingly at the myriad colors and shapes stretching under him. Then it is easy to sink slowly into the new world and become a part of it. But whether diving off the rocky Maine coast or in the Bahama Islands, most people want to take a crack at getting a fish underwater.

The undersea fisherman can now find an already large, and still growing section of the sporting goods industry catering to his every whim . . . at a price. The equipment problem in underwater angling is threefold, namely, safety, comfort, and suitability. For most people a fourth criterion might be added: economy. To fulfill all these aims will be difficult for the absolute beginner who has never even swum underwater for more than a few seconds, but common sense coupled with the advice in this chapter should enable almost everyone to get the correct outfit the first time around. After getting the right gear there is still the problem of using it correctly, and this too will be discussed, but only practice makes a good fisherman.

The current hot spots for underwater fishing in America are Southern California and Florida. Of the two, Southern California is more highly organized with clubs, associations, laws, and 'national' contests to determine top spearfishermen of the year with large trophies awarded. But if the reader has a choice of where to take his two weeks vacation underwater, he should select Florida, for these are the waters most rich in marine life and color, and most abundant in big fish. Aside from these two highly publicized spots, much active fishing is being done elsewhere. The entire New England coast has its share of enthusiasts as does New Jersey and other Atlantic states. The Gulf of Mexico is rather poor generally, being so flat, but some activity goes on, while even in lakes, rivers, and other inland waters, fish are being taken on the spear. But lakes and rivers cannot be fished indiscriminatly, since they are closely governed by state laws as to what fish can be killed in this manner.

Figure 49. H. Kendall with a Tautog speared off Rockport, Massachusetts. The water here is cold and fairly murky, but many fish can be found around piers and wrecks.

Once the fisherman has decided on his area (see Chapter X) he next needs to think about the kind of fish and the underwater conditions. Cold, murky waters require special equipment that warm clear ocean waters do not, and large fish require special gear. Some of the following questions must be answered before purchasing of equipment begins:

a) Is air supplied diving equipment required?

b) Is a warmth-giving suit required?

c) Is a spear gun required?

Since it is impossible to list all diveable waters in the Western Hemisphere in this book, descriptive examples will be given when gear is considered and one or two representative areas will be mentioned.

DIVING EQUIPMENT

Many pages have already been devoted to an exposition of the principles of every type of shallow diving equipment. The pay off is, of course, in the correct use of this equipment, or, in the case of spear fishing, whether it should be used at all. The most popular underwater breathing equipment in use at this time is the Aqua-Lung. As already noted, the Aqua-Lung has certain design deficiencies which can be corrected in part by the user, if he wishes to take the time to do so. The Desco lung is also used for fishing, as are all other self-contained units on the market. Now, as self-contained equipment falls into two basic categories: recirculating and throw-away, a practical problem arises at once as regards underwater fishing. This is the nearness of the diver to a source of compressed air. In Southern California, this is no problem, since most sporting stores can charge Aqua-Lung or other tanks quite readily, but in the Florida Keys, Bermuda, the Carribean, or Baja California a recharge may be difficult or impossible to get. Thus the diver may be better off with a recirculator, since he can carry a 125 cubic foot cylinder in his car filled with oxygen that will keep him going for a month or so of heavy diving. But with this increased mobility the diver now is limited in depth due to oxygen poisoning, and he may not be able to get down to the big fish. Fortunately, this problem usually works out quite well. Where high pressure air is available, deep dives are needed for big fish, since many other divers are working over the area. For outlying places where oxygen must be carried, the fish are unsophisticated, and the diver can stay within 30 feet or so of the surface and do everything he wants.

If self-contained gear is definitely indicated, two other solutions are possible. One is to obtain a Cornelius or General Electric high-pressure compressor to charge the air bottles and operate it from a gasoline engine. The other is to take enough spare bottles to allow for all the necessary diving. Obviously, rather than waste money on many extra cylinders, the serious diver would do better to make his own charging unit which he can carry and operate easily. As charging a bottle takes time, one or two spare tanks must be carried in any case so the compressor is charging while the diver is in or out of the water. It is doubtful if the purchase of a motor compressor rig is justified for the diver working close to a source of commercial compressed air as a compressor is expensive and somewhat complicated to maintain.

But the undersea fisherman does not have to depend on self-contained equipment. As noted in the chapter on mask diving, the free-swimming diving mask, using floating hose and a regular diving compressor is a most versatile rig. One hundred and fifty feet of hose will allow the diver to cover well over an acre of territory in 30 feet of water working from an anchored boat. The diver can swim on the surface or just underwater, dive to his prey, and be no more hindered by his line to the surface than if he were trailing a thin rope. Compared to throw-away gear, there are no air supply problems, nor are there

Figure 50. The Bel-Aqua front entry rubber suit and rubber snorkel. The suit is closed by tying with a piece of surgical elastic and the flap stuffed under the weight belt. (Courtesy Bel-Aqua Co.)

any depth limits due to oxygen sickness as in the recirculators. However, the fisherman thus equipped will need a larger boat than if he were using self-contained equipment and this may be a real problem in some out of the way spot unless a boat is readily available.

These then are the choices of underwater breathing equipment for the fisherman. Helmets are simply not suitable for 90 percent of fishing since the diver cannot swim or maneuver out of an upright position with a big fish. The question still remains, when is diving equipment necessary?

Part of the answer to this question depends on the preferences and finances of the individual enthusiast. Possibly the beginner would do better to start with a simple face mask and fins and see how he enjoys the sport. Generally, the more adverse the conditions, the more helpful diving equipment becomes. Off the rocky portions of New England for instance, men do fish with no air supply, but they are experts who have plenty of cold water experience under their belts. It is harder to maintain one's wind in cold water, and diving equipment does help on this score. Also, when the bottom is invisible from the surface, frequent dives must be made blindly by the diver with no air supply, whereas the man with air can get down right to the bottom and cruise along.

Since underwater fishing is only one of several enticements for underwater diving, most spearfishers usually end up with some form of diving equipment, for while it is possible to take large fish without diving gear, it is more difficult to take photos, investigate wrecks, and observe marine life with only a lungful of air. For those who plan to take a vacation in California or Florida, the choice is a simple one, for it is possible to rent Aqua-Lung or other self-contained equipment from local sport stores and try it out without expending 100 dollars or more. Once the fisherman has decided that some form of air supply is necessary, the following summary may help him make up his mind.

Type	Number Bottles Needed	Where Used	Outfit Price
Throw-away store charged	2-3 70 cu. ft. for one full day of active diving	Near large cities	$200. and up
Throw-away (Self-charged with compressor)	2-4 70 cu. ft. for fairly continuous diving	In non-populated areas	$350. and up
Throw-away with spare bottles	2-3 70 cu. ft. per day of diving	In non-populated areas	$75. plus $75. per bottle
Recirculating with spare oxygen	One 125 cu. ft. cylinder per 4 weeks	Anywhere under 35 feet depth	$100. and up
Mask-Compressor	None, but compressor instead	Anywhere that boat of 15' or so is available	$100. and up

It should be noted that each type of gear has other advantages and disadvantages for fishing which will be considered under fishing methods.

DIVING SUITS (WARMTH GIVING)

Regardless of whether the spearman decides on air-supplied equipment, he should give careful thought to the purchase of a rubber suit of some sort. As already noted in Chapter I under "Heat Transfer", the addition of a suit and underwear is of great help in preventing heat loss from the body. The authors believe that for the casual athlete

Figure 51. Two interesting suits by Engineering Development Corporation, 305 American Trust Company Building, Berkeley 4, California. These suits are not water-proof but of sponge rubber with laced construction for good fit. The manufacturer claims they are warm in the coldest water and less cumbersome than suits with underwear worn next to the skin. This is a new firm which was located too late to include in Appendix B. It is headed by the well known scientist, Dr. Hugh Bradner.
(Courtesy EDCO)

suits may be an aid in the following waters: Southern California, the Great Lakes, inland waters of all types, New England and the Atlantic Coast as far south as Georgia, and the Gulf of Mexico. Suits may be generally dispensed with in the Carribean area including Southern Florida, Baja California and most of the Mexican coast, and Bermuda in the summer. Certain places such as Bermuda and Florida may require suits in the colder times of the year. It is better to have a suit and not use it than to be cold after only a few minutes of diving.

The main question one always raises about the several brands of rubber suits is, quite naturally, do they leak? An examination of Table II in Chapter I shows that an air space between the skin and rubber is over twenty times more resistant to heat loss as the same space filled with stagnant water. A leaky suit then will admit water into the air space and increase heat loss greatly. Most of the frogman type suits will leak a little around the face since it is not possible to lace the head section so tightly that the cheek-rubber seal is absolutely tight, but if only a little water gets in, it will not make too much difference.

As to which suit of the several illustrated in this chapter will prove best for any individual, the authors can say only that the reader should, if possible, try a couple and see which are the snuggest and most comfortable. The Navy uses a back-entry one-piece suit with hood. This is a rugged suit, but requires help to enter and leave. The Pirelli suit on the other hand, has no hood, and comes in two sections so the user may get in without help. The Bel-Aqua has front entry and a hood. The self-entrance feature is a good one, but should not be the only criterion in purchasing a suit. The Navy suit has an air exit valve on the head similar to the Desco, while the Bel-Aqua does not, depending on air escape around the face to clear the suit of excess air. The Bel-Aqua solution appears to be the best if the suit is to be used only with a snorkel or Aqua-Lung, since the head valve can admit water at the surface where there is no pressure differential to maintain closure. The Bel-Aqua suit will not be suitable with surface supplied diving equipment such as air supplied diving masks, since these seal tightly over the whole face area and therefore prevent any air escape at this point. The same applies to the Pirelli mask (discussed in a later section) which fits over the entire face. If the reader is planning to be in California or Florida, he should defer buying by mail, since it is better to try a suit on, and suits are readily available in these two localities.

Most brands of suits come in two types, one with short arms and legs, and one with long. There seems to be little reason for getting a short suit other than the fact that it permits greater maneuverability. For this feature, the user may have to pull the short arms and legs very tightly over his limbs, thereby cutting down circulation to the body parts that need it badly. The wearing of underwear may also be more difficult around the thighs with a short suit. Also the long suit has feet so that there is never any constriction on the legs when swimming. The main disadvantage of long suits is their bulk and bouyancy which requires the diver to wear several weights so that his bouyancy will be neutral in the water.

Figure 52. The Pirelli rubber suit for free swimming. This suit is in two halves which are split at the waist and donned just like a shirt and pants. (Courtesy U.S. Divers Co.)

As noted in Chapter I, wearing underwear between the suit and skin creates an air space which is excellent insulation. The thicker the space, the warmer the diver, but the more weights he must wear to sink. Some divers dispense with the rubber suit and use only long underwear which is exposed to the water. When this gets wet, it acts as a reservoir of stagnant water between the sea and the skin. As illustrated in Table III, this is about five times as effective as skin alone in preventing heat loss. Other divers use only a rubber shirt, which is not waterproof, but simply fits fairly tight around the trunk and arms. This allows a stagnant water layer to sit between the skin and rubber, and acts like the underwear alone. A European sponge rubber tunic (not waterproof) also holds a layer of stagnant water. All these types of insulation have varying degrees of effectiveness and thus are useful within certain temperature ranges, depending upon the individual preferences of the diver.

It should be remembered that all 'Frog-Man' type suits are of thin rubber, and much more fragile than the working diver suits such as the Desco. They are not suitable for bottom work using heavy equipment, nor are they good for clambering over rocks and coral. Since the suits are not cheap, they must be handled with care in and out of the water. Washing with fresh water is necessary after diving is completed, and sprinkling talc inside the suit after carefully drying it will keep the rubber from sticking to itself and deteriorating. Standard tire patching material is suitable for rips and tears, but a garage applied hot patch may prove more lasting. Experience has indicated that on long suits, the feet may wear out where they join the leg rubber. Close watch should be kept on this area so that patches can be applied over weak points. Suits should never be stored for any length of time folded into a bundle, but should be hung up in a dry, cool, dark closet.

Should a suit be torn underwater, there is no immediate cause for alarm since water will generally not enter too quickly. A suit filled with water, however, could drag on a diver's endurance as he swims for shore, and thus could be quite dangerous. For this reason the authors recommend most strongly that any suit wearer obtain a Res-Q-Pac or similar life preserver, and never attempt diving activity without carrying one. Also, it might be noted that the weights worn by a suit wearer are counteracting the bouyancy of the water-free layer between the suit and body. When this fills with water and the bouyancy is destroyed, the weights produce a negative bouyancy. Should the suit tear and fill, and the diver is without a life preserver through oversight or foolishness, *his first duty is to drop his weights*. Never try to get into shore under these conditions with the feeling that weights cost money, and you can make it in without loosing them. They don't cost that much.

SPEAR GUNS

When Guy Gilpatrick and other sportsmen first began spearing fish in the Mediterranean, they used hand spears of 10 or more feet in length. These were suitable until such spears cleaned out all the unwary and slow moving fish. At that point the underwater weapon makers began to develop more potent weapons. Rubber band, compressed gas, spring driven, and cartridge propelled harpoons began streaking about underwater until in some places it is as dangerous to go underwater when a spear fishing crowd is out as to wander through the woods on the opening day of deer season. The use of high powered

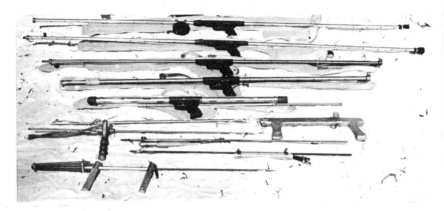

Figure 53. A galaxy of undersea guns. From top to bottom; Cressi Cernia, Cressi Torpedine, Cressi Siluro, Cressi Saetta, Cressi Mignon, experimental CO_2 cartridge gun, Deluxe Hawaiian Sling, stainless push button sling, simple Hawaiian Sling, two handle four strand gun. The first four Cressi guns are spring powered and the last one rubber powered. All guns available from the Florida Frogman. (see Appendix B) (O.R.A. Photo by Raepple)

guns creates a rather vicious circle. The more guns the less fish. The less fish the more powerful are the guns needed to get any and so on. Fewer and fewer gogglers are using hand spears, and readily accesible diving areas, particularly in Southern California, are being depopulated of easily shot fish.

The most common type of gun is rubber powered, of which several makes are illustrated. Most manufacturers make claims for these guns which are frankly fantastic. In Chapter I we noted that a spear fired underwater can be expected to have 900 times the drag as one fired in the air, yet makers claim 'effective ranges' underwater of half those on the surface. Few shots should be taken at a range of greater than five feet, and the fisherman who can't get this close is not much of a stalker. Rubber guns of the two strand Arbalete type, are suitable for fish up to 15 pounds or so, and for lobsters which cannot be taken with the hands alone. The guns can be cocked underwater with some effort, and most have a safety of sorts.

Probably the most powerful rubber powered gun is the four strand Arbalete which packs a pretty mean punch. Cocking all the rubber in this gun at once is not possible so that each pair of elastics must be set up separately. Of similar power to most two strand guns are foreign made spring guns. These have a barrel containing a powerful compression spring. The spear is placed in the barrel and thrust down over the spring by using a 'loader' which folds out of the harpoon head. This loader is illustrated in the spear head section. One such spring gun is now available in the United States under the product name 'Cressi'. While the spring guns are more streamlined in the water, it would appear that due to their rusting qualities, they would not compare favorably with rubber guns of the same power. Also, the rubbers are easily replaced in the Arbalete and similar guns. Care must be taken with used rubber, since one spearfisherman has already been partially blinded when an elastic broke and whipped back into his eye. Since most shots are taken with gun-holding arm extended, this will not generally be dangerous.

A fish of over 10 pounds is very likely to bend and twist the steel shaft from a gun into pretzel shapes. The serious fisherman is thus very foolish to buy his spear shafts from dealers. The spear heads should be purchased and the shaft made from proper size stainless steel or monel which can be threaded and worked into a proper spear. This is somewhat cheaper, and monel is much tougher than the mild steel used in many commercial spears, and neither stainless steel nor monel rust.

Compressed gas guns are often used for really large fish up to 100 pounds, and for fish with tough hides such as shark. Some fishermen reject the guns since they claim the burst of gas out of the muzzle frightens fish. Other gogglers find these gas bubbles an attractive feature when out in open water where large and possibly dangerous fish congregate. Again, the gas gun does not give a long accurate range, but its hitting power is large. Short, thick darts can be used, that go completely into a large fish and fix him forever to the harpoon line. Using such short darts is often wise, since they are virtually non-bendable when the fish begins to fight. Some gas gun fishermen do not use a harpoon fixed to a line, but let the dart shoot freely, hoping to kill the fish at once. This is very unwise. All current gas guns use carbon dioxide under a pressure of 800 psi to drive the spear, most having a large cylinder that will hold ten or more shots. The *Barracuda* uses standard Sparklet soda-making cartridges, one shot to the cartridge. One of the biggest disadvantages of gas guns other than the *Barracuda* gun is that each shot has less power than the last due to the dropping off of the cylinder pressure. Also, the total available expansion of the gas is decreased with increasing depth (Boyles law). Also since the pressure of a gas varies directly as the temperature, the available pressure energy decreases as cold water chills the gas cylinder. Great care must be taken with all these guns as they will disembowel a man with ease.

Figure 54. An underwater rubber spear gun by Desco. This awsome artillery is equipped with a small look-box so the gun can be used from a boat and aimed through the surface. It is cocked by a handle, the rubber being too much to set up by hand alone. The fishing reel for holding line is seen on the Cressi guns as well. (Courtesy of Desco)

The most powerful rubber band guns, such as the four strand Arbalete and the CO_2 gas guns will take a big Jewfish or other such heavy bodied slow moving fish running to hundreds of pounds, although such a catch must usually be made with two or more divers firing into the fish from close range. Big shark and manta ray running to the hundreds of pounds class cannot be taken safely with current equipment, unless a large number of divers are present and they are expert and coordinated in their actions. Realizing this, several California divers working the Gulf of California where such large monsters abound use a gas gun or large Arbalete with a special spear whose head contains a .38 calibre blank. When the spear strikes, the cartridge explodes, driving a short spear deep into the fish. The spear-heads are cocked only by firing, according to reports on the weapons. This seems almost too complex for a sport that began with native divers having only googles and push spears, and it would appear that a properly designed gas gun should be able to do as well at close range as the blank cartridge driven dart. The taking of a large shark would seem to be the ultimate of spear fishing, but it is nothing for any but the most experienced and hardy men, using air supplies, and well accustomed to tight corners.

Recent tests on guns conducted by the Bottom Scratchers and Kelp Kings were reported in "The Skin Diver". The target was 10 feet from the gun and made of plywood. The following results were obtained.

Equipment	Penetration
Two strand Arbalete	$\frac{1}{4}$ "
Four strand Arbalete	$\frac{1}{2}$ "
CO_2 Cartridge gun (Barracuda)	$\frac{1}{2}$ "
Six strand Typhoon gun ($\frac{3}{8}$ " shaft)	$\frac{3}{4}$ "
Six strand Typhoon gun ($\frac{5}{16}$ " shaft)	$\frac{1}{2}$ "
Cressi spring gun	$\frac{3}{8}$ "
Six strand Typhoon gun with .38 powered head	through $1\frac{1}{4}$ " target

These results are not surprising, but they do not give an adequate picture of penetration into a fish. Tests in soap would be more nearly like actual conditions. The spring gun is intermediate in power between a two and four strand gun, while the power heads are well beyond anything else in penetration power. These same tests noted that wire leader was preferable to nylon line on the spear. Naturally, the smaller the diameter of the trailing line, the less resistance it will have.

SPEARHEADS

"The Skin Diver" recently carried an interesting article by Mr. Rodney Jonklass on spearheads. The illustrative material (Figure 55) and information here is abstracted from this work, since it was extremely informative and useful for all underwater spearfishermen.

Spear heads can now be purchased in a variety of shapes and sizes to fit individual fishing needs. The oldest and most traditional of spearheads is the two, three and more pronged gig with a fixed barb on each point. This type of head is only suitable for very fleshy fish which might pull off a single spear and is very hard to drive into a firm fleshed target. They are seldom seen now except on very long poles in shallow water where flounder and halibut are prevalent. Most heads are now single, and either two or three edged or round. The three edged points penetrate furthest and are most desirable, though they must be kept sharpened.

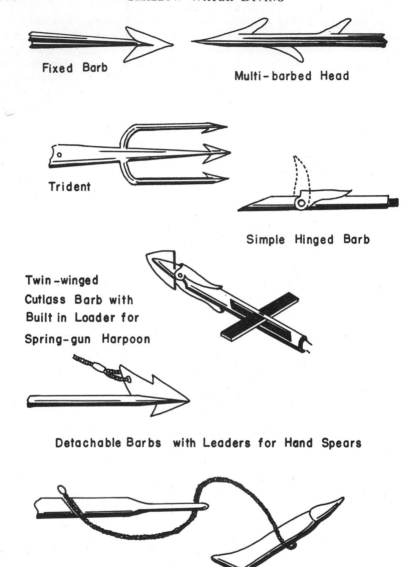

Fixed Barb

Multi-barbed Head

Trident

Simple Hinged Barb

Twin-winged
Cutlass Barb with
Built in Loader for
Spring-gun Harpoon

Detachable Barbs with Leaders for Hand Spears

Detachable Barb with Leader and "Extension" for Harpoon

Figure 55. A selection of spear heads courtesy of "The Skin Diver." These heads are discussed in the text. Generally the trident is for the smallest of fish, the fixed barb comes next, then the multi-barbed and hinged barb heads, with the largest detachable and hinged barb heads being used for the biggest fish.

Some heads have disappearing winged barbs that fold into the head with only enough sticking out to open them once in a fish. Others, such as those commonly sold with the Arbalete, have barbs that fold back on the shank of the spear and are held there by a ring which is pushed back on contact. This frees the barbs which are extended slightly by a rubber spring. As the fish tries to pull off, the barbs open out and jam in the flesh. Using these heads, it is important that the spearman check his barbs to see that the ring is properly in place, or the spear will penetrate poorly.

When penetration is of prime importance, a barbless, very thin head is used with the line affixed in the middle of the head. Once in the fish the pull on the line pulls the head sideways so that it will not pull out. These heads are also good because the line is affixed directly to the head without any wire attachment or other potentially weak link in between.

The spring gun, such as the Cressi, requires a special kind of head for loading. This head has a hinged bar which folds out of the head or shaft and which is used to push the spear down against the spring. Some heads use this loading bar as a barb as well. The spear must never be shot with the loader open for it will not penetrate.

Most spearheads fall into the above mentioned catagories and differ mainly in details of construction. Whatever the type of head, it must be securely fastened to a line so that the line will break before the head comes off. Many commercially available heads are weak at this point and must be worked on to make them suitable.

OTHER EQUIPMENT

Masks: The modern diving mask is something that should be in every swimmer's possession, whether he fishes or not. Not only does it permit seeing underwater, but it teaches poor swimmers proper breathing through the mouth. Which mask to buy is a question best settled by inspection in the local sporting goods stores. But the authors do not recommend any of the cheap masks which have a thick rubber rim with no flap of soft rubber to spread over the cheeks and forehead. The saving of a couple of dollars with such a mask will often result in pain, headaches and general discomfort. The French 'Squale' and 'Champion', the Voit 'Custom', and the Sea Dive 'Deluxe' are all good masks with liberal rubber to fit comfortably around the face. Less expensive masks made by American companies are generally not suitable being rigid and hard. The question of comfort will be stressed to the point of obsession in the following sections, since masks, fins, and other less expensive items should be purchased with only comfort and utility in mind. All the commercial gear is suitable technically, but an

uncomfortable unit is completely useless regardless of its other quali-
fications. The reader should keep in mind that what, in the sports
store is only a minor tightness, will become a major pain after only a
few hours of sun, salt water and rubbing.

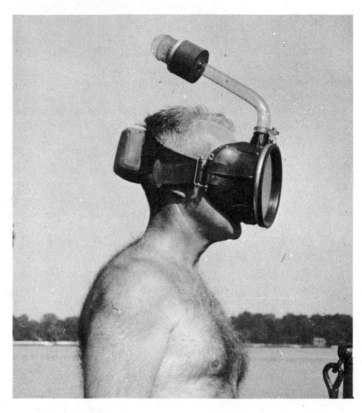

Figure 56. The most complex swimming mask on today's market; the Pirelli. The
mask covers both mouth and nose, has an integral snorkel with cork float closure,
and a comphensating chamber on the back of the head to bleed air into the mask.
This mask would be excellent if adapted to use with Aqua-Lung. The mask could
be pierced to admit tubes, and a shut off would be needed on the lung for surface
breathing. (Courtesy Fenjohn Co.)

Snorkels: A snorkel is simply a plastic or rubber tube leading
from the mouth back over the head through which a swimmer breathes,
enabling him to keep his face underwater as he swims. The advantages
are two fold, the first being that he can watch everything happening
underneath him, and the second being that he can swim with the
face down all the time rather than raising it periodically to breathe.

The snorkel is thus an aid of considerable magnitude to an average swimmer, provided he uses it properly. Several snorkels are available from manufacturers and dealers each having its special advantages. For diving that is not done in kelp or thick seaweed, the 'double curved' snorkel is good, since it is more difficult for water to get around the upper curve, than into a straight pipe open at the top. However,

Figure 57. A display of spearfishing equipment by the Florida Frogman. Left rear mask is a Cressi with cork snorkel closure, center rear is a plain snorkel, and at right a standard Aqua-Lung. The two masks to either side of the shell are Squale masks with very soft rubber lips around the face. The knives float and the snorkel in the foreground has a ping-pong ball for closure if the end goes under a wave during a breath. Just in front of the shell is Res-Q-Pac. (O.R.A. Photo by Raepple)

the upper curve will catch on weed, and the tube may be pulled from the mouth dragging a mask with it. A simple straight rubber snorkel is probably best for kelp diving since it will not tangle. Other snorkels have ping-pong balls which float up plugging the entrance to the snorkel when it is under water due to a wave, thus preventing water from getting into the mouth. Any snorkel will not take water in a dive when the breath is held since air in the mouth and snorkel will simply be compressed, and will not let the water bypass it. Where the automatic sealing feature is most useful is in sighteseeing from the surface on a rough day where the swimmer may be inhaling as a wave splashes over him, because the closure will prevent gagging on inhaled sea water.

In use the snorkel mouthpiece is gripped between the teeth and the tube is affixed to the mask strap between the ear and eye. The angle at which the tube inclines over the water is important. It should be about 30 degrees off the vertical with the top slanted towards the diver's feet when in normal (face down) swimming position.

Several swimmers have taken standard masks and permanently affixed tubes to them, but this means that all breathing is done through the nose, which is tiring as well as conducive to bad swimming habits. A rather interesting mask-snorkel combination is shown in Figure 56. This Pirelli equipment is probably the most elaborate and expensive mask on the market. Instead of using a ping-pong ball to close the tube in rough water, Pirelli uses a cork float arrangement which is more rugged and permanent than the ball. Unlike other masks this one covers the mouth as well as the nose and eyes. The swimmer thus has to depend on the snorkel at all times, and must expel any water that gets into the mask through it. This mask also has a compensating chamber at the back of the head to equalize pressure inside and outside the mask on deep dives. This rig was greeted with mixed emotions, and is probably not suitable for any but experienced gogglers who can spend an hour or so without needing to take the mask off.

Fins and Other Accessories: Swimming fins are, of course, a basic necessity for all fishing. Whether self-contained equipment, air supplied diving mask, or simple face mask is used, fins must be procured. As with masks, fins are selected on the basis of comfort alone. As noted in Chapter I, the difference in performance (swimming speed) between a good set of fins and a bad set is not large, so that there is no sense in selecting fins on the basis of how fast you will go. All American and foreign fins give about the same speed increase, between 30 and 40 per cent. What is important is that the fins fit like a second skin, that they can be worn over sunburned and raw skin, and that they do not chafe and produce sores. The type of fin best suited to fulfill all these important conditions is one that fits over the foot like a glove so that no ridge or edge of rubber is holding the fin in place. Some American and foreign fins are designed to fit with a hard rubber edge bearing on the top of the foot. This edge will surely chafe the foot, and produce a line of sores that will not heal in salt water. Such a fin used for only a few days can virtually incapacitate a diver, and ruin a trip. The authors have found the 'Frog Feet' fins manufactured by Sea Net Company to be generally satisfactory. These fins also have the adjustable strap feature which is very desirable for prolonged use.

since even the best fins will chafe a little, and relief can be gained by
loosening the strap. For some reason the manufacturers of equipment
have not produced a fin that fits like a shoe so that the entire bottom of
the foot is protected by the fin. In Southern waters this can be annoying, since it is not comfortable to wear both sneakers and fins, and the

Figure 58. Mr. Woody Dimel of the Los Angeles Neptunes and a 58 pound stingray
taken off Catalina Island. Mr. Dimel, a skilled and enthusiastic fisherman, is wearing
a front entry suit and a wide view mask by the Spearfisherman. The mask is equipped
with a water purge device over the nose. The gun is a four strand Arbalete. (Photo
by Marx Scott)

diver must thus take his chances with the sea urchins and stinging plants if he wants to both swim and walk. One solution is to obtain so-called Japanese Tabe Socks from the Universal Sales Company. These are snug fitting socks with thin rubber soles that should protect the heels sticking out of the swim fin. When purchasing fins, the user should remove his shoes and try them on over his stockings. If there is any area of pressure or slight pain the fin is unsuitable for serious diving, and must be discarded. Should any part of the foot begin to hurt and show red sores similar to blisters, some sort of bandage should be placed over the area at once for further rubbing will open the sore and cause it to grow deep and painful. Also constant immersion in water will prevent even the smallest cut from healing.

Aside from masks, snorkels and fins, many other accessories are available for the diver-fisherman. The depth guage has already been mentioned. Weighted belts have also been discussed in other chapters. Generally a full protective suit will need around 10 pounds of weights or more if thick underwear is worn. An adjustable belt is good for a beginner with weights that can be added or taken off. Learn the slip knot illustrated in Chapter V for weight-belts, and always use it.

Knives of many sorts are on the market. Most of them float, and unfortunately, most of them also rust quite rapidly. Since it is easier to clean an ordinary piece of steel and keep an edge on it than steel which is chrome plated, the simplest knives are the most suitable. Chrome plating on commercial knives does not stop rust. A double edge is an attractive feature if shark fighting is intended, but not really necessary. Knives should always be worn in tropic waters if for no other reason than the confidence they give the wearer.

Abalone irons are for California divers who enjoy this state's great delicacy. They can be purchased, or a standard tire iron will do the job almost as well.

For fishing off shore where a boat is not used, many gogglers use inner tubes with burlap bags hung down in the hole. The tube permits a tired swimmer to rest as he chooses, and the bag holds the days catch of abalone, lobster, or fish. The European divers have a custom of stringing fish through the mouth and gill on a loop of wire worn at the waist so that the diver lugs his dead and bloody fish at his side as he swims around looking for more. This appears to the authors to be a most foolish and risky business, at least in Florida and Mexican waters. In all probability when a Barracuda comes after fish hung in such a manner, he will not strike or injure the diver, but if the water is murky as it often is at the turn of the tide, even Barracuda can make mistakes. That a 'cuda' will come eventually is inevitable, so fish handled in such a manner means the diver is counting on the good behavior of a most sharp-toothed fish. It would be much better to take each catch ashore or to a boat than do this. Using the burlap bag is not really safe in southern waters, as the blood still gets into the water, and the swimmer paddling his tube home may be attacked. Therefore it is suggested that those who wish to keep fish with them in the water procure some thin rubber sheeting and make a bag of it using a good grade of rubber cement. This bag, suspended in an inner tube and containing a little water will keep fish and lobster fresh but will not allow blood to get into the water.

Figure 59. An exciting action picture of Gustav Dalle Valle taking on a shark off Haiti. Mr. Dalle Valle is one of the great undersea fishermen of this time and has taken many large shark on the spear. He also instructs amateur spearmen and sight-seers in the marvelous water off Port Au Prince, Haiti. His address is Box 923 of that city. (Courtesy O.R.A.)

Mits that fit over the hands do not help swimming to any great degree and in any case prevent proper handling of spearing equipment.

For use from a boat, when a wide area is to be explored, a viewing box for seeing underwater is most useful. Several are available, but they are expensive for such a simply made object. Any diver should be able to turn out his own from a wooden bucket with the bottom cut out. A piece of glass is cut at the glaziers to fit the widest end of the bucket; it is jammed in, and neoprene cement dripped over the glass and wood inside and out. Carefully used, this will reveal large patches of bottom clearly.

The final item is a must for all free swimmers and for divers who are not tended from the surface. It is the already mentioned Res-Q-Pac. When squeezed the wings inflate instantly, supporting all but the heaviest men or those with too much equipment. Since the gadget can

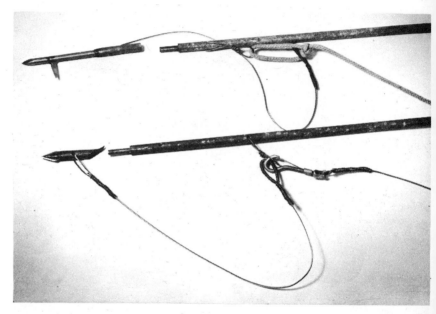

Figure 60. Two spear heads designed and built by the Tampa Tridents. The upper unit has a swinging barb and the lower a removable head that swings at right angles to the line inside the fish. Both heads come off the shaft so that the fish may be fought without the encumbrance of a long shaft. Photo by Burton McNeely. (Courtesy the Tampa Tridents)

be clipped to a strap, belt, or swim suit, it is always handy. This is a particularly necessary item for Aqua-Lung with no emergency air reserve, which as noted, do not give much warning when they give out.

FISHING METHODS

Much has been written on how to spear fish and a consideration of the currently available information shows that everyone has his own favorite methods. One basic fact can be stated at once however, namely

this: *always get as close to the fish as possible*. There are two main reasons
for such a rule. One is that no spear gun is very accurate at more than
10 feet or so, nor does it have much power at greater distances. Hitting
a small fish at 10 feet or more takes more luck than most fishermen
can boast. The second reason is just as important. Long shots at fish
wound more than they kill. A greedy and inept goggler can wound dozens of fish in a bad day and leave a bloody trail over hundreds of yards

Figure 61. Put yourself in this picture! An "Aqua-Lunged" diver goes for a fish.
This sort of thing is sport with a capital S.

of good bottom. Now if there is one thing fish do not like it is blood in
the water. An area treated in such a manner for a couple of weeks will
no longer have any fish at all, and the local surface fishermen will be
extremely unhappy, and justifiably so. Also such a practice may attract
Barracuda or shark to the diver with unfortunate results.

Of course it is an easy matter to say 'get close to the fish' but the
question of how to do it still remains. Considering the various types
of gear in order of their complexity, let's examine some of the possible
techniques.

Using the basic mask, flippers and hand spear, the spearfisher is taking the 'classic' approach to underwater spearing. These are the tools used by the first Europeans who undertook the sport, and they will serve well, if one can find a good area. Such spots still do exist in the Carribean, and Baja California, but even here skill will be required. The fish spear is usually 10 or more feet long, made of one inch wood or thinner steel and tipped with a steel head. These heads can be purchased from the Sea Net Company, the Florida Frogman, and others in a variety of configurations. The best is a so-called needle point with a disappearing barb. Since ease of penetration is of primary

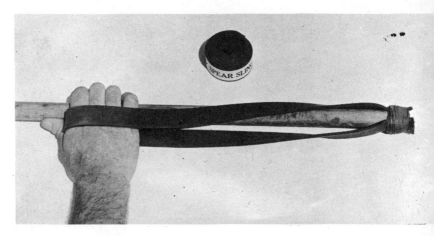

Figure 62. A simple rubber sling for the hand spear obtainable from Bel-Aqua. This photo shows the position of the hand in grasping the spear and rubber for a shot. (Photo by Julius Down)

importance with hand spears, the use of a fixed barb or multi-pointed spear does not seem very attractive except for bottom flounder whose flesh is soft and easily torn.

There no longer seems any reason to use a hand spear as recommended by Guy Gilpatrick in his original book on goggle fishing. That method is simply holding the spear, swimming down, and jabbing. Rather, the spear is augmented by a piece of surgical rubber tubing (inner tube rubber is just as good but may chafe the hand and wrist) which is affixed as shown in Figure 62, with the tube fitting around the thumb as shown. When a strike is to be made, the spear is pulled back and gripped by the hand with the rubber under tension. The swimmer gets a normal breath of air either by raising his head, or through his snorkel, and dives on the fish. This dive can be made in various ways depending on the circumstances. Either an ordinary surface dive is done with the accompanying splashing as the feet go up in the air and the body pivots downward, or the swimmer can sink until he can pivot over without a splash. Swimming down to the fish must be done rapidly using feet and free hand. Approach from behind him if possible, but don't hesitate. Once within range, the hand holding the spear shaft relaxes allowing it to shoot foreward ˙to the extent it was pulled back under tension, usually two feet or so. If you have gotten close enough to the fish you will take him, but do not depend on the thrust of the spear to sink the barbs. Follow up by jabbing with the arm so that the fish is pinned against the bottom by the thrust, and jab hard until he is firmly on the spear.

Many California divers are still taking fish with such rubber powered spears, but they have a hard time competing with the many gun-armed skin divers. In some cases the long hand spear may be an advantage, particularly when fishing in the surf close to shore. The diver here swims just past the point where the breakers start to curl over, and holds his spear pointing down towards the bottom as he swims. If a fish is spotted he usually jabs at him using the rubber to thrust the spear downward into the fish without making a dive. Taking such a fish with a gun would be difficult from the surface, particularly in roiled water which may deflect a spear in its flight.

A further modification of the rubber powered spear is the Hawaian sling spear. See Figure 53. This is a hollow tube with rubber around the back. The spear is pulled through the tube under tension and allowed to shoot foreward and free into the water, attached of course to the sling by a line. Somewhat more range is possible and the spear is usually smaller. Using both these spears in deep water requires a diver to swim down to the full depth and very close to his fish. Generally, the fisherman will be swimming on the surface peering down into the depths through his mask and breathing through the snorkel. When he sees his fish he dives as described before and swims downward. With all but the Pirelli compensating mask, the pressure will force the mask against the face causing some pain. This can be relieved by snorting into the mask through the nose, thereby supplying more air in the cavity, and equalizing the increased pressure. In the Pirelli, a collapsible chamber on the back of the head does this for you. The chamber collapses rather than the mask, since it is the less rigid, and feeds air in until it is empty and flat. Nearing the fish, the spearman will usually be seen by his prey, and the fish may run and escape. More likely, he will dodge beneath some rock or into some seaweed. This requires a rapid change of direction on the part of the spearer, and a quick revaluation of the fish's position. All this may require extremely rapid movements, particularly since 30 seconds may be the maximum underwater duration for the swimmer.

If a spear gun is used in place of the hand spear or sling spear, the technique for smaller fish is very little different from what has already been described. The rubber powered gun will have to be cocked while in the water, and this can usually be done, although it requires effort. The swimmer will have to assume a vertical position in the water, get a good breath of air, and then sink under water while he sets up the rubber bands. The gun's grip is best placed against the groin and, with both hands grasping the elastic, pull them back in one quick movement to the cocked position. You may sink several feet during the

Figure 63. The Janna CO_2 gun distributed by the Florida Frogmen. (O.R.A. Photo by Raepple)

operation but this does not matter. This is NEVER done next to a boat or near another swimmer. If you miss the cocking notch on the spear it will shoot upwards, easily impaling a swimmer above you or someone in a boat overhead. Once the gun is cocked it points toward the bottom as you swim along looking down. The line affixed to the spear head is held by snaps on the gun's side so that it pays out easily when necessary but does not entangle everything during a dive. Some foreign made guns have a fishing reel as a part of the mechanism. The line is wound on the reel which plays it out on a shot. Such a reel could easily be attached to any gun such as the Arbalete or Sea Net models if tangling seems to result from using the simple clips.

Just because you have a powerful gun does not mean you can get halfway down to the target and let drive with the spear a la Wild Bill Hickock snapping shots at rustlers from the hip. All shots should still be made within three feet of the target if possible, and the bigger the fish, the closer you get. The aiming point on a fish is just behind its gills. Forward of this the spear will not penetrate the hard bony gill plates, and aft, the meat will be ruined. If you inspect the catch of a good spearman you will always see that each fish is holed in almost the identical place.

Once the fish has run to cover, you have a chance to place your shot or jab correctly by following him and placing the spear tip right on him before letting go. With a gun there is no need to pin him as with the spear, but if you should observe an expert in action you will see that very seldom does his spear leave his gun, he is that close when firing. With larger fish it may be best to shoot and jab simultaneously to insure maximum penetration. The spear heads used on the Arbalete gun must penetrate two and a half inches before the collapsed barb is in the fish, and with such minimum penetration would probably still pull out. Therefore, sinking the spear at least four inches will prove necessary and in the thick hide of a shark this can be most difficult. When taking on a big tough fish it is best to have at least two or three men with guns going down. Send the best shot in first closely followed (but not from behind) by the second man. If the first spear takes hold, the second man shoots his and the others follow suit, thereby getting several lines to the prey. Then he can be bridled by the swimmers and held in control unless he is simply too huge. As noted, commercial spear shafts bend surprisingly easily on fish weighing over 10 or 15 pounds and extra shafts are necessary in big fish waters.

Another technique used in Baja California and Florida is the use of a float of some sort affixed to the spear line. This may be an inner tube on the surface which is towed by the swimmer until his dive. As he goes down he trails a line behind him affixed to the tube and when the fish is impaled it plays against the tube, and the diver is free to return for a breath. In kelp or heavy weed this line may become entangled. An experienced skin diver, (Jack Prodanovich) suggests the following rig to obviate the difficulty. He has a deflated Mae West life jacket in a bundle clipped to his suit or trunks. When the fish is fast, it pulls on the line to the Mae West and jerks it clear of the clips and diver. The CO_2 inflation valve is rigged so that this pull activates it, and the Mae West inflates and bobs to the surface, clear of the diver, but fast to the fish. All this is getting gimmicky, but for large fish it is necessary when diving equipment is not used. When one considers that a big shark is a much more violent individual than most

Figure 64. A Cape Cod lobster is taken on a spear. Often these shell fish will hole up and be impossible to dislodge unless speared.

African big game, and that the so-called sportsmen who stalk lion or buffalo in the veldt have arsenals of huge power, it is hard to begrudge a diver any slight help he may get from gadgets. The complexity of such inventions must not be such that they foul and tangle half the time they are used, since this is simply dangerous and foolish.

Some remarkably big fish have been taken by non-air supplied swimmers using CO_2 guns or heavy Arbaletes. Spear-fishermen in Florida take 500 pound Jewfish and the reader can rest assured that larger catches are always being made. There is of course no need of complicated equipment for pan fish and small catches.

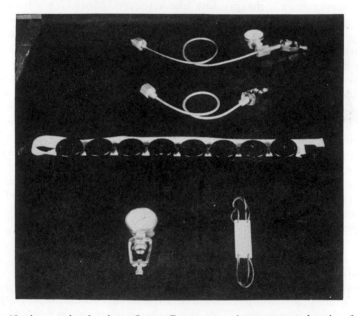

Figure 65. Accessories for Aqua-Lung. From top to bottom; two charging fittings, the weighted belt with one pound iron weights, a small pressure gauge with yoke for checking tank pressure, and the wrist depth gauge. When using this belt be sure to knot the free end once weights are on lest they fall off during diving. Also, this belt must not be used without the slip knot described in the previous chapter. (Courtesy U.S. Divers Co.)

The CO_2 gun used in conjunction with catridge powered heads is the most powerful weapon available. It is needed for the largest sharks, manta rays, and possibly Jewfish running over 200 pounds. Again the gun must be used at close range, but when used thusly it has enormous muzzle energy. For big time fishing, the CO_2 gun owner should have some 'drivers' precision machined for his gun barrel. These are simply short lengths of steel rod that fit snugly in the barrel behind a short spear. The snugger the fit, the greater the gas pressure and the higher the muzzle energy. The driver may be lost on a shot if the spear actually leaves the muzzle, but this is generally not so on large fish where the spear tip may actually touch the hide before firing. This may appear to be uneconomical, but it must be remembered that the CO_2 gun allows the use of short spears that will not bend in a big fish since they may go completely into him, so one spear may last throughout a season's fishing. Wire line may be necessary, or still better, aircraft shock cord which is both tough and elastic. Don't skimp on the vital link between spear and float or diver, since a big fish may not die when hit, and may snap a meagre line like a thread. Most CO_2 guns do not have anything more than a trigger which feeds gas into the chamber as long as the trigger is pulled. Thus, to conserve gas, the gun must be triggered quickly, and the trigger not held. The loud blast of gas in the water may scare fish, so short sharp triggering is doubly important. However, when a big one comes nosing around, he can often be scared away by the noise of the gun being fired slowly (without a spear). At the time of writing, explosive heads are not on the general market, but when they become available they should prove to be sufficient for anything which swims, short of a Whale Shark.

The reader still may feel that no great secrets have been revealed, but the fact is that there are no real secrets to successful spear fishing. Skill and practice go together and a certain amount of physical endurance is no hindrance. Later on we will consider certain specific fish and methods of taking them, but only by getting into the sea often will the novice take everything he shoots at.

THE USE OF DIVING EQUIPMENT

The majority of spear fishers still do not use air supplies simply because they are complicated and expensive as compared with the simple mask. But it should be remembered that while fishing can be successful without diving, many other underwater activities cannot. Photography under water demands an air supply and dives without diving equipment deeper than 20 feet or so are not safe for any but experts. There is a current trend to see who can go the deepest under his own power for no other reason than to make some kind of a dubious record. This is most foolish. There is a growing collection of semi-invalids in Europe who have wrecked themselves by over-diving to great depths. Beyond 30 feet a swimmer with full lungs is no longer bouyant due to the collapse of his lung cavity under pressure. He thus has to fight his way back. The deep swimmer often has nose bleeds, and the interior of his nose may become a mass of clots. He may rupture his eardrums due to the necessity of rapid descent, and the strain

Figure 66. How about some shell fish for dinner? Not quite as inexpensive as a clam rake, perhaps, but who ever saw a clam flat that looked like this?

on the heart is tremendous. Very much of this sort of inane activity will enlarge and damage the heart valving mechanisms and lead to an untimely demise. Japanese women go to over a 100 feet, and Greek sponge fishers go even deeper, but few of them live to be 70. The real sport in undersea activity is the taking of big fish, not stupidly straining the body beyond its proper balance.

Of course with diving equipment none of the above complaints appear, for air or oxygen is fed into the lungs to maintain them in their normal condition and descents can be leisurely for those with ear pain. The reader who has read carefully the chapters on equipment should be able to evaluate the various rigs as far as undersea fishing is concerned, but the special advantages and disadvantages will be noted. Remember that the place of diving, the method of getting there, and the availability of compressed air locally all play a part in equipment selection. This phase has already been discussed in this chapter. The would-be equipment purchaser should thus weigh these aforementioned suggestions with those yet to come, and try to reach an optimum solution based on his own capabilities, his diving location, and the type of fish expected.

The throw-away self-contained characterised by the noted Aqua-Lung is most commonly used today, and is generally the simplest. As noted in the self-contained chapters, in such equipment the rate of use of air is in proportion to the depth and exertion of the diver. Thus cruising along at 30 feet means that the diver must come up twice as quickly as if he were just beneath the surface. Since charging air bottles costs money and time, the optimum use of such gear is to swim along the surface just as though a mask and snorkel were used, and to dive only when something interesting is seen on the bottom. The Aqua-Lung and all other American units of this type are not giving the best possible efficiency of air saving since they do not permit breathing atmospheric air easily on the surface. By incorporating the Pirelli idea in Aqua-Lung, namely affixing a snorkel and valve to the mouth piece, the overall saving in air will be great. The authors believe that average air consumption can be cut in half by this relatively simple device so that instead of using two tanks in an average day, one tank will prove enough. At $1.50 a tank charge, it wouldn't take many days of diving to pay for such a modification. Also, the diver will not need as many spare tanks at $75 apiece. This modification of existing gear is fully covered in the self-contained chapter. There can be no doubt that the bubbles from a throw-away unit frighten and disturb fish, but the degree of fear may not be much except for the most skittish undersea inhabitants. Also, since the equipment is often used in a dive, the fish does not have a chance to become too wary before he is impaled. Before using any throw-away gear, the reader should read over the chapter on them carefully, and learn all their tricks and dangers.

The recirculating self-contained has just the opposite disadvantages from the throw-away. Since it usually has a valve admitting oxygen that must be operated manually, a rapid dive to high pressure will tend to decrease the volume of the breathing bag before more gas can be admitted, thus making the diver short of breath. This is particularly true in fishing where the hands are occupied by the spear paraphernalia. Probably the best solution is simply to hold your breath on the dive and forget about valving in oxygen until the spear has been released. However, the recirculator permits spending all the time down on the bottom where the fish can be taken without diving at all,

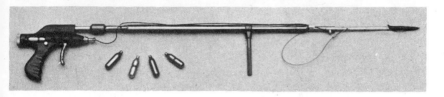

Figure 67. The Barracuda single shot CO_2 gun. The gun has a safety and clips to hold the spear line. A single barbed head is shown on the spear which pivots when in a fish. (Courtesy Metal Formfab Corp.)

providing the spearman has a gun or at least a rubber driven spear. Walking or swimming along the bottom is a tricky way of fishing for the element of surprise is usually lacking. Often the diver can take a heavy bar of metal and pound on rocks and coral laying open small crustaca for fish chum. Staying in the vicinity until the fish congregate will usually insure a catch of smaller fish, though the big ones are not so easily attracted. When a wreck is located, it will usually be the richest place in the area for large fish. If it is in bad condition, the diver may have to swim down among the ship's plates searching for fish and ready to fire at a moment's notice. A depth gauge is a must for recirculators since the oxygen poisoning matter cannot be disregarded and this effect represents the main disadvantage as far as recirculators are concerned. Of course dives to 50 or 60 feet can be made after fish providing the swimmer does not stay there longer than a few minutes, but it is easy to forget and have the symptoms of oxygen poisoning in deep water before realizing you have remained too deep too long. Thus a habit of checking (the depth guage) constantly is necessary for all recirculator users. The other disadvantage of recirculating equipment over throw-away is its complexity necessitating more skill in use and more practice. The main advantage is its lack of bubbles for fishing and its easily portable oxygen supply.

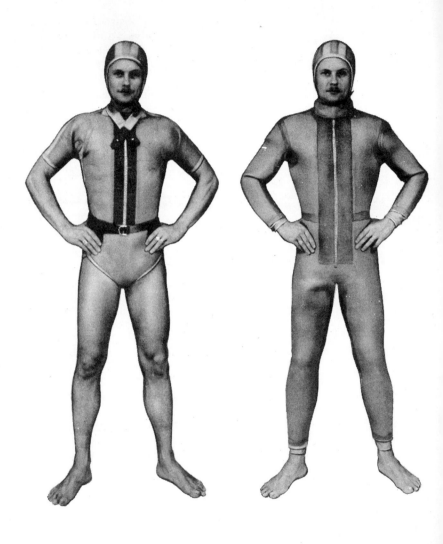

Figure 68. Two swimming and diving dresses. These units are the so-called 'mid-Season' tunics for spearfishermen. They have zipper fronts, are made of rubber, but are not completely watertight. The theory being that the little water that is trapped between suit and skin will be a warming layer. (Courtesy La Spirotechnique)

The use of diving masks with no safety line ('free swimming with air supplied masks') had been little utilized, but the authors have found this a completely satisfactory method of taking fish. The free air hose must float as explained in the mask chapter so that wherever the diver swims the hose will be going to the surface directly above him. Using the diving mask equipped thusly the fisherman can either dive on his prey or stalk him on the bottom. The main disadvantage is the fact that his wanderings are limited by the hose length. It might appear that tangling would result when more than one diver is in the water, but such does not happen very often since the divers usually have no trouble keeping their lines free of one another. Swimming with the hose is no trouble and in fact it is usually not even noticeable, until you are following a nice fish and are brought up by the too short hose. If the divers are experienced, and a large volume tank with 60 psi maintained at all times is connected between the compressor and the hose to the diver, only one person need be in the boat with two or three divers over the side. Instant warning is given in event of compressor stoppage by the different sound of the entering air and everyone can easily get to the surface while the volume tank exhausts air. One observer must always be in the boat however, to watch for other boats, check on equipment operation, and generally keep an eye on the hose lines in case someone should get in trouble. For fishing purposes a valve at the mask is necessary, not·only so that the shallower diver is not taking all the air, but so that it is possible to shut the air off completely when approaching a fish. This feature on the mask gives it the advantage of a recirculator for a few moments of stalking on the bottom, although of course the breath can be held with a throwaway self-contained to produce the same effect. A general listing of the various types of diving equipment listed in this book may prove useful with their salient features emphasized.

Gear	Type of Fishing	Advantages	Disadvantages
Non-air supplied mask	All types within 30 feet of surface	Simple, cheap,. portable	Can't go deep, exhausting
Diving helmets	None	None	Can't swim or dive
Throw-away self-contained	All types	Simple, can go deep, fairly portable	Requires compressed air source
Recirculating self-contained	All types within 30 feet of surface	Very portable oxygen supply	Complex, not good for rapid dives
Air-supplied mask	All types	Simple, no high pressure gas	Not portable, limited diving area covered

This table can be used in conjunction with the one noted earlier in the chapter regarding portability and availability of air or oxygen to

Figure 69. Gustav Dalle Valle catches a turtle in Haitian waters. If firmly held at the back of the shell, a turtle can be steered by the diver towards the surface. Photo by Philip Nash. (Courtesy Gustav Dalle Valle)

select the proper outfit. Whatever outfit is used, the reader should read carefully those sections of the book covering his gear and understand it thoroughly. Do not believe any advertising or write-ups which say that this or that equipment is fool proof. No mechanism or device is secure against a fool, and a fool is someone who is too stupid to learn to use the equipment properly.

CONSERVATION

Offhand, one would say that there could be no conservation problem in underwater fishing, the ocean being a rather large and populous place. That this is definitely not the case has become most evident in Florida and California.

Essentially, most fish can live within a certain range of water depths and those fish classified as shallow water types are found in water depths of 20 to 200 feet or so. Usually such a fish will prefer a shallow reef since it tends to be richer in food supply, unless conditions in shallow water become intolerably frightening. An inexperienced and greedy fisherman turned loose on a tropical reef easily can become the frightening factor that will drive fish further into the open sea, into deeper water, making them inaccessible to other spear-fishers. This is due to two main causes. One is simply overfishing. Some Florida spearmen have taken a half a ton of smaller fish in one wild weekend over a small area of reef and sold them in Miami at good prices. One can easily imagine conditions in the fishing area while these fish hogs did their devious work. CO_2 blasts, many dead fish, blood in the water, larger fish attracted and maddened by the slaughter, in short a nightmare for the small edible fish unlike anything ever before experienced. Add to this the second factor, namely, the wounded fish thrashing about after the greedy gogglers have left, and it is not hard to see why fish begin to look for a region that the gogglers cannot hit.

Florida fishermen who use conventional surface methods have been extremely upset over spear-fishing, and the possibility of stringent restrictive legislations are likely at any time. Thus, all thinking underwater fishermen should do their best to curb needless slaughter and promote sportsmanship among all spearfishers. Clubs can do a great deal of good along this line, and it is gratifying to see that California clubs have taken intelligent and reasonable attitudes towards legislation relating to underwater fishing. The use of diving equipment is now illegal in California for the taking of lobster and abalone, a move that most clubs felt was warranted in spite of the hardship it forces on inept or amateur divers.

Unfortunately, some divers have voiced rather strange ideas about legislation protecting the bottom from over-fishing. The attitude of

Figure 70. A pictorial summary of underwater fishing methods; I—A diver in shallow water surface-swims and shoots flounder from the surface. II—A skin diver makes a conventional surface dive (A) and prepares to hand spear a fish against a rocky cliff where he can pin him. III—A skin diver sinks under (A), flips over and swims down (B), and after shooting a large fish releases his floating gun and prepares

to finish the fish off with a knife (C). IV—A throw-away equipped diver sinks in the water (A) and dives on a large fish with his CO_2 gun. As his spear strikes the fish, a Mae West attached to the spear line inflates to play the fish (B). V—A surface supplied mask diver swims after some fish. VI—A recirculator (no bubbles) equipped diver stalks a fish from behind a rock.

the few seems to be that since all undersea fishermen are heroes engaged in supremely dangerous sport, they should be permitted an entirely open season on everything that swims including trout, salmon and other fresh water fish. The objections to such an attitude are too numerous to consider in detail here, although a few are worth mentioning.

1) As noted, overfishing and careless (wounding) fishing will drive fish into deeper and inaccessible water.

2) A given area can support only a very few large fish (such as Jewfish) and once it is cleaned out, restocking could take many years, providing it can occur at all with the few fish left.

3) The slaughter of one particular type of edible fish in an area could conceivably upset the ecological balance, and disturb the entire bottom life profoundly.

4) Trout and other fresh water fish frequent small pools which could be completely looted by a single spearman in a day, since the fish cannot escape up or down stream in periods of low water.

It is up to those divers who love the sport to denounce their fellows who are either unwise or greedy. The authors suggest the following rules of conduct for diving clubs and individuals who wish the maximum of sport with the minimum of restrictive legislation and bad feeling. Don't forget that the surface fishing equipment industry is a giant compared to spear fishing, and no group of spearfishers can hope to beat the tackle industry, charter boat operators, and fish and game associations, in a knock down fight.

1) No fish taken by spear should ever be sold. Clubs should institute the most stringent punishment of members who violate this rule.

2) Fish should be taken for two reasons only, a) Pure sport (i.e. shark, ray, etc.) b) Edibility (i.e. Jewfish, Snook, Mackeral, Flounder, etc.) Thus small, inedible fish are not legitimate targets for the sportsman.

3) Reasonable limits should be decided on. One large Jewfish per man per day would not seem unfair. A poundage limit on small edible species should be established.

4) No prizes in contests should be awarded for number or total poundage of fish taken, since this encourages unthinking over-fishing. The true sportsman is the man who brings in a big shark, Jewfish, Barracuda, etc. not the one who gets 50 pounds of perch.

5) Inedible fish highly prized by surface anglers (best example, the Tarpon) should not be taken by spearmen under any circumstances, since other types are just as sporty underwater.

6) Every undersea fisherman should acquaint himself with the types of fish to be found in his area, so that only edible small fish will be taken. Many books are available (See Appendix C) and an introduction is given to fish spotting in the next chapter.

If Florida fishermen follow the California example, it may be that the situation will stabilize with reasonably good fishing for all, and no tears from the surface fishermen. But if the few false prophets who advocate wide open slaughter are followed, real sportsmen may find themselves without a sport.

SPEARFISHING CLUBS

It has been noted that with the boom of underwater sport, has come a large number of clubs consisting of from a few to 200 or more members. In California, the active clubs have formed an association which in turn is affiliated with the Ocean Fish Protective Association, a powerful sportsman's group with lobbying and other functions.

There are pros and cons to joining a club, but certainly the pros are predominant, since as with any organization, it is not necessary to follow in all its activities. One big factor for club members are prize contests, 'championships' etc. which are most often open to clubs. Also, being in a club allows the individual to put his point of view as regards conservation and fishing conduct before interested people, and perhaps get things done. Large clubs, such as the Los Angeles Neptunes perform certain services for their members such as trying out all new commercial equipment, and issuing data on its worth. This is a useful service indeed in a field that is growing in expense and complexity and in which dangerous devices may appear at any time. By talking over diving situations with the 'old hands' sensible procedures can be learned, and bad habits avoided.

Probably the most useful thing of all for a club member is the fact that he can usually find a diving partner when he is going fishing. It is important that no free swimming far from shore with or without diving equipment be undertaken by a solitary man. But the average skin diver may have difficulty coordinating his vacation periods with the few friends he may have who are interested in the same field. If he belongs to a club he should usually be able to find someone heading for the same area and thus both divers can operate under the all important 'buddy system'.

The important thing is to have fun, enjoy the undersea, and stay within sensible limits as regards exertion, size of fish attacked, and depth of dive.

Chapter VII

THE OCEAN AND ITS INHABITANTS

The study of the oceans, their currents, waves, and bottoms, and the fish and other life that live in them can be divided into three main catagories. These are; *Oceanography*, the study of the physical nature of the sea, *Marine Biology*, the study of the sea's inhabitants, and *Marine Geology*, the study of the topographical nature of the bottom and its rocks and history. Of these three scientific fields, the first two consider topics of interest to the shallow diver, the third dealing generally with deeper phenomena and more specialized material than the average diver wishes to consider.

Some data from Oceanography has already been considered in this book relating to underwater sound, radio wave propagation, and the temperatures and pressures beneath the sea surface. The subfield of this ocean science which has the greatest of practical utility for the average diver is *Coastal Oceanography*, which deals with inshore wind waves, breakers, currents, and surf. All divers have been or will be involved in one or more of these phenomena so a review of information on them should be well worth considering. The authors cannot, of course, go into detail on any research in these highly technical fields, which might be undertaken by divers since such a discussion would have no interest for the average reader. But it might be noted here that the use of diving gear in Coastal Oceanography can and undoubtedly will provide rapid answers to some problems, as well as providing means for the rapid placement of measuring instruments.

Marine biologists are concerned with many diverse matters, many of them of little use to a diver. Rather than procede on a lengthy exposition of ecology, cellular structure, etc. only a few interesting observations from this field will be made plus a short consideration of various fish, their habits, and their potential as prey for the underwater fisherman.

Current emphasis in Marine Biology and Oceanography has been on deep water work with little practical interest to divers. A return to the study of shallower areas will probably be forthcoming as the necessity of harvesting more and more food from the sea becomes increasingly obvious. The shallow waters of both the northern and southern seas may someday have to feed many people and a thorough understanding of the ecology and fish populations of these waters will be needed.

One aspect of Marine Geology might be mentioned in passing, namely tidelands oil. Divers are actively employed by many oil companies in the search for fuel in the shallow waters off the coasts of the Southern United States. Perhaps not only our food but our heat and light may someday come in substantial measure from the sea.

WIND WAVES, CURRENTS, AND SURF

The study of the sometimes violent dividing line between land and sea is both a practical and fascinating one. Structural engineers who design shore installations of any sort require every scrap of information they can get in this field, for the destructive surge and flow of the ocean against the land can produce unbelievable strains in man-made devices. Similarly, a mask equipped swimmer or self-contained diver who has to come and go through surf and operate in currents and waves should know and understand the forces around him.

Wind Waves: When a steady wind blows over a water surface a portion of its energy is transmitted to the water which gradually builds up waves which in turn gradually increase in velocity. Thus the energy transfer from wind to water goes in part to building up the height of the waves and in part to speeding their travel. The height of a wind wave as it approaches a beach or shore line will in general depend on two things, the wind velocity over the water and the *fetch* of the wave. The fetch is defined as the length of the stretch of water over which the wind blows. The relationship between wave height (H), wind velocity (W) and fetch (F) can be expressed roughly as

$$H = k \, (W^2 \times F^{1/2}) \qquad (11)$$

where k is some constant. Thus doubling the wind velocity will increase the wave height by a factor of four. Also, waves rolling in from a storm in the open sea where the fetch may be a thousand miles will be much larger than waves built up in a narrow bay a mile or two wide. This is one reason why ships seek an anchorage which has an upwind spit of land or breakwater cutting the fetch to only a few hundred yards rather than hundreds of miles.

Another characteristic of wind waves which is of interest to those who must work in amongst them is the steepness of the wavefront. It is much more pleasant to conduct diving operations from a boat that rises and falls on long rolling combers than one that leaps about in a sharp, steep chop. To consider this question it is first necessary to establish an expression for the velocity of a surface wave. The well known formula for the case of shallow water is

$$c = (g\ D)^{\frac{1}{2}} \tag{12}$$

where c is the velocity of the surface wave in feet per second, D the water depth in feet, and g a constant (32.2 feet/sec²). This tells us

Figure 71. The spiny lobster of California, a popular prey for skin divers. The lobster must not be taken by diving equipment but only by lung power. (Courtesy of The Skin Diver)

that in shallow water the velocity of a wave depends only on the depth of the water. (This formula is only applicable for the case where depth is less than one half the wave length, but will hold for most open, coastal water.) Now we can evaluate the criteria for the steepness of a wave. When the ratio of wave velocity (c) to wind velocity (W) is small, the steepness expressed as the ratio of wave height to wave length is large, while a large c:W ratio gives slight steepness. For those who may have lost the sense of these formulations, a useful table is provided:

TABLE VII

Fetch	Wind Velocity	Wave Height	Water Depth	Wave Velocity	Steep-ness	State of the Sea
short	small	small	small	small	slight	calm, slight chop
short	small	small	larger	larger	none	calm, rollers
short	large	large	small	small	large	steep chop
short	large	large	larger	larger	slight	moderate rollers
long	small	moderate	small	small	slight	moderate chop
long	small	moderate	larger	larger	none	small rollers
long	large	great	small	small	great	violent chop
long	large	great	larger	larger	small	great rollers

The above table gives in qualitative language what can be expected under varying sea conditions. If, for instance, an onshore wind (long fetch) is creating a bad chop, we can see from the table that if the wind swings offshore (short fetch) the chop will remain bad, though the wave height will be less. The only way the chop can be flattened is for the wind to drop or the water to become deeper, i.e. the tide to come in.

One other factor which influences the height of wind waves has not yet been mentioned, namely the time elapsed since the wind began to blow. When the wind first starts to blow over a sea surface the waves build up rapidly, but their height increase falls off as time goes on. As an example, it requires five hours for a 50 mile an hour wind to raise waves eight feet high, but after five more hours the waves have increased only four more feet to a total of 12.

So far we have considered aspects of wind waves which are mainly of interest to those on the surface, but the most important conclusions which have special interest to divers will now be noted. As every diver knows, surface waves affect the undersea like a wind that blows periodically in two opposite directions. The diver on the bottom sees the ferns, fish, and his own body swaying back and forth in phase with the passage of surface waves. When a surface wave moves along it forces the water particles within and beneath it to move in elliptical paths. Obviously, the water cannot simply travel with the wave for this would mean that all the water in the ocean would arrive at a coast and innundate it, something that does not happen. Each water particle stays in its own particular area of ocean and moves in a vertical oval path as each wave front passes. If we examine the shape of these oval paths while descending downward

Figure 72. Dr. Nelson Mathison of the Los Angeles Neptunes with 110 pound Garropa (a typical member of the grouper family) taken off La Paz, Baja, California.

toward the bottom we find that the ovals become more flattened close to the bottom until just over the bottom the water is moving in straight lines, back and forth in a horizontal path. But more important than this is the fact that the further down we progress from the surface, the smaller the ellipses become and the less the surface wave is affecting the undersea. Quite obviously, if we can determine the depth at which these ellipses are practically non-existant, we will know how deep we must go to be in calm water, or if, in a given situation, we will find ourselves being badly swayed by passing waves. Fortunately, there is an excellent answer to this question which can be depended upon to give good results in most situations. The rule is: if the depth of the water exceeds half the distance between two adjacent waves, there will be negligible swaying effects on the bottom. That this is an extremely useful rule can be shown by the following example.

Suppose diving is to be conducted in a seaway of very heavy swells. Watch the sea surface and try to estimate the distance between the longest successive wave crests. Suppose it is roughly 50 feet. Then even without diving we know that in water greater than 25 feet deep the effect of the waves will be small and the diver will be able to work on the bottom unhindered by the annoying back and forth motion of the wave surges. In some confused seas it is difficult to judge the length between wave crests, but it may be possible to time the period of the wave, that is, the time interval between successive waves, taking the largest as the ones to measure. If this is possible, the depth beyond which no effects are felt can be computed from;

$$D = 2.55 \ T^2 \tag{13}$$

where T is the time between crests in seconds and D is in feet of water. For example, suppose the time between waves is three seconds, then T^2 is nine, and D will be 2.55 times 9 or 23 feet.

Another conclusion can be drawn from all that has been said. In examining Table VII, we see in general that comparatively deep water produces rollers, that is, long waves, and shallow water produces choppy or short waves. But, from the preceding discussion, long rollers will be felt at a greater depth than short chop. Therefore it can be generally said that while rolling swells are more pleasant for those in the surface boat they are a nuisance to the diver who must work in deeper water to escape their effect, while a steep chop is bad on the surface but does not penetrate very far underwater. By learning the interrelationships presented here and coupling this knowledge with practical diving experience, the reader should be able to predict bottom conditions for a given sea quite accurately.

In cases where undersea photography, or precise technical work is to be done on the bottom, it is important to know if bad swaying effects are present, for if they are, it may be necessary to use heavy weighted belts and more tenders, etc.

Breakers and Surf: When a wind generated wave approaches shallow water the velocity of travel decreases as the depth decreases. Since the time between waves does not alter, it follows that the distance between crests must also decrease. It is said by oceanographers that when this occurs, the wave is 'feeling' bottom. That is, the frictional drag on the bottom of the wave is changing its shape and characteristics. (A wave feels bottom when its wavelength is twice the water depth as discussed in the previous section.) As the wave velocity decreases, the energy of velocity is partially transformed into added wave height so that shallow water waves grow taller as the bottom shelves, the crests becoming narrow and steep, the troughs wide and flat.

Since the forward velocity of the wave is continually decreasing, the water in the wave crest eventually achieves a speed greater than the overall velocity of forward progress and the crest tumbles over the front of the wave or the wave breaks. A short steep wave that comes into shallow water with an already steep front will break soon after it feels bottom since it does not need much decrease in velocity to become unstable, whereas long rollers will move well inshore before breaking. Surf on exposed portions of the Atlantic and Pacific coasts is characteristic of extremely long waves coming in over great distances and forming long, regular lines of surf that begin at a constant distance from shore. In bays and inlets under high wind velocities the entire area may be irregularly pocked with small breaking waves indicating that when the wave was formed it was short and steep and extremely unstable. It should be noted that the relations in the previous section do not hold true in very shallow water when a wave is beginning to crest. In such water it is very easy to see where the bottom will be roiled up by noting where the waves begin to steepen and where the wavelength is decreasing.

In regions where the bottom shallows and then grows deeper, such as reefs, waves will break over the shallow portion offshore and then subside and continue inwards, breaking a second time on the beach. Long surf that may begin many yards from shore and thunder inwards with continual white crests (such as in Hawaii) is formed by a flat bottom just shallow enough to make the wave unstable. Since the bottom does not shelve upward appreciably, the wave does not lose its energy at once, but expends it gradually as it rolls inward. In some cases surf may exhaust itself before reaching shore, the disturbance arriving on the beach without white caps or froth.

It is important to note that the violence of breakers and surf depend on two factors. One is the total energy in the wave as it approaches the shore, and the other is the character of the bottom where the wave breaks. Wave energy is manifested in two aspects, wave height and wave velocity. This can be deceptive in the case of very long rollers which do not appear to be very high or steep, but which are moving at high velocity, for when they reach shallow water and break they may form violent surf as their velocity energy is consumed. It is therefore unwise to approach a beach from the sea simply because only low waves are in evidence off shore. In fact, a sharp chop offshore generally characterizes milder breakers than very long, low combers moving at high speed. If the bottom shelves very rapidly the total energy of a wave will be transformed into crashing surf with sudden violence while a beach with a gently sloping bottom will usually have gentler surf starting way out and rolling inward. It is often possible by examining Coast and Geodetic charts to predict the type of breakers over a stretch of beach by noting how close together the depth contour lines are placed at waters edge. Very little wave energy is lost in friction, most of it arriving at the beach in the form of surf and breakers.

Aside from selecting a section of coast that has minimum surf disturbance, the free-swimming diver is also vitally interested in the processes occurring in a breaking wave, since he may, through design or accident, be inside one. As already noted the water masses in a wave travel in oval paths with the plane of the oval perpendicular to the bottom. Thus we would expect if looking at the cross section of a breaking wave to see the crest traveling forward with high speed, the bottom of the wave receding or standing still, and the average motion of the whole wave being slowly forward. To attempt to swim outward at the crest of a wave would thus be foolish since the swimmer would be fighting a high speed mass of water. Everyone who swims in surf knows that when a wave is breaking one dives quickly beneath it and swims strongly outward. As the surf crests over, there will be a slight surge of bottom water toward the beach followed by a general movement toward the open sea, pulling the diver with it. Even the largest breakers can be crossed in this manner, but coming back through them to shore is another matter.

Once outside breakers, it is difficult to judge their position and violence until one is actually caught up in the tumbling crest and smashed to the sand. This is partially due to the inability to judge the wave energy from a seaward direction as noted previously. A man equipped with free swimming diving gear is probably best off near the bottom, watching the water surface over him. After a wave has broken it may be impossible to swim inward due to the backwash, but as the next wave starts to build up, the water next to the bottom will be moving slowly and the diver can pull towards shore. If the water is breaking into water deeper than two or three feet, it will not matter if the wave comes down on top of him, providing he is scraping the bottom, but should the bottom shelve so quickly that the wave breaks over exposed sand, any attempt tó reach shore will be risky. Thus before swimming in breakers or surf a careful observance of the conditions is necessary, keeping in mind that the return to shore is much more difficult to do successfully than the swim out to sea.

Figure 73. One of the most astonishing sights in the movie, UNDER THE RED SEA, is this forty foot whale shark. Hans Hass and his fellow divers made a minute photographic study of this beast as it cruised by close under the surface. Although this fish is docile, anything this big must be watched since a tail flip could break a man's back. (Courtesy RKO Radio Pictures)

When using throw-away equipment with heavy air tanks strapped to the back, great care must be taken in rough water lest the tank or regulator strike the diver's head and injure him. Possibly a strap through the crotch will hold the tanks down on the back.

Tides and Currents: There are many phenomena of surf and breakers inshore that are not yet explained. Undertow is one, and, in fact, its very existence is doubted by some oceanographers. Rip currents that flow out to sea through breakers and that carry swimmers with them are not understood, though there is no doubt that many bathers have been drowned in freak currents during rough weather. Doubtless the complex of current patterns inshore will not be explained until actual surveys have been made by skilled free-swimming divers.

Because such currents exist, diving or swimming on a strange coast can be dangerous if the wind is strong. Possibly the best advice to diving gear equipped swimmers who get caught in such currents is to change depth and try and find water that is still, or at least moving in the direction desired. It does not seem generally possible that an entire mass of water can be moving out to sea continuously unless the current circles back into shore at some other point. If changing depth does not get the diver out of the current he should ride it on the theory that it may bring him back to shore or at least lose its power far from the beach. Any current will be smaller right down at the bottom since there is frictional drag here, and escape should be made by swimming to this region. If there is plenty of air in the rig, any diver should be able to escape even the worst rip currents if he stays cool and searches for a way out.

Aside from local inshore currents, all divers are interested in widespread currents in deeper water due to the tide and other factors. In a harbor or other restricted waterway, a change in tide often forces water to rush through the entrance with considerable velocity, making diving operations difficult or impossible. A general rule in such cases is that diving is best undertaken right at high or low water. There have been cases of currents so strong that a diver in full suit has been stretched out on the end of his life line like the tail of a kite.

Currents due to tidal action are tremendously complex in general and it is usually not possible to predict current action in any area without proper tables prepared by the Coast and Geodedic survey or similar agency. Sometimes a current will be moving West on the surface and East on the bottom and its velocity may rise or fall with increasing depth.

One aspect of tides which is of interest to all divers and most particularly undersea fishermen and photographers is the marked change in visibility that can occur with a tide change. Often in Florida the water will be clear as crystal until high or low water and at the turn of the tide become murky and silty in a matter of minutes. This is apparently due to the combination of tidal currents and reef currents which clash under certain conditions and stir up the bottom badly. It is very important to the diver arriving in a strange locality to find out the tides at which this occurs, since fishing often becomes impossible or at least somewhat dangerous due to Barraccuda and other predatory fish. Sometimes a change in tide will sweep cold

Figure 74. A forty pound white sea bass taken off Catalina by Mr. Woody Dimel, proving that big fish are present in this area for those who know how to find and spear them. (Photo by Julius Downs)

ocean water over a reef and produce a marked change in temperature in a very short time.

MARINE LIFE

The amount and variety of life in the seas continues to astound those who study it. There are rich and fascinating rewards to the naturalist-diver who studies the fish and plants of the bottom from an underwater perspective. The subject is too vast for any but the most skimpy account, but the interested reader will find references in Appendix C to help him begin his study. Those fish and plants which have some interest to divers and spearfishermen will be briefly reviewed in this section.

STINGING CREATURES

In tropic waters it is fairly easy to touch or step on some plant or animal that can leave a nasty sore spot. It is important in such waters to wear something covering the entire foot under swim fins if any walking on the bottom is necessary. Here are a few representative specimens to look out for:

Portuguese Man O'War: A floating jelly-like fish about one foot long with vivid purple and reddish tints, this creature looks like a large blob of translucent plastic floating serenely on the surface. Beneath it hang tentacles that can be up to 30 feet in length and which will raise bad welts on the skin if touched. Found as far north as Cape Cod, the Man O'War must be avoided.

Sea Urchin: A pure black handful of spines, the urchin does not actually have stinging cells. If stepped on or bumped the needle sharp spines enter the flesh where they may cause infection. Removal of the spines is difficult. Found in great abundance in rock crevices off Florida and in all tropic waters.

Jelly Fish: Many varieties of jelly fish are found in all waters and only some will sting. Beware of particularly large specimens since these can be dangerous if blundered into carelessly.

Sponges: Most sponges have sting cells which they need to trap food in the many passages. Generally, the sting of a sponge is not serious, but they should be handled with care.

Coral: Beware of cuts on coral for these can be very painful and may not heal for months. In the Pacific many servicemen caught coral fever from cuts while swimming, though this does not seem to happen around the waters of the United States. Coral underwater is very sharp and the flesh may be soft from exposure to water, so move carefully over reefs and broken bottom.

Bristle Worm: A bright pink worm a few inches long found in tropic waters. It has a covering of white spines which will give a painful sting if the worm is handled.

Figure 75. A good sized Barracuda taken by the Tampa Tridents Club of Florida. If the diver stays clear of bloody areas in the water he need not fear these impressive teeth. Photo by Bill Friend. (Courtesy the Tampa Tridents)

Sea Anemone: These bright, flower-like creatures grow attached to the bottom and can be found in all colors and many shapes, though usually they look like a small bunch of flowers in a large thick vase. The 'petals' can give a nasty sting.

FISH

Every spear fisherman should acquaint himself with the different varieties of fish in his area, so that he will not kill inedible species needlessly. Here are a few of the more common types.

Striped Bass: The 'stripers' are a sport fish ranging the length of both coasts of the U.S. They are often found in surf just beyond the breaking point of the waves, but are protected against spearmen in some areas by rather ridiculous local laws.

The Mackeral Family: Also sport fish and often the target of spearmen. All types of Mackeral are very fast in the water and some species will jump 20 feet through the air when running a school of bait.

Scup: A flat sided panfish caught in most waters, it is found on the bottoms in weed or kelp and around rocks.

Tautog: This fish is also found on the bottom with the Scup, but is larger running to five pounds or more. The Tautog is a heavy bodied, dark fish which usually finds its way into chowders.

Snapper: The Red Snapper is perhaps Florida's most succulent fish, often going at steak prices. It is flat sided with a reddish tint and is very shy, usually running under weed when frightened.

Snook: This is a very sporty fish that runs to 50 pounds and moves rapidly when disturbed. He has a pointed head and a black stripe running the length of his body, and can be found around wrecks and in coral regions.

Flounder: This thin, flat fish is found on both coasts and usually lays on its side on the bottom. They are often not seen until stepped on when they undulate away like a skimmed plate. Can be taken easily with a hand spear but you must have sharp eyes.

Tarpon: This fish supports a multi-million dollar tackle industry. It is also inedible. Florida clubs have agreed not to take the fish by spear under any circumstances and all visiting spearmen should abide by this agreement.

Barracuda: The behavior of this fish underwater is extremely puzzling. He will swim directly up to a diver and circle him at a distance of only a few feet, a most disconcerting action for the novice diver. The 'cuda has, apparently, an insatiable curiosity so that the spearman can take him by backing up, thereby enticing the fish in very close. If shot cleanly the 'cuda dies quickly, but a big one will run like a shot from a cannon if hurt and may severely jar the shooter before the line breaks. A man dragging behind a boat in Barracuda waters will often attract the fish, and dragging is not safe for this reason. Flashy jewelry is also out of the question since the 'cuda might strike at the glitter, especially in water that is murky. Barracuda run up to six feet in length, although three or four is more likely.

Jewfish: This fish is a member of the prolific grouper family and there are several species found in Florida and California. The Black Jewfish runs very large, up to 600 pounds, but several have been taken by spearmen. The big ones hide in wrecks and coral caves and may be hard to spot. When hit by a spear most groupers will run for their hole, and once into it, may be difficult or impossible to dislodge. Therefore, any attack on a fish of this type must be carefully planned so as to steer him from his lair after the strike is made. A big jewfish may charge a man underwater like a bull, but these attacks do not appear to do any damage other than to the divers nerves. Some Florida undersea workers spot a big one on the bottom, swim down, and pop a large hook into his mouth. The hook is connected to several strong arms in a surface boat who dislodge the fish by brute force. Perhaps this could be called sport, perhaps not.

Moray Eel: The Moray grows to six feet in length with a body as big as a man's thigh. It hides in holes with only its head poking out, and since the head is much smaller than the body, it is easy to mistake a big Moray for a small one. Once the spear is deep in his head the mistake rapidly becomes apparent, for a large Moray can shake a spear quite vigorously with diver attached. Some fishermen claim the eel will leave its hole when speared and come up the spear shaft after the diver, and the beast is probably mean tempered under any circumstances. The casual diver should never poke his fingers into holes underwater and he very likely will never be bothered by Morays.

Rays: The Sting Ray runs to 100 pounds and is poor to eat. It is often speared for sport, however, and can put up quite a struggle. Watch out for the tail barb, which can inflict a bad wound. The largest of the ray family is the Manta which can go to over a ton. This enormous fish jumps at times with a smack heard miles around, and a large one has not yet been taken by divers, though one probably will be eventually. The whole family has a low order nervous system and can thus be very active, even when hurt badly.

Shark: Along with the Barracuda, the shark has a bad reputation, although most divers will find them rather skittish in shallow water and difficult to approach. One skin diver has been attacked and killed by a shark so their danger aspect cannot be ignored. Blood in the water is the thing that may cause trouble so never use a fish ring in shark waters, and come out if cut. Of the many varieties, the White, Leopard, and Tiger seem the most feared. In Florida some divers say the Blackfin is dangerous and will not go into the water with one around. Since all shark are heavily muscled, they make fine opponents on the spear, though a big one is nothing for the amateur to take on. Apparently shark around the Pacific Islands and off the Great Barrier Reef are much hungrier than their American relatives for bathers are attacked in this region fairly often.

Octopus: This beast is apparently rare in American waters, since few are taken. Should a non-air supplied diver be caught by a good sized octopus, say with a spread of five or six feet, he would be in real trouble. Even in a case such as this, a sharp knife would end the contest rapidly. The chances of being snared by these creatures is practically nil, unless one is investigating the interior of a wreck. When speared, the octopus may crawl up the handle or line so be careful.

Lobster: There are three general varieties of this delicacy found in New England, southeastern American waters, and in California. Only the New England species have claws, but all are hunted by underwater fishermen. In cases where the lobster hides deep in a hole, it may take a spear thrust to get him out, but this kills the lobster and may ruin the meat, since these creatures should be cooked alive. Lobster expert Bill Barada in the *Skin Diver* suggests the following method for taking California lobster: Big lobster ('Bugs' to the Californians) are as often found in very shallow water as in deep, just outside breakers in grass and lurking in nooks and crannies. To find them you must get right down on the bottom and when one is seen go right up to him with arms wide apart. The idea is to attract the lobsters attention with your face and when in range grab hard with both hands before he runs. The feelers come off so grab at the body and use good heavy gloves for this work. The Northeastern variety has more armament than his cousins in warmer water, so this method gets a little risky used on a 10 or 15 pounder with six inch claws. Lobster can travel at surprising speed backwards when frightened, but usually hide out in little caves where they are hard to see.

Abalone: This shell fish is found only in California and, like the lobster, cannot be taken in this state with diving equipment. The Abalone has one shell, the other side clinging to a rock wall or reef underwater. A big Abalone is nine inches across and there are several varieties to be found. The Abalone fisherman goes equipped with an iron pryer of some sort and noses around rocks until he finds one, then

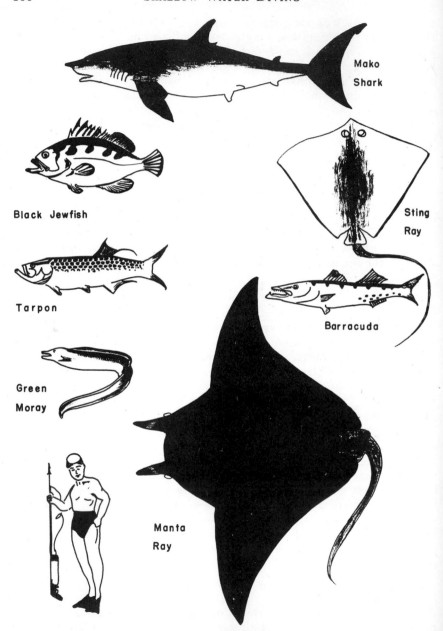

Figure 76. Some representative American fish. The fish are drawn to two different scales. The man on one page and the head on the other give the rough scale of the

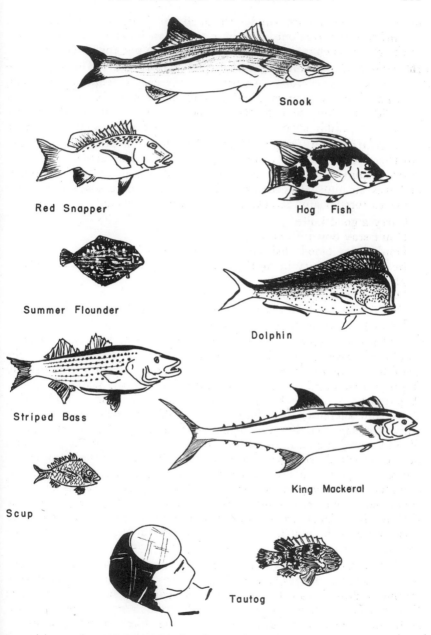

Snook

Red Snapper

Hog Fish

Summer Flounder

Dolphin

Striped Bass

Scup

King Mackeral

Tautog

fish on each page. All these fish except the Tarpon are legitimate targets for the spearman.

inserts the Abalone iron under the shell and jerks the shell fish loose. For lobster and Abalone, it is best to use an inner tube as described in the previous chapter with a bag in which to put the catch.

Parrotfish, Angelfish, and other tropic fish: These brightly colored fish are generally inedible and very easy to approach and kill, offering even the poorest goggler little sport. The authors urge that they be left alone to beautify the bottom and that the diver concentrate on edible species and big game fish such as shark and rays.

Precautions in Tropic Water: The diver off New England and Northern California is completely safe from fish attack. The last shark assault on a swimmer off Cape Cod was in the early thirties, and was an unusual occurrance. The following is a suggested safety guide to forstall any attacks on underwater workers.

Carry a good knife.

Don't stay down if cut.

Don't carry bloody fish around with you in the water.

Be especially wary in murky water since this is when a Barracuda might make a mistake.

Don't go poking into dark crevasses.

Don't wear bright jewelry, or flashy bathing trunks.

Don't drag in the water behind a moving boat.

Shark repellant is of dubious worth, but in bad shark waters would be certainly worth having. It can be obtained through the Fenjohn company. Blasts from a compressed air gun will usually frighten a shark off, or, lacking one, shouting in the water may help. Apparently, a diver who is swimming can turn inside an attacking shark and therefore hurt him with a knife without being touched. This of course sounds nicer on paper than it would be in the water. Should a predatory fish decide to take on a man underwater, it would be the Barracuda that would do the most damage for these fish are so quick that it would not be possible to prepare for them. The low casualty rate in waters surrounding this country as far as divers is concerned proves that dangers from fish are not large. Actually, the shallow diver must learn to use his equipment and when he can do this correctly, he will be ready to face just about anything the sea can hand out to him.

Fish Noises: One of the most interesting research problems of the recent war was the recording of fish noises underwater so that submarine hydraphones could be corrected against them. In Chesapeake Bay, bewildered listeners heard sounds from a new underwater installation which were described as being like bullfrogs, crickets, monkeys in a zoo, etc. Scientists soon found the noise to come from a species of small fish known as Croakers. They also noted that as the season changed from Spring to Summer, the noise decreased in frequency taking on a more bass quality. Quite obviously the Croakers were maturing and their noise chambers getting larger.

While the Croakers produced sound in the low frequency region (around 700 cycles per second) small shrimp known as Snapping Shrimp, were active in the high frequency region (10,000 cycles per second). These tiny shrimp made a sound by snapping their big claw rapidly together which was heard by soundmen in every theatre of the war. The Navy made a collection of these sounds on records to train their student sonarmen.

Many other marine animals make noise underwater. A school of porpoise will make weezing and grunting noises that sounds surprisingly like conversation. The diver who is equipped with a throwaway unit or a surface supplied helmet or mask will not hear much of this since the escaping air noise deadens anything else around him, but the underwater swimmer or recirculator user can stop and listen for a while and often pick out all sorts of marine noise. What the purpose of all this jumble of sound is, no one has yet been able to determine, but perhaps the mystery will be solved by divers at a future time.

Chapter VIII

COMMERCIAL SHALLOW WATER DIVING

Diving as a profession is costly and unpredictable. The high cost of equipment and the high wages paid to qualified men prevent salvage companies from handling anything but the most complex and expensive undertakings available. Even in depression times, the average salvage operator cannot afford to waste his time on small jobs, such as recovering outboard motors, finding and unfouling moorings, raising small sailboats, clearing propellors, etc. Tasks such as these are usually done from the surface or not done at all. A two or three man salvage team can profitably take on these jobs and fill in the gap between the boatyard operator, dragging a grapnel for lost gear, and the fully equipped salvage corporation, raising a cargo ship.

This chapter is intended to benefit those wishing to use diving as an aid to an already established business, as well as anyone interested in setting up a complete shallow water salvage concern of his own.

PLANNING AND OPERATING

Before buying any equipment, the prospective diver should investigate the possible markets in his area. A large crowded harbor may seem fruitful at first glance, but after the immediate needs are taken care of, the business can fall away to nothing. For this reason, shallow water diving is particularly good as a summer occupation, but often unsuitable for year round employment. Since the minimum starting capital will be well over $100, at least this amount of business should be in plain view at the start. The best harbors are 40 feet or under in depth, fairly warm, and not so deep in mud that everything on the bottom goes out of sight.

Helmets are suited for only the simplest kind of jobs such as hull inspection and pier work, where the diver does not have to bend over or lie down. The mask is so much more versatile, that anyone starting out for serious work should purchase a mask outfit. The Teco or Desco mask, Desco suit, five to eight cubic foot a minute compressor driven by a four cycle gas engine, weighted belt, and 100 feet of hose make up an all-purpose basic outfit that can be built upon as the need arises. Hand pumps do not supply enough air for a working mask diver. As new jobs are discovered, auxiliary equipment may become necessary, but there is little point in spending money until the need actually arises. With this outfit, diving can be done from a small skiff in a sheltered waterway, providing the compressor is not heavy and bulky. If considerable traveling is to be done from one harbor to another and financial prospects seem bright, a small boat is worthwhile. Such a boat, 15 feet or more long, highsided, broad beamed, and stable, should have room for all the equipment with plenty to spare. Some provision for getting the diver in and out without undue strain must be added. Inboard or outboard power are equally satisfactory, but the motor should easily throttle down to one or two miles an hour. Don't use a boat that can't take a beating, since diving is not a friend to nice varnish and paint jobs.

LOCATION OF OBJECTS

The type of job requiring the least amount of skill and equipment is the location and recovery of lost objects on the bottom. These can be anything from a diamond ring to a one ton mooring. As far as the fee for such jobs is concerned, no hard and fast rule should be made. The factors determining price are: worth of the lost article, how accurately its location is known before the search is begun, its size, the condition of the bottom, etc. Work can be done on a time basis or a job basis. Payment by the hour is usually best for jobs where the chance of success is small such as the finding of jewelry. If two men, diver and tender, work, 10 to 15 dollars an hour is about minimum. Naturally, the chances of finding the object should be explained to the customer, and some arrangement made as to the maximum amount of time to be spent in searching. If the object is worth three or four hundred dollars or more, a bonus for finding of 10 or 15 percent of value, or some sort of minimum fee can usually be agreed upon. While five to ten dollars apiece per hour may seem like good pay, the divers should remember that the work is irregular and there may be many days without an hour's diving time.

As far as larger objects such as outboard motors and moorings are concerned, it is usually best to work on a straight no-find, no-pay basis. This is because they are easier to locate because of their size, and usually not worth as much to the owner as jewelry or a wallet. On outboards, a fair reward is one-third of the salvage value, while on moorings, one third to one half their new value can usually be asked. Always remember that most people will hesitate to call a diver until they have grappled or otherwise searched themselves, and you probably represent the difference between recovery and abandonment of the object. These are only suggestions, and many other factors will help determine the final price for a given job. Boatyards and men who handle moorings are often ready customers for the shallow diver, and their business is best solicited by maintaining a fixed, fair price for a given type of job, and conducting all business in an honest aboveboard fashion. Often these men can give valuable advice as to the location of lost and abandoned equipment, and keeping on their good side pays off in tips.

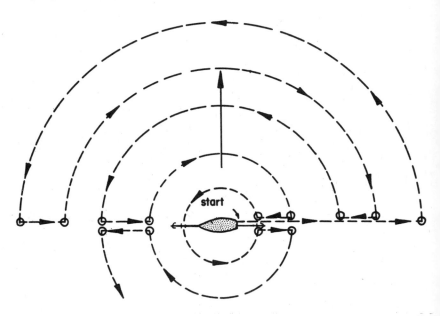

Figure 77. Diagram of circular search conducted from an anchored boat. Each circled dot indicates where the tender signals with one pull to the diver. By consistently keeping his lines taut and remembering where he is in the pattern, the diver always covers new ground. Some new signal must be devised to notify the diver that he has gone under the boat and is searching on the up-current side. The heavy arrow shows the direction of current flow.

As soon as work is begun, the divers will undoubtedly find lost objects other than the one desired. What to do with these is a touchy subject. Often the harbor master or some such person will remember the object and its owner. In this case the owner should be called and the object offered to him at one third of its value. If the owner declines to pay or isn't interested, the object may revert to finder who can sell it for whatever it will bring. The question of legal ownership is decided by the ticklish question of whether the original owner has abandoned search or not. Sometimes, in the case of a mooring, the owner will claim he knows the location and can find it whenever he wishes. In a case like this, the only thing to do is take off your bouy and leave the mooring on the bottom. To protect yourself against fraudulent claims of this sort, which seldom turn up, take bearings on the object without bouying it, or use an underwater float to mark it. The owner will then be unable to spot the location from shore, and be easier to deal with. If the owner no longer lives in the vicinity, it is safe to assume that search has been abandoned. Often a man familiar with the harbor will give locations of abandoned gear which is later found. The ethical thing to do then is to offer him the object at 1/3 of its value, and if he does not want it, make some arrangement to give him a commission on the final sale of the article. In all cases, *try to find the owner*. This protects the diver, not necessarily from law suits which would be ridiculous for such small amounts, but from hard feeling on the part of all concerned.

When working in a strange harbor, especial care should be taken, for there is always someone who resents a newcomer, and is annoyed that someone else has the ambition to look for abandoned gear and make money at it. Such people are usually more shrewd and lazy than dishonest, but they sometimes revert to common theft, and the divers, if they must leave an object for some time, after locating it, should protect themselves. Assuming the object is heavy, this can be done by bouying it with light cotton line which will break before anything comes to the surface. Most pilfering is done at night, and this will usually save the object, providing cross bearings have been taken on it before it is left.

There are several methods of searching. They will be considered in order of their utility.

Circular Searching: For locating small objects on any type of bottom, the following method should be used. Anchor the diving boat bow and stern with ropes taut, and send the diver over. He then reports to the surface on the extent of bottom visibility, and the search is carried out in the following sequence, controlled by the tender.

Tender (after diver is on the bottom)—one pull on the lines. When he receives this signal, the diver goes out in a straight line until the tender has paid out all the line and hose. Tender—one pull. At this point the diver stops, turns 90 degrees to his left, and begins to search moving foreward. The tender holds the lines, and the diver moves so as to keep them tight, that is, in a circle. If there is any current, it is best to work a 180 degree arc down current, and when the diver reaches a point where his mud is being swept over the search area the tender gives—one pull. The diver then turns to his left 90 degrees and comes slowly inward along his lines, the tender pulling them in until roughly twice the visibility distance has been covered.

Tender—one pull. The diver again turns 90 degrees to his left and makes another half circle, and this sequence is continued until the diver is under the boat. Then the up current semi-circle is searched in the same manner, starting at the boat and working outwards. This method of searching is simple, having only one signal and continual repetition of motions on the diver's part, and is particularly suited to shallow diving. It is useless however, unless the location

Figure 78. Diagram showing bottom 'plow' in use. A wire propellor cage is necessary unless the tender can be sure to keep lines completely clear of the prop.

of the object is known fairly closely. When looking for anything, try to get the person who knows the most about the location, who was there when it was lost, to come out in a boat and point out the spot. More time is wasted in searching due to heresay stories than to any other cause.

Distance Line: This method is suitable only for large objects on a flat, clear bottom. A large weight on the end of the descending line is dropped straight down from the anchored boat. The diver goes down and affixes a long line to the weight six inches to a foot above the bottom. Then he goes out as far as his lines permit, and holding the distance line just off the bottom, he starts a circle. When the distance line brings up, the diver follows it until he comes upon the obstruction.

Dragging the Diver: This is best when the object is large, its position doubtful. Three men are required. The diver goes over with a weight attached to a rope. One man tends the diver's lines and the other runs the boat's motor. The diver is towed over the bottom at low speeds, the weight keeping him down. A more useful modification of this technique is to tow a hooked drag on the bottom with the diver clinging to it. This is best done with a low power outboard motor, since the drag can catch and stop the boat while the diver inspects the find. Such a method is particularly effective when looking for moorings on a rocky bottom, since the diver can quickly determine what the drag has snagged and clear it if it is a rock, beer can, etc. The drags illustrated in this chapter have proved useful with and without a diver, and are best suited for finding chain in muddy bottoms. When 'plowing' the bottom in the manner described, it is vital to arrange signals so that the diver can regulate his speed in accordance with the condition of the bottom and the visibility. One pull for slower, three for faster should suffice. Two pulls always means, 'pull me in'. Otherwise the diver may come upon a rock too rapidly and be injured. Generally two miles per hour is the maximum safe speed in an average harbor. A good signal indicating the location of a worthwhile object is a series of short pulls on the lines. When this signal is received, the search is stopped at once, and the diver can inspect the find at his leisure.

Other Search Methods: The hard way to do a thing often attracts people, but don't overlook the chance of finding a lost object by simply looking for it from the surface. If the water is clear, a glass bottomed box will often save time. Sometimes a muddy harbor clears up in the late fall of the year, and bearings can be taken for the following summer's diving. Another trick is to pour a little olive oil on the water on a calm day. If properly done, the bottom can be seen at considerable depths.

HOISTING GEAR

Finding a lost mooring can be accomplished with the basic outfit, but often such heavy weights are more valuable delivered to the buyer. If diving is done from a good sized boat, a four or six fold block and tackle could be rigged to heave heavy objects off the bottom. A little easier way would be to purchase a surplus bomb hoist of 1000 pounds capacity or more, and rig it to haul over the bow. A chain fall is also a possibility, but is most useful when working from a pontoon

Figure 79. The Desco salvage lifting bag for hoisting heavy weights off the bottom. Air is admitted at the top and excess air escapes at the neck. (Courtesy Desco)

arrangement, right down through the middle of the work scow. Probably the simplest way to get a large weight off the bottom is to put a heavy piece of wood amidships across a skiff with a chain on each side fastened to the weight. This is done at low tide, and when the tide comes in, the weight comes up. Usually, several tide changes are needed to get the object far enough in shore to be of any use to anyone, and a much simpler method is to use fifty-five gallon oil drums, easily obtainable at around $4 apiece from the local garage. One

Figure 80. 55-gallon oil drums welded together. Notice the globe valves on top to let out the air when sinking. The compressed air inlet valve is visible at the bottom between the drums. It is connected to a manifold that goes to each drum. The water outlets are also visible at the very bottom of each drum.

such drum sunk and attached to a mooring and then blown out with air from the diving compressor, will lift over 400 pounds. Two lift close to 900. The drums should be rigged so that they float lengthwise in the water with the weight tied underneath. A plumbing globe valve to let the air escape can be brazed at the top with the drum's large bunghole at the bottom. When the drums are sunk, the water comes in this hole and the air escapes through the valve at the top. If two drums are used together and blown through an air manifold, it should be at the bottom by the filler hole. After the drums are sunk and secured by chain or heavy rope to the work, the top valves are checked to make sure they are closed, and the air into the bottom turned on. If more than 5 cu. ft./min. is being delivered by the compressor, the diver can stay with the drums and regulate their bouyancy by means of a needle valve attached directly to the drums' manifold. Although they are somewhat awkward to handle, it only takes a little practice to get them almost floating on the bottom and then tow them to the desired spot. Once the drums are all set, the diver keeps clear and the drums clear themselves of water and rise slowly to the surface. If two drums are used, the outfit may have a tendency to upset so that one drum is higher than the other. They can be quickly righted if the diver will screw on the bung of the higher drum so that all the air is forced into the lower one. There is no reason why a number of drums could not be used to lift a small boat, if such a job were ever offered.

The Desco people make an extremely useful looking hoisting device which is extremely simple and well adapted for the small operator. These are *lifting bags* made of heavy rubberized canvass and shaped like an old-time hot air balloon. They are in every sense an underwater balloon in operation as well as shape for they are attached when collapsed to the object to be raised, and then air is pumped into them until enough bouyancy is obtained to make the lift. Since the air in the balloon is expanding as the balloon rises from a high pressure region (Boyles Law) there must be an escape hole at the neck of the bag to vent the excess air. The bags are pumped from the top through a standard fitting. These units come in three sizes having lifting capacities of one, three and eight tons, and weighing respectively, 25, 65, and 175 pounds. The only disadvantage to such a rig is that the suspended object hangs quite far down underwater and would thus be difficult to bring into shallow water, whereas the drums will hold a mooring, properly slung, only three or four feet under.

UNDERWATER LIGHTS

Lights underwater are generally used by professional divers when they are at great depths or working in deep shadows. In shallow diving, unless the day is very overcast, there is always plenty of light. There is however, a lack of visibility, due primarily to the continual churning up of the bottom by tides and swells. An underwater light, then, is useless in shallow depths unless the diver anticipates night time descents. If night diving is desired, a standard automobile sealed beam headlight, run from a storage battery will do a satisfactory job. Desco manufactures a five cell flashlight which is pressurized to withstand 300 feet of water, and which would probably prove to be suitable for average needs.

UNDERWATER JETTING

Sometimes moorings and other large objects will become imbedded so deeply in the mud, that they can withstand a direct upward pull of several tons. This is due partially to the weight of mud on top of them, but mostly to the suction underneath. A jetting nozzle is then useful to tunnel down under the object and get water between the object and the muck. This tends to break the suction, and, if an upward pull is being exerted while the jetting is done, the object will often pull out. The water jet can also be used to dig objects out of a

Figure 81. Drag hooks for locating chain in soft mud. The wing-like projections are for the diver to grip when he is towed along the bottom. The iron weights help maintain negative bouyancy.

muddy bottom. The digging works best when a fairly good current is running to clear the debris away. Other uses for the jetting nozzle are, sinking pilings, tunneling under small boats so that lifting chains can be placed, and also for pumping out boats after they are raised. To sink pilings with a stream of water, the divers need only put the piling in its proper position, have one man on the surface heave down and wiggle the post while the diver holds the nozzle next to the piling's bottom and directs the stream downward. When hefting a small sailboat off the bottom, always check the bouyancy tanks first to see if they are sound. If there is damage so that the tanks cannot hold air, a canvas patch must be placed inside, so that the pressure of the expanding air will make a watertight seal. This work is usually done last after the jetting nozzle has cleared enough space underneath the boat to put lifting chains, and hoists and drums are pulling upward with their full force. When lifting a sailboat, don't neglect the possibility of affixing at least part of the lifting gear to the mast which will withstand a great amount of upward pull. It should be remembered that anything coming up from the bottom is in a condition of unstable equilibrium. That is, as it rises, the air inside expands, blows out more water and gives it more bouyancy. This could blow out a patch if there is no place at the bottom for the air to escape. It also means that something coming up from a good depth will arrive at the surface with considerable velocity, and if the salvage boat happens to be over it, considerable financial tragedy could result. Also, with a hose, air lines, life lines, etc., all funneling to a common point, the diver will have to take care that he doesn't turn his lines around the others, and find himself being dragged to the surface like a fly in a spider's web.

Large salvage companies use high pressure water pumps, throwing thousands of gallons an hour, but the average shallow diver will find a six or seven hundred gallon an hour pump able to handle most small jobs. The authors have used a gear pump of 600 gal./hour capacity, powered by a one horsepower Briggs and Stratton. Ordinary garden hose carries water and a simple adjustable nozzle does the jetting. There is not enough back pressure to necessitate using the holes pointing backwards to equalize the thrust of the forward water jet. A far better outfit than this, if it can be obtained, is a surplus 'Handi-Billy'. These little gas driven portable pumps were used by the Navy for fire fighting, and come in two sizes. Either one will straighten out a one and one half inch hose. These pumps will require some man-handling on the diver's part, and sometimes a large stake, lashed to the nozzle and firmly imbedded in the bottom will give the necessary stability. If the diver has machine shop facilities available, he should be able to make a professional nozzle from stock with compensating holes. Morse sells a nozzle with adjustable back pressure. Such a nozzle will travel a considerable distance into the bottom with very little urging.

The physical reason why such pumps are hard to handle stems from Newton's Third Law, 'For every action there is an equal and opposite reaction'. Thus, a nozzle that is ejecting a stream of water with a large thrust will be pushed backwards by the force of the water in the same way that a gun is shoved against the shoulder by the thrust of the bullet. If part of the water stream is deflected backwards, it will tend to shove the nozzle forward and counter, at least in part, the backward movement. If the same amount of water goes backward as goes forward, the nozzle will stay in the same place, providing the streams have equal velocity. The compens..ing nozzles are designed to provide this backward thrust and aid the·diver.

DIVING TELEPHONES

If complex underwater operations are in prospect, a set of telephones may be a help. For naturalists and others who may wish to keep a

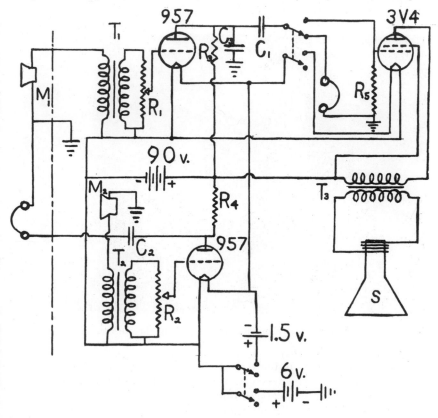

Figure 82. Homebuilt diver-telephone set illustrated in text. The following circuit elements are used: C_1 and C_2; .2 microfarad, 150 volt. C_3; .01 microfarad, 150 volt. R_1 and R_2; .5 meg potentiometers. R_3 and R_4; 50 K, ½ watt. R_5; .5 meg, ½ watt. T_1 and T_2; carbon button mike to grid transformers. T; Speaker output transformer to match 3V4 to 4″ p.m. speaker. A battery; Burgess #4F, B battery; 2 Burgess # M30, mike battery, 4 std. Flashlight cells. Microphones are lip or throat type for diver, type T 17 B for surface. Earphones; High impedance type. The dotted line identifies the three wire cable to the diver. The total B battery drain is 2 ma. with phones and 8 ma. with speaker. Both channels are always open and the tender has optional use of phones or speaker. The cable carries only four volts so is not dangerous and does not need to be heavily insulated.

running account of their underwater experiences, telephones are invaluable with a helper on the surface taking notes. The best gear for use with telephones are helmets, and masks with the special Desco suit. They cannot be used with a mask alone, since the water will enter the ear passages and make hearing difficult as noted in Chapter I. A throat mike, easily obtainable from any radio store, is perfect for diving, since it is small, light, and out of the way. In a helmet, any kind of ear phones are suitable, but with a standard

Figure 83. Small, one diver telephone constructed by the authors. (see circuit this chapter)

suit, a small pair of phones that press into the ears become very uncomfortable as the pressure increases. With the suit, the best phones are the large, oversize ones mounted in foam rubber. They are about four inches in diameter and very comfortable. On the surface the tender wears an identical headset and handles the volume controls on the amplifier. The accompanying circuit diagram, (figure 82) is for an amplifier constructed by the authors, which has worked well using the Desco suit. Telephone outfits of varying expense and complexity are available from a number of manufacturers. The telephone cable should be waterproof and affixed to the lines by adhesive tape at intervals so that it hangs in shallow loops. Speak slowly and distinctly. Valve down the air if it is noisy in the helmet or mask.

CUTTING EQUIPMENT AND TECHNIQUES

Underwater cutting is a fairly advanced art for the beginning diver. It is possible, however, that some of ·those undertaking diving will have at their disposal a standard cutting torch, regulators, hose, etc. It is fairly simple to convert the standard cutting torches to underwater use. If continual use is to be made of a torch underwater, it is best to purchase one designed for the purpose, but for occasional use, a converted one will perform satisfactorily. The gases used for cutting on the surface are most commonly oxygen and acetylene. However, acetylene is explosive in the absence of air when used at pressures of over 12 psi. This limits the depth at which acetylene

Figure 84. The Desco underwater cutting torch. The three control valves meter air, oxygen, and acetylene or hydrogen, and the small handle spurts pure oxygen over the work. (Courtesy Desco)

can be used underwater to 24 feet. If hydrogen is substituted for acetylene, there is no depth limit, but hydrogen is not as efficient a fuel.

An ordinary cutting torch has three controls. Acetylene (or hydrogen) and oxygen valves control the flow of these gases to a mixing chamber and then through several small holes in the tip to give the preheating flame. Once the work begins to give off small sparks, the lever (third control along the side of the torch) is depressed to send a jet of pure oxygen over the work. The preheated metal catches fire in the oxygen-rich atmosphere, and burns, thus starting the cut. The proper use of a cutting torch requires some practice in adjustment and in the actual cutting. This information is readily available from many sources, and will not be discussed in detail here. Cutting underwater is essentially the same as cutting on the surface, except that the extra air comes from an air cuff placed around the tip rather than from the atmosphere. This air cuff is supplied by compressed air from a surface diving compressor. When using acetylene underwater, another device is needed for the protection of personnel. This is a flash back arrestor. Construction details are given in Figure 86.

When using acetylene and oxygen, the torch is lighted and set properly on the surface. The gas regulators are set on the normal surface pressure plus .445 times the depth in feet. The diver takes the torch down burning, and if everything has been done properly, there should be little need for adjustment on the bottom. The pressure in

Figure 85. Small diver telephone outfit manufactured by Byrd Commercial Diving. Most rigs of this type can be used with one or two divers.

the air cuff should be several pounds above the pressure at the depth the torch is being used. If there is not sufficient air in the bubble to keep the torch from blowing out, increase the compressor output. If the air from the torch does not seem to form a bubble, the clearance between the torch tip and the air sleeve is too large or improperly shaped. (See Figure 86). This clearance is quite important in forming a proper bubble, and it is wise when adapting a surface torch for underwater use to make the clearance adjustable. In order to ease the diver's job when visibility is poor, the air cuff should extend far enough ahead of the torch tip so that it can lay on the work and the end of the small blue preheating flames will just touch the work. The portion of the cuff ahead of the tip is filed down at intervals so that gases and slag can escape from under the flame. When hydrogen is used,

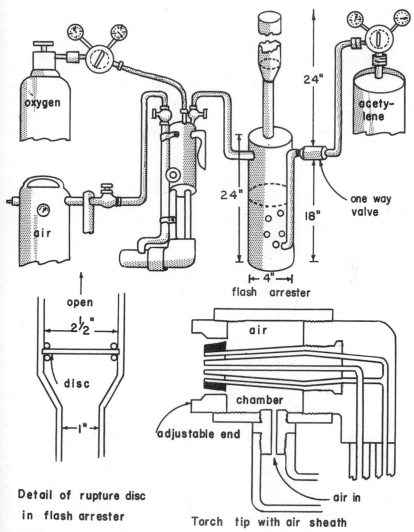

oxygen

acetylene

air

24"

24"

18"

one way valve

flash arrester

4"

open

2½"

disc

1"

air

chamber

adjustable end

air in

Detail of rupture disc
in flash arrester

Torch tip with air sheath

Figure 86. Gas circuit diagram for an underwater cutting torch outfit. Notice that the acetylene flash arrester is made from 4 in., 1 in. and 2½ in. pipe, the first two sizes are in 24-inch lengths and the 2½ in. pipe is long enough so that the whole assembly is higher than anyone standing around the device. In action, this arrester works as follows: If the torch backfires, pressure rises in the large bottom section of the arrester, forcing the water back up the pipe to the one-way valve where it stops. The excess pressure bursts the rupture disc and flames escape out the 2½ in. pipe. The rupture disc is made of .005 in. aluminum, tinned with a soldering iron on both sides, with a thin paper gasket on the bottom. If hydrogen is used instead of acetylene, the entire arrester assembly can be eliminated.

the following pressures are recommended for the gases. Hydrogen—
55 psi at 10 feet water depth. Add five pounds for each 10 foot increase. Oxygen—75 psi at 10 feet water depth. Add five pounds for
each 10 foot increase. Air in the cuff—same as the hydrogen pressure.
This will require very fine tolerances in the manufacture of the cuff
and considerable amounts of air. Some experimentation will be necessary with whatever torch is available.

Hydrogen and acetylene regulators and hose connectors all have
left-handed threads and are marked as such by an indented line
around the middle of the fitting.

Anyone attempting surface or underwater cutting for the first time
should obtain a manual explaining the principles and techniques.
A completely surplus outfit can be obtained for a little over $50.
A new one runs closer to $100. This includes regulators, hose, and
torch. Anyone who is seriously interested in diving would do well to
invest in an outfit, including a welding torch, since these tools will
prove invaluable in equipment construction and in general surface
usage. Underwater welding is expensive, requiring high amperage
electrical equipment, and also a high degree of proficiency. Anyone
interested in this advanced phase of underwater work can find references in the back of this book which will give complete details on it.

UNDERWATER JOBS

Aside from locating and lifting objects off the bottom, there are
any number of other jobs underwater that can be accomplished by a
shallow diver. These vary all the way from inspection of hulls to the
removal of lead and bronze from sunken wrecks. When establishing
a price for such undertakings, it is often wise to find out how much
they would cost if a diver were not employed. Find out, for instance,
how much it would cost to haul a boat out of the water to clean its
bottom or unfoul its propeller. You can then make a competitive
estimate on this basis, or refuse the job if it doesn't seem worthwhile.

Hull and Propeller Work: Sometimes a boat will strike a rock
and the owner will wish his hull inspected for damage. Such a job
pays little, but is quick and easy to do. A stage of some sort must be
rigged so that the diver can stand or sit under the hull. It can usually
be made from a stout plank, suspended from the vessel's side by rope.
The hull should be checked for plank cracks and sprung seams.
Sometimes repairs can be effected underwater, but any work of this
sort requires a man who knows ship repair as well as diving. Cleaning
a hull underwater is a dirty job, but can usually be done with some
profit to the divers. The main charm of doing this sort of work is
that the customer's boat is out of action for only a short time opposed

to the several days it might take to haul it on a marine railway. When a large boat fouls its propellers, the job becomes a natural for the shallow diver. Here again a working stage must be rigged under the stern. If rope is fouled, it can be cut away with a sharp knife, but cable may require a torch or hack saw. Hack sawing underwater is not as difficult as it sounds, although it requires considerable work. The blade on the saw should be reversed so that it cuts on the draw, since this is easier for the diver. If the screw must be turned over to help clear the mess, great care should be taken for the diver's safety. In fact, power boats in a crowded harbor represent one of the primary dangers to a man working on the bottom. A large sign posted on the work boat may help as well as a megaphone. If nothing else keeps a speed maniac from cutting over the diver's lines, a few medium sized rocks might suffice in an emergency. Never take chances with a crackpot in a fast boat. Get the diver aboard.

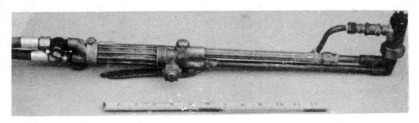

Figure 87. Standard cutting torch converted for underwetar use. Air sheath on tip, air tubing and an air control valve at the handle were added.

Pier Work: All sorts of carpentry can be done profitably underwater on piers and floats. This type of work is best paid for by the hour at the same rates described previously. The main difficulty in underwater carpentry is with jobs that require the use of body weight such as using a brace and bit in hard wood or handling a sledge. If the diver is held down only by a negative bouyancy of 10 or 15 pounds, he will have trouble exerting any force on tools that require it. If many jobs of this sort are anticipated, a special heavy belt might be a worthwhile investment. A negative bouyancy of 50 or 60 pounds should do the trick. When mounting a large number of weights, it is wise to run shoulder straps from the belt, so that there will be no sagging to chafe the suit.

Use of Power Tools: The most easily adaptable type of power tools for underwater work are those which operate by air pressure. Pneumatic drills, riveters, hammers, etc. are available on the surplus market. They require a large air supply however, and the average diving compressor cannot hope to supply both the diver and a pneumatic tool underwater. Should the diver have available a compressor supplying more than 10 cu. ft./min. he will find the following air tools available from Desco: impact wrench (for tightening or loosening nuts), chipping hammers, wire brush and grinder, ⅞" drill, reciprocating wood saw (requires up to 60 cu. ft./min.) diggers, rivet busters, etc. All these tools require an inlet air pressure of 90 psi plus a great deal of air.

Blasting Underwater: There is no reason why a well equipped, competant shallow diver cannot undertake the job of clearing a channel of rocks or other obstructions with explosives. Unless the divers are licensed explosive experts, they will have to employ someone who is. Ordinarily the diver will descend and survey the job to be done. He will then report his findings to the explosive expert, who decides the best way to do the job, makes up the charge to be used, and instructs the diver on proper placement. The explosive used underwater must be insoluble and unaffected by water, or else enclosed in a watertight container. Commercial dynamite may be used if it is fired within 24 hours of immersion. Ammonium Nitrate explosives, and Nitro-starch can be used only in watertight containers. Usually, the size of the charge necessary to do the job if it were on the surface will suffice underwater, but some skill in this sort of work gives the best results. Firing is best done by an electrical system rather than fuse. Always remember: *All divers must be out of the water before firing.*

Other Jobs: Aside from actually working on the bottom, there are other ways to make money from diving. Sight-seeing and fishing parties can be taken on underwater jaunts for pay. If this sort of thing is done as a business, the equipment owners should be very careful to protect themselves fully from any lawsuits in case of accident. Usually an affidavit releasing the divers from any responsibility will take care of this matter. When diving with inexperienced persons always have an expert with each novice.

One possibility for making money is to offer your services to the bureau of fisheries in your state. Often they will be interested in employing divers at moderate pay to make surveys of existing shell-fish in various areas. Information on the whereabouts of beds could be sold to fishermen, but a much better way to use this information is to exchange it for tips on the location of lost and abandoned equipment on the bottom. There is a possibility of employment by various scientific institutions, and this sort of work could be tremendously interesting. It would not pay well at all, however, since most of the employers will be operating on a meager budget themselves. Inevitably the old daydream o treasure hunting rears its head. Most of the gold and silver bullion is unfortunately at great depths, well out of the shallow diver's sphere of influence. What there is, or was, at less than 60 feet, has long since been removed. After scoffing however, there always seems to be someone who turns up with a box of gold moidores, and you wonder if perhaps there isn't something there after all. If you're the type that likes to bet on 17 to 1 shots at the horse races, perhaps diving for treasure is the answer.

Figure 88. 15 foot assault boat used for shallow diving operations. It is outboard propelled and very stable. Any diving boat should be able to support a weighted diver on its rail without tipping badly.

SETTING UP THE BUSINESS

Most coastal locales have gotten along without divers for a long time, and many will feel that they can get along a lot longer. The first job of the beginning divers is to convince those who work around the water that many tasks can be accomplished quicker, cheaper, and better by employing a diver. This really can be done only by contacting personally those who might be interested. Letters are often disregarded, since the recipient, who has survived many years without using diving, feels that nothing new can be gained by employing a man underwater. This is a large hurdle to overcome, but once a few jobs have been successfully completed, the customer will start to pass the word that his business has benefitted by the introduction of diving. Business calling cards should be sprinkled liberally about to anyone who might conceivably use your services. Many jobs will be passed along by word of mouth, and a notebook to jot down names, locations, rumors, etc., will pay off handsomely. Politeness and a willingness to explain the secrets of the trade to anyone who might care to listen can coax the more reticent old timers into offering information on the location of this or that lost in the 'big storm of '23'.

If much traveling around is planned, it is important that the equipment be insured against theft and fire. This is easy to do for a boat and motor, but finding a company that will write any sort of a policy on diving equipment will prove somewhat more difficult. The insurance is also liable to be expensive. Eight percent of value for six months protection was one quotation given the authors. If there is any doubt about the honesty of strangers among whom you are working, it is still worth while.

VALUE OF MATERIAL FROM THE BOTTOM

Here is a list of common salvageable articles with their probable condition after various lengths of time.

Outboard Motors: If the motor was properly lubricated, it is worth recovering after two or three months submersion in sea water. A new ignition system and carburetor parts will be required. Probable cost of parts: $25. After six months to a year, any motor is of doubtful value. All aluminum parts will be partially dissolved due to local electrolytic action. The propeller, shafting, and stem may be worth getting. Probable value: $10–$20. After a year in salt water, forget it. In fresh water, longer periods than these listed may be withstood with little harm.

Moorings: Concrete block moorings are cheap and easy to make and valuable mainly for the attached chain. Block alone worth $4–$5. Chain that is still usable worth 1/3 to 1/2 new cost. Chain can survive in a muddy bottom with little loss in value up to 15 or 20 years.

Iron mushroom moorings are worth up to half their new value or up to 12 cents a pound. The only part of a mushroom that goes bad is the eye, which is purposely made weak. If the shank has been out of the mud and in the water, ten years will usually dissolve the eye and make the mooring useless. However, if the eye has been under mud, twenty years or more may not devalue the mooring too much.

Anchors: Usually these last up to four or five years, but galvanizing goes after a year. Old style stocked anchors are good for junk only, although a large one might have value as a lawn decoration. Patent anchors such as the Danforth and Northill are worth up to a dollar a pound.

Scrap Metals: Iron is barely worth recovering if there is several tons lying around. Two or three cents a pound is usual. Lead varies between nine and fourteen cents a pound, and the market changes often. A lead keel is often the most valuable part of a sunken boat. Copper, brass and bronze get from twenty to fifty cents a pound. The shafting and propellers of a boat are always worth going after.

Other Materials: No rope that has been on the bottom any time at all can be trusted. Wood also deteriorates quickly. Watches, field glasses, and other precision instruments must be recovered quickly or electrolytic action will destroy them.

Chapter IX

SPECIAL DIVING APPLICATIONS

The current emphasis on the use of diving equipment centers around four main applications, undersea fishing, commercial diving, scientific investigation, and underwater photography. These first three phases have been considered in one way or other in the previous three chapters, and the fourth has received fairly complete attention in the companion book to this one, *Underwater Photography*. But this is by no means all that can be done with underwater equipment and this short chapter will consider some further possibilities.

SIGHTSEEING

No matter what else the diver may be doing underwater, he will quite naturally be looking at the sights around him. In southern and Gulf Stream waters this can be a full time job as Dr. Beebe and others have pointed out in their writings. In fact, it may be in time to come that more people will dive simply to sightsee than for any other reason. Glass bottom boats now do a good business, but this is not much better than being in an aquarium. The observer in the water is actually a part of the show and can examine objects at his leisure.

The simplest sightseeing equipment is mask, snorkel, and fins. Much can be seen by just easily kicking along the surface with perhaps an occasional dive to get a closer look at some object. For a more detailed examination of the undersea, an Aqua-Lung or similar throw-away unit is good, providing it is modified with a snorkel as described in Chapter V. Since the observer is not exerting himself too vigorously, he will not require much air underwater and using the snorkel he can husband his air by staying on the surface while looking at things. One 70 cubic foot tank will give a good day of leisurely sightseeing. The authors envy those readers who have never been down in the Gulf Stream or Florida water, for the first few hours of such an expedition are a never to be forgotten experience which no amount of subsequent diving can ever dim.

LIFE SAVING

All beach administrators, lifeguards, Red Cross safety officials, and others interested in water safety should give careful thought to the use of self-contained diving apparatus for rescuing of drowning persons. Only one kind of equipment is suitable for this work, namely throw-away gear of the Aqua-Lung type. The gear should be arranged in the following manner since speed of use is a premium in this application. Take the unit and find how much weight is necessary to allow the diver to swim rapidly and comfortably at his maximum speed. This should be just enough weight to completely counter the bouyancy of the gear in the water so that diver has the same floating ability with the rig on as without it. This should be done with full air supply since such a life saving device must obviously be fully charged after each use even though only a portion of the air is used. The weights should be affixed to the straps of the gear itself with no weighted belt being used. Standard buckling devices should be replaced by a single snap buckle that is large and quickly fastened. The gear (taking Aqua-Lung as an example) should now be arranged thusly: Two straps fit over the shoulders like a parachute harness and a single snap catch on a third strap connects the two in front. Besides the lung itself, a mask and fins are kept with it at all times.

When an emergency occurs, the guard puts both arms through the shoulder straps, snaps the front catch, and runs for the water adjusting the mask on his face. At the water's edge the fins are slipped on and the guard enters the water. Never attempt to walk with fins on since it is very time consuming and awkward, and even in the shallowest water swimming is much faster. The mouthpiece should be put in the mouth before entry into the water lest it fill with water and choke the diver.

Care must be taken with Aqua-Lung that too vigorous an entry into the water does not bump the regulator against the guard's head or misplace the assembly on his back. When entering surf it is best to get out to knee deep water and start swimming. As the wave crests over, duck down and keep going as close to the bottom as possible. The back wash here will take the diver out past the breakers where he wishes to go. Once actually into a heavy sea, the diving-gear-equipped life guard is much more in control of the situation than the best swimmer alive, for he can move rapidly several feet underwater relatively undisturbed by wave action or white caps. Usually, greater speed is possible underwater in any case since the swimmer is not creating waves which waste his energy.

Upon reaching the trouble area, the diver can surface to establish the nature of the situation and then approach the drowning person underwater. No elaborate holds or breaks will be necessary for such a rescue, for the diver is able to carry the struggle underwater and can see everything well through the mask whereas the rescued person is essentially blind and can only strike without purpose. The situation

Figure 89. A scene from the Hans Hass motion picture, UNDER THE RED SEA showing myriad baitfish. Scenes similar to this one are found in Florida around wrecks. (Courtesy RKO Radio Pictures)

is even more attractive in the case of a foundered boat where several non-swimmers may be in trouble. This is an extremely dangerous situation for even the most skilled guard who may be overpowered and pulled under if he directs his attention to only one swimmer. But the diving-gear-equipped guard moves into this arena underwater, selects his target, and guides him to the overturned boat without ever breaking surface. Several Res-Q-Pacs attached to the guards lung straps can be used to great advantage in such a situation, for the guard can inflate one as he gets up to one of the struggling swimmers and get him onto it. Any such support usually quiets the most panicked non-swimmer and the guard can continue to others giving each one a pair of inflated water wings. Since all this can be done from underwater, the others in the water need not even be aware that a guard is present, making an attack impossible.

Much of this advice is based only on an extrapolation of the capabilities of a good diver, since little work has been done on this diving application. It does not appear generally possible to use diving equipment for all water rescues, nor does this appear desirable in the majority of cases. In calm water off crowded beaches where most rescues are close to shore the non-diving-gear-equipped diver will be able to work more rapidly and often, but in times of heavy surf and rough water where undertow or seaward currents are operating, diving gear may not only save swimmers' lives, but the guard's as well. Also, off resorts where there is a chance of rescues of several persons at once the use of diving gear will mean that fewer guards will be necessary to handle the possible situations that may occur. Tests should be conducted in bad water using skilled divers and swimmers to determine the merits of this type of rescue and standardized methods for rescues established. Too little has been found out about conditions in surf and every year bathers and small boat sailors are killed in bad weather and coastal water.

The question may arise as to which size of air bottle should be used in a lifesaving rig. If we take three cubic feet a minute as the absolute maximum for a man exerting vigorously, then a fully charged 35 cubic foot cylinder will give between 11 or 12 minutes. For rescues in surf and inshore water, this should be more than sufficient time. If long swims are necessary the 70 cubic foot bottle will be better. The smaller the bottle, of course, the less cumbersome is the equipment and the more easily it is stored.

Should life guards be trained in the use of this equipment, it must be remembered that a drowning swimmer may get his hands on the air tubes. Since these have great resiliency there should be no damage if the guard closes with his opponent and goes down, but there is the possibility that the mouthpiece will be torn from the guard's mouth,

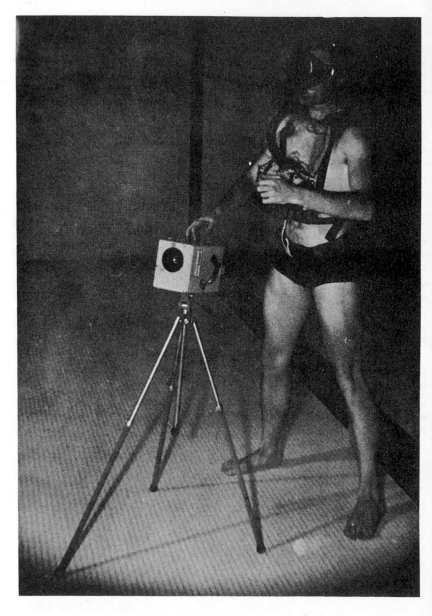

Figure 90. Diver-photographer on bottom of a swimming pool, preparing to take movies of swimmers. Notice the complete lack of bubbles from the recirculator.

creating a dangerous situation. If actual tests show this to be the case it will be a simple matter to design a special mouthpiece that will fit into the entire mouth and be gripped by all the teeth. Before such a mouthpiece could be torn from the teeth, the tubes will have broken. Using a mask fitting over the whole face does not appear wise since it would take more time to put on and impairs the flexibility of the system which must be kept simple.

Once a person has been lost in the water, diving equipment has been used for many years to recover the body. For this reason, most police and fire departments keep diving equipment on hand. At times this gear has been used to effect unusual rescues involving people trapped out in the water or in cars and other cavities beneath the surface.

COACHING SWIMMING

The authors have made several hundred feet of movies of college swimmers taken from beneath the surface. These pictures show clearly any defect in style particularly in rapid turns which are often obscured from surface viewers by bubbles and froth. Diving equipment thus offers the swimming coach an excellent view of his team in action where many obvious mistakes become glaringly apparent. While a few pools have underwater windows for this purpose, a diving helmet or mask permits the coach to get directly under a swimmer and study him at his leisure, either in mid-pool or at a turn.

Usually a hand pump is sufficient to supply air for pool use since the water is never over 10 or 12 feet deep and the diver is not exerting himself. Also handpumps are much cleaner than motor driven equipment, and not so liable to mar tiles. The equipment is also useful for pool cleaning and inspection and for teaching rescue holds and breaks to novice life guards.

UNDERWATER SPORT

Aside from spearfishing, the use of diving equipment offers other possibilities for exciting action sports in the water. Some divers in Europe and America have been using 'undersea aquaplanes' for some time, consisting of a flat board to which the diver clings while being pulled by a motor boat. By gripping the board properly, it can be pointed up or down to act as a 'waterfoil' which allows the diver to rapidly change his depth as he skims along. A more elaborate device has the diver lying on a large wedge shaped craft with rudder and elevator controls so that he can perform simple acrobatics at the end of the tow line. While this sort of sport is most exciting, it is not for the beginner since the rapid depth changes require quick ear adaptation, something that comes with practice for many people. Also, only the clearest water is suitable for rapid towing lest a rock end the 'flight' in tragedy. For such entertainment, the most obvious equipment is a throw-away self-contained.

A diver who has exactly neutral bouyancy in the water can perform any number of spectacular acrobatic manouvers, impossible on land. All the known aerobatic stunts, barrel role, chandel, immhelman are easily done by an underwater swimmer, suggesting the possibility of mock 'dogfights' between fin equipped divers. Lazily twisting about

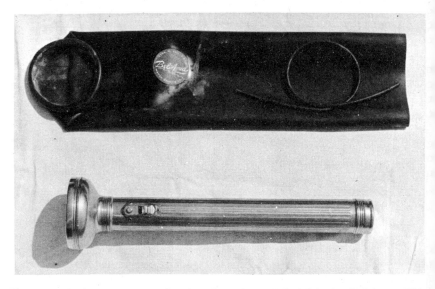

Figure 91. A simple waterproofing bag for a five cell flashlight by Bel-Aqua. This is suitable for cave diving or for investigating dark and shadowy places around reefs. (Photo by Julius Down)

underwater in a pool or in warm water is a delightful experience, and doubly so when some form of diving gear is used so that breathing is easy and natural.

PROPELLED DIVING

During World War II some of the most astonishing feats of arms were accomplished by diving-suited men riding self-propelled underwater craft. The Italian efforts in this direction have been well documented and Davis goes into considerable detail in *Deep Diving* describing tiny British submersibles and manned torpédoes known as X-Craft,

Submersible Canoes, etc. Occasionally, a well equipped amateur diver has undertaken the construction of a self-propelled underwater vehicle of some sort with varying degrees of success. Such a project could only be worthwhile if undertaken by someone with large machine shop facilities plus an ability to use proper engineering methods in the design. An underwater craft must be designed with care if it is to be stable under all conditions and if it is to function soundly for any length of time. The general form of most amateur projects has been a torpedo shaped unit on or in which a self-contained equipped diver sits and operates the craft. Just what use such a tiny submarine has other than joy riding is questionable, since it cannot go much faster than a good underwater swimmer and certainly cannot equal the speed of a surface-towed sled or undersea aquaplane.

One rather interesting device now made in Germany consists of a motor on the surface connected to a wire-caged propeller by a flexible coupling, the prop being affixed to the swimmer's middle. In theory, this allows the swimmer to become a true human submarine towing the motor on the surface behind him.

All these devices are costly to buy or make and not much more than gadgets. The considerable speed possible to the diver with only a pair of six dollar swim fins does not make a complex underwater propulsion unit appear very practical.

CAVE DIVING

Sir Robert Davis in *Deep Diving* mentions the activities of English cave investigators or 'spelunkers' who used recirculating equipment to probe deeply into large caves. D. Rebikoff in *L'Exploration Sous-Marine* also goes into considerable detail in discussing cave divers in France.

Although there are many enthusiastic spelunkers in America, this form of exploration has not been tried to any extent. There are many caves scattered all over the United States having submerged caverns and passageways leading to underground areas untouched by men, possibly for all time. Even the most widely explored caves, such as those open to the public in Missouri and elsewhere, have mysterious streams that disappear into rock walls, hinting at further secrets still unseen. The challenge is very inviting for the most daring spelunkers, though certainly an extremely steady nerve is required to venture into a pitch black waterway with no free surface whatsoever and of unknown length.

English cave divers have made a wise choice in selecting recirculating gear for their travels, for this gives maximum duration with minimum bulk of equipment. Often it will be necessary to walk and clamber deep into a cave before diving begins so that a throw-away with its heavy air bottles would not be suitable. Aside from the recirculators, spare oxygen, and extra soda lime, the divers should have lights (waterproofed), rubber suits and thick underwear, small slates with attached chalk, depth gauges, and water tight rubber bags. Once the diving area is reached, two divers can make a preliminary survey of the path underwater, always allowing plenty of reserve oxygen for

Figure 92. A busy scene on the bottom during the filming of a training movie. Three types of equipment are in evidence. On the left, the deep water suit, in the center a diving mask, and on the right an open helmet. (Official U.S. Navy Photograph)

a return to the starting point. If an open space is found, spare oxygen and soda lime can be placed in the rubber bags and ferried to the next room in the cave. Generally, four men represent a minimum team for this work, two underwater and two in reserve. Should a man be stranded deep in a cavern by loss of oxygen or malfunction of equipment, his buddy should go back for help. In this way two man teams can work from cavern to cavern, always leaving spare oxygen and soda lime on each step of the route.

Depth gauges are absolutely necessary for this work since it is impossible to estimate depth of water due to lack of a water surface at the cave roof. Naturally, if the explorers must go deeper than 35 feet to clear an obstacle, the attempt must be abandoned with oxygen equipment. Waterproof containers for flash lights are obtainable from the Bel-Aqua company and others. In the event that a mask-compressor unit is used, so that the diver is trailing lines behind him, a sealed beam headlight will be suitable.

Figure 93. A scene from the movie, "The Frogmen", showing a three tank Aqua-Lung. (Courtesy U. S. Divers Co.)

Every cave diver should carry a small slate at his belt with chalk attached so that he can note down the steps of his journey and times spent underwater. It is also suggested that each diver have a reel of tough cod line that can be attached at the jump off point and trailed behind to mark a path for others to follow or the diver to return over. These lines can be left in place for future expeditions and should prevent anyone from getting lost in a labyrinth of passages. To get lost in a passage filled with water would be a terrifying and dangerous matter.

Such an operation as is described in this section is nothing to be taken lightly for it requires men skilled in both cave investigation and diving, who also have very steady nerves in unusual situations. Progress must be slow and the investigation of a large cave with many underwater tunnels could take months of time. Preliminary practice with the equipment in a swimming pool is mandatory and the assimilation of the necessary gear plus spares would be expensive. It should be clearly stated that the English have lost men in this sport, even though they appear to have undertaken the matter methodically and with great care. It is difficult, however, to conceive of a more adventurous type of exploration.

Figure 94. A group of Navy UDT personnel come ashore near Wonsan, Korea. Mine sweeping is the main UDT job in Korean waters, which are cold. Note typical back entry dress of the Desco type (Frog Man dress). (Official U. S. Navy Photograph)

DIVING IN THE ARMED SERVICES

Some of the finest divers in the world have been graduates of U. S. Navy training, which now uses a great deal of shallow water equipment. Most readers are undoubtedly familiar with Navy diving work through the writings of Captain Ellsberg, Tom Eadie, and others. The Navy diver works under varying and unusual conditions and does many odd and dangerous jobs, yet his casualty rate is much lower than civilian divers simply because he and his tenders are forced, by regulations, to observe the most stringent precautions. The reader of this book can take a lesson from the Navy's fine safety record and never try to cut corners with faulty equipment or careless work underwater.

Though the Navy deep sea divers have been working along for years at many spectacular jobs, they have recently been challenged in the publicity spotlight by a more recent group, the Underwater Demolition Teams. The exploits of these shallow divers is too well documented to bear much discussion here, though it might be noted that a reserve team has recently been formed in California having many young spearfishermen as recruits. The UDT has been using Aqua-Lung in its training and has apparently found it serviceable except for the obvious wake of bubbles left by any throw-away unit. This has certain, obvious tactical disadvantages and the Navy is now considering rebreathers for missions where bubbles must not occur. The British with their 'P parties' and other underwater commando units appear to be ahead of the United States equipment-wise since they have designed a large number of different rebreathers using air, and various oxygen-nitrogen mixtures for depths greater than 35 feet. The recent UDT actions at Inchon and elsewhere along the coast of Korea may point up the need for further research and engineering on shallow water equipment and produce some interesting units which may eventually filter onto the civilian market. It is not unlikely that, in the event of war, many of the readers of this book will find their way into some form of service diving job. A complete understanding of the principles and methods of diving should then prove most useful.

Chapter X

THAT UNDERWATER VACATION

We cannot all live in an area close to beautiful underwater scenery and big, spearable fish. But the majority of Americans can, with a little perseverance, use a two weeks or longer vacation to have one of the great adventures of all time, exploring the undersea and hunting its inhabitants. There are three good to excellent diving areas available to United States citizens equipped with a car. Two of them, Southern Florida and Southern California are reached by fast roads and have complete tourist accommodations, sports stores, etc, The third, the peninsula of Southern California (Baja California) is in Mexico and is in large measure unexplored and untouched by skin divers. Roads and tourist cabins are horrible, however, so a trip to this region can be almost an expedition into fairly primitive country. This chapter will also consider check lists of equipment for various modes of transportation, addresses of useful stores, and many other items designed to make the trip exciting and memorable.

MILEAGE AND TRAVEL

The potential underwater adventurer living in the East Coast area should quite naturally head for Florida. Since the average vacation starts on Friday night and ends two weeks later on a Monday morning, there are some 16 days in which to go, dive, and return home. A 1500 mile jaunt is perfectly possible in this space of time, provided the diver has helpers at the wheel and all concerned are young in spirit. Thus the New Englander can leave on Friday evening, arriving in Miami on Monday without any fast driving, but with steady travel. He then has nine or ten full days of underwater fun before returning. This same general schedule can apply to the Western diver as far as a trip to Southern California is concerned, and an examination of the map of the United States shows that very little of it is not within driving range of one of these two areas. Should plane or train travel be taken, even more time is availadle but generally a car will have to be hired at the destination since both Florida and California are big states and the diving areas are not easily reached by public transportation. Baja California is reached by driving through Southern California to Tijuana, and then southward on the peninsula. This is not a simple two weeks trip except for those who are very close to the border to begin with. The roads in this part of Mexico may not be in good repair so an old model station wagon, pick-up truck, or Jeep will prove most suitable. Once the vacationist is well down on the peninsula, he may have to leave the road and cross fields to get to the coast, searching for a bay or inlet. Before making this trip one should consult AAA or other automobile agency, procure maps, and be well stocked with provisions. If you like seafood you won't need any meat, that much is guaranteed in Baja California.

Figure 95. Mr. Dalle Valle takes a Mako Shark at Cap Haitian, Haiti. He is using the Cressi spring action gun in this fine picture of spearfishing's most exciting and critical moment. Photo by Philip Nash. (Courtesy Gustav Dalle Valle)

SOUTHERN FLORIDA

Miami is the focal point for underwater sportsmen in this area. Several stores (see Appendix B) in this area will prove to be cooperative to the stranger and carry all necessary underwater equipment. Air tanks can be charged at most stores listed. Little need be said about tourist accommodations in the Miami area since they are this city's life blood. However, the diver may decide not to stay in the immediate vicinity since better underwater areas are available elsewhere. The city of Tampa on the West coast and about halfway down the Florida peninsula has considerable spearfishing activity and clear water. But the Florida Keys are the American Mecca for underwater sights. Here are miles of shallow reefs, big fish of a dozen species, wrecks and galleons (six Spanish ships found in the last two years) and, in summer, 85 degree water. Here is indeed the prescription for adventure.

The Keys are reached through Miami, Key Largo being the first large Key on the Overseas Highway some 35 miles to the south. Tourist cabins abound along the Keys and there are many small marine yards where small boats may be rented. The northern shore of the Keys, which fronts on the so-called Florida Sea is very shallow and completely unsuited to any kind of underwater activity. But the south or ocean side has a reef some four to seven miles off shore and running the full length of the Keys that is fairyland itself. The visiting diver can establish himself on Key Largo, Marathon Key, or one of the other larger islands that form the chain and begin his trips out to the reefs. Be sure to stay on a Key that has an ocean side boatyard so that no time is wasted getting started in the morning. The local people will explain how to get out to the reef which is clearly marked along its entire length by automatic lights. Twelve to fifteen foot boats rent for around $3.00 a day with motors $5.00 or more. It is therefore important for the economy minded vacationist to bring his own outboard (at least 7½ horsepower). The trip out takes a little over an hour and the boat should be anchored just seaward or just inshore of the lights. A geodedic chart will help (see end of this chapter) since it spots wrecks and rocky bottoms. Do not anchor over the very blue water since these are generally featureless sand. Look for green-brown water that is perhaps 20 or more feet deep and has both sand and coral reef. A look-box, described in the fishing chapter, is very useful in spotting the best places to investigate underwater and a simple sounding line will insure that the first dives are not made in too deep water. Since the Key reef is well offshore, the trip out should not be made unless the weather is good and the sea moderate. There are many wrecks dotting this reef and an effort should be made to dive over at least one of them, since the sights are usually spectacular. Often the boat yard operator will help in spotting wrecks for you, and having a chart is most useful in this regard. If fishing is the prime object, do not bring in hundreds of pounds of fish since all resort people are very touchy and may refuse any further help. Do not spear or kill Tarpon in this area under any circumstances.

Ordinarily, Florida is a winter resort area, but for this special type of vacation, the summer will prove superior. The water around the

Keys is warmer and clearer in the summer, rates are less on housing and boats, and it is much easier to obtain help from the local people who are much less busy. Contrary to popular belief, Florida on the coasts is cooler in summer than New England and New York. The nights are actually cold at times, and the days mild and enjoyable. Water temperature runs well into the eighties and a rubber suit is

Figure 96. The authors preparing to go underwater over a Florida reef. Swimming with the surface supplied mask was practiced here and proved to be very successful for examing small regions of the undersea.

not necessary for summer diving. The main drawback in the Keys are the hordes of mosquitoes that swarm over everything after the sun has set. This can be very unpleasant except that a full day of underwater swimming is most tiring and the divers are usually in bed and asleep before the flies are out in full force. All cabins and motels have screens but a good anti-mosquito dope will be needed if after dark traveling is done.

In general, the Florida Keys area is the best and most easily reached underwater playground in America. Even the rankest amateur will be able to get many fish and lobster and the expenses in the summer are low. The main drawback is the distance that must be traveled to reach the reefs, for the first four or five miles of water south of the Keys is dull and unexciting. Off Tampa, Fort Lauderdale, and other coastal cities, diving can be done from rowboats or even from shore. These areas are more heavily fished and not quite as spectacular generally as Key water. Many readers may prefer to stay nearer the large cities and devote only one or two days to undersea sport. Some inquiry at diving supply stores will be necessary to select a suitable and convenient area that can be reached without too much over water travel. It might be noted that south of Saint Augustine on highway A-1-A is Marineland, the largest single tank aquarium in the world. To those who are planning to dive in Florida water for the first time, a visit here may prove useful since they will see most of the species of fish in a natural setting that they will wish to identify in the ocean later on. Usually attendants are present to name the fish for interested parties. Although Marineland is interesting and worth a visit, it cannot hope to compare with open sea diving. Swimming underwater in the midst of thousands of Amberjack or Angelfish can never be duplicated in any acquarium.

SOUTHERN CALIFORNIA

Like Florida, much of this area is devoted to tourist trade so the vacationer in this area will have no trouble with accommodations. Undersea fishing is considered to begin north of Los Angeles, becoming more and more widespread as one goes south. Laguna Beach is a focal point located some 50 miles south of Los Angeles on the coast. In this area are several private and state-run camp sites where the less well off vacation seeker can pitch a tent or park a trailer at a moderate fee. This makes Southern California a 'poor man's vacationland' in a very real sense and the area is thus unique compared to most other built up resort areas. The non-Californian is often unpleasantly surprised by the relatively cold water along most of the coast line. Where in Florida one can stay in or under the water for hours at a stretch without noticing the cold, such is not possible in Southern California water. The non-athletic type should therefore definitely take or purchase a rubber suit for serious diving whether in winter or summer. Winter diving in the Laguna Beach region is a very rugged matter even with a full suit.

Except for the waters around Catalina Island, most of the fishing areas can be reached easily from shore, although a rubber boat or tube is necessary for all but the strongest swimmers. High surf runs along most of the beaches and most serious spearfishing must be done close to rocks and breakers. It is therefore unwise for a poor or weak swimmer to plan on any fishing in this region unless he will be accompanied by an expert. Even getting through the surf into deeper water may at times be a problem (see section on this in Chapter VII). Equipment can be purchased in many stores in the Los Angeles area and in other towns to the south, and the compressed air bottles can

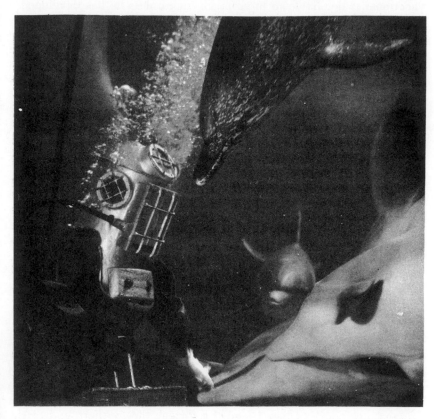

Figure 97. A diver at Marineland feeds the tame porpoise in the big tank. Sometimes a porpoise will pass a diver at close range in the open sea, but these curious beasts do not offer any harm. (Marine Studios)

be charged at many stores. Proprietors of equipment stores should be consulted as to good areas and as to what type of equipment is currently taking fish.

Further south near San Diego the water gets a little warmer but much of the sea coast is featureless with no rock ledges or cliffs. Also much of the coast is unavailable being owned by the U.S. Government.

Most of the fishing activity is centered just south of Los Angeles and around Catalina Island.

The California diver is competing with many other of his fellows wherever he goes. It is not unusual to see 10 or 20 spearmen working one patch of offshore reef or rock ledge. With such intense competition, considerable skill will be required to get the larger fish, and the casual vacationer is not liable to have much luck unless he has developed a technique already. In some areas the orange Garibaldi fish are plentiful, making the undersea look like a gigantic goldfish bowl and the long kelp and weed give the undersea an eerie appearance. The visibil ty is generally not as high as in Florida nor is the scenery as spectacular, but there is still plenty to wonder at and enjoy. There are fewer wrecks off the California coast, but the diver can find many tidal caves and current etched rocks along the shoreline that make striking undersea vistas. Beaches are magnificent and the above water scenery is large and impressive.

Catalina Island is reached by ferry from Los Angeles and Balboa. The waters surrounding it are not hit quite as hard as those off the mainland and most recent large catches in the area have been made off Catalina. Accommodations here tend to be expensive, a boat may be needed, and full information on where to fish should be obtained before going over. A few charter boats are operating in the area for spearmen and smaller boats can be rented. Information on matters of this sort is best obtained from sports stores or the magazine *The Skin Diver*, which is published every month in California and devoted to spearfishing (see Appendix C).

BAJA CALIFORNIA

The peninsula of Southern California is one of the few virtually untouched regions in North America. It is part of Mexico, but is not really connected with the main portion of the country except by bad roads in the Mexicali, Calexico region. Thus, most journeying into the peninsula is done through California and across the border at Tijuana, just south of San Diego. La Paz, at the southern end of the peninsula is a current favorite spot for spearmen who can afford the trip. Apparently the ocean side water well down the coastline is very cold so suits should be taken. The narrow bay formed by the peninsula and the mainland of Mexico is quite shallow and should prove to be warmer, but there are not as many roads leading to this side. The many bays and rocky headlands have large numbers of fish including some big shark, ray, and other tough fighters. Lobsters can be picked off the bottom in shallow water by the dozens and Abalone are common. Most of the hundreds of square miles of this region are deserted except for an occasional sheep herder so the vacationer must be self sufficient for the entire time he is there. Naturally, charging lung tanks is impossible.

Before making the trip to this area, the diver should spend some time in consulting the various agencies that can give him information on conditions. These would include automobile service agencies, tourists bureaus, the Mexican consulate, skin diving stores and clubs, etc.

Figure 98. An interclub contest off Palos Verdes at Los Angeles. This is typical California water. Notice that all divers in the picture are using either a one-man rubber raft or an inner tube. (Courtesy of The Skin Diver)

The magazine *The Skin Diver*, has carried several accounts of trips to the western side of the peninsula which will help the stranger become acquainted with the problems he will face here.

OTHER AREAS

New England, New York, New Jersey: For those who cannot get away, there is diving to be done in these northern waters, although the scenery is not as colorful or varied. A full suit is mandatory and diving equipment is usually necessary for successful fishing. The best spots off the New England coast line are over wrecks where fish congregate. It might be noted that there are many, many wrecks in

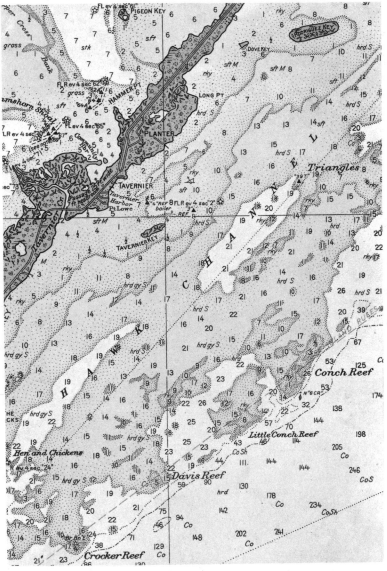

Figure 99. A portion of Nautical Chart 1249 showing the seaward water off Tavernier Key, just south of Key Largo. The line of reefs along the bottom of the illustration is the region for diving and underwater fishing and runs along the entire length of the Keys. Those unfamiliar with charts should study this example carefully and learn all the symbols and their meanings. (Courtesy of the U.S. Coast & Geodetic Survey)

this area that have never been found or investigated, although most of them are probably flattened by storms. While the chance of finding any valuables is slight, wreck hunting is exciting and results in interesting souvenirs. Some of the water off Cape Cod is surprisingly colorful if one knows where to go. Charts are a help here. The shore lines of Connecticut and Long Island are quite dull and dirty as far as water is concerned. Some spearing is done here and off New Jersey, but the heavy industrialization of the area make it tend towards polution and filth. Lake diving is becoming popular in northern states, particularly in Minnesota, but laws generally forbid taking edible fish in these waters by spear.

Bermuda: Doctor Beebe did much diving in an open helmet off Bermuda. The Island's position in the Gulf Stream gives it shallow bottoms that surpass the Keys in many places. Tremendous coral growths have created fascinating bottom formations and the sea life continues to attract the marine biologists. Unfortunately, Bermuda is relatively inaccessable to the diver with much equipment and there does not appear to be any dealers or compressed air sources as yet available on the island.

The Carribean Area: This is the dream area for everyone in North America who likes to dive. Warmth, visibility, richness of life undersea, and astonishing growths characterize most of the reefs and inshore water. All the islands have good water, but Jamaica is currently popular with the international spearfishing set. Fine color movies have been made off Nassau. If you can afford it, this is the region for you.

Other Countries: Where in the world? The Mediterranean where spearfishing among western nations began. Impressive undersea scenery, cold water, and many enthusiasts. The islands of the South Seas where coral lagoons have water so clear you can see down 100 feet. Where shark will take a speared catch in the blink of an eye and where pearl oysters lie waiting. The Great Barrier reef off Australia is thought by some to be the most spectacular in the world. The fish here are virtually unknown and you might have a species named after you. The shark are always hungry and take bathers time and time again. Hawaii, another undersea paradise with sea caves, and black volcanic rock punctuated by the brilliant flash of fish. And what about places like Easter Island where the ancient roads of a lost civilization run down into the sea . . . or Pitcairn where Captain Johnson of the YANKEE and his crew of 'round-the-worlders' dive over the sunken BOUNTY . . . or off Heligoland where a diver recently found stone walls similar to those described in Plato's description of 'Atlantis'. There is much to be seen and much to be done beneath the sea.

CHARTS AND MAPS

For those who do not actually live in a good diving area, but who have to travel a considerable distance, the problem of where to dive is perhaps the most difficult to settle. As already noted, various stores and local people are of help, but they usually find it hard to explain where the best undersea areas are and how they are reached. It is

Quality of the Bottom

1	Grd.	ground	32	Fr.	foraminifera
2	S.	sand	33	Gl.	globigerina
3	M.	mud	34	Di.	diatom
4	Oz.	ooze	35	Rd.	radiolaria
5	Ml.	marl	36	Pt.	pteropod
6	Cl.	clay	37	Po.	polyzoa
7	G.	gravel	39	fne.	fine
8	Sn.	shingle	40	crs.	coarse
9	P.	pebbles	41	sft.	soft
10	St.	stones	42	hrd.	hard
(10a)	Sp.	specks	43	stf.	stiff
11	Rk.	rock	44	sml.	small
(11a)	Bld. (s)	boulder (s)	45	lrg.	large
12	Ck.	chalk	46	stk.	sticky
13	Qz.	quartz	47	brk.	broken
14	Co.	coral	(47a)	rky.	rocky
(14a)	Co. Hd.	coral head	50	spk.	speckled
15	Md.	madrepore	51	gty.	gritty
(16a)	Vol. Ash.	volcanic ash	53	fly.	flinty
17	La.	lava	54	glac.	glacial
18	Pm.	pumice	56	wh.	white
19	T.	tufa	57	bk.	black
20	Sc.	scorice	59	bu.	blue
21	Cn.	cinders	60	gn.	green
22	Mn.	manganese	61	yl.	yellow
23	Sh.	shells	63	rd.	red
24	Oys.	oysters	64	br.	brown
25	Ms.	mussels	66	gy.	gray
26	Spg.	sponge	67	lt.	light
27	Grs.	grass	68	dk.	dark
28	Wd.	weeds	(69)	Ca.	calcareous
			(70)		

Figure 100. The quality of the bottom as specified on Nautical Charts. This is very valuable information for the diver since it gives a clue as to the visibility underwater in an area and the type of fish and marine life expected. (Courtesy of the U.S. Coast & Geodetic Survey)

thus very necessary that the visiting diver procure charts of the general diving area before he talks with the experts so that they can mark down on the chart good sections of reef, location of good boat rental agencies, and other related data. Regardless of how good a reputation an entire region may have, the visitor should not think he can go anywhere and find interesting bottom, for this is almost never the case. Even in the Carribean there are vast stretches of dull sand bottom or thinly scattered weed.

Fortunately, there are several excellent sources of information on bottom conditions, tide and current data, harbors, towns, etc. Best of all are the usual nautical charts prepared by the United States Coast and Geodedic Survey. To the diver who understands these charts will go rich rewards in successful dives, for they contain a wealth of information. These charts cover the inshore waters surrounding continental United States, Puerto Rico and the Virgin Islands, Alaska· and the Aleutians, and Hawaii. There are a few small boat operators who pride themselves on doing navigational work using road maps only, but for diving, road maps and maps handed out by marine oil and gas companies are entirely useless and will waste more time than nothing at all. The road map navigator usually wrecks his craft anyway.

The Coast and Geodedic Survey also handles tide and current tables for the above listed areas. These are a help to serious diving work although local publications may give more detailed information of an immediate area.

Another set of very useful publications put out by the Geodedic Survey are the "Coast Pilots", hard cover books containing detailed sailing directions and harbor data for the waters surrounding the already mentioned areas. The books give details of all bouyage and lists of available charts, as well as waterways, dangers, etc. The main body of each book is a running commentary on a section of coast, minutely detailed and packed with interesting information. These books are particularly valuable for the diver who is traveling in his own boat.

Using the Charts: Included in this chapter is a sample section of a Survey chart and some symbols that appear on such charts that are of especial interest to divers. Notice that the quality and nature of the bottom is noted on the charts, a most useful fact since it is obvious that where mud and ooze are specified, diving will be poor. The most optimistic notations are white sand, rocky, coral, and boulders, all of which indicate an irregular but clean bottom where fish are liable to congregate.

Of special interest to the sightseer or fisherman are underwater obstructions such as wrecks, large rocks, reefs, etc. These are always interesting objects usually offering the most spectacular scenery in an area. The small portion of chart shown in this chapter is a typical section of the Florida Keys and the reader will note the wealth of detailed information that is given.

The mere spotting of potentially interesting objects on a chart does not, unfortunately, guarantee their instant location at sea. This requires seamanship and a knowledge of inshore navigation, since a wreck completely out of sight is not an object one steers for by eye.

Dangers

1	Rocks which do not cover; with their elevations above M.H.W.	**15**	Wreck of known depth
2	Rocks that cover and uncover, with heights in feet above datum of soundings (*uncovers 2 ft *(2))	**16**	Sunken wreck, not dangerous to surface navigation or over which the depth exceeds 10 fathoms
(3a)	When rock of 2 is considered a danger to navigation	**17**	Foul ground
(4a)	Sunken rock	**18**	Overfalls or tide rips (tide rips — Symbol used only in small areas)
(4b)	When rock of 4a is considered a danger to navigation	**19**	Eddies
(4c)	Shoal sounding on isolated rock replaces symbol (②Rk)	**20**	Kelp, any kind (Symbol used only in small areas)
6a	Sunken danger with depth cleared by wire drag (Feet or fathoms) (21Rk 21Wk 21Obstr)	**(20a)**	
		21	Bk. bank
		22	Shl. shoal
		23	Rf. reef
10	Coral or rocky reef (below datum of soundings) See A-11g	**24**	Le. ledge
		25	
11	Stranded wreck (any portion of hull above datum of soundings)	**27**	Obstr. obstruction
		28	Wk. wreck
12	Sunken wreck with only masts visible (masts)	**(28a)**	Wks. wreckage
		33	cov. covers
14	Dangerous sunken wreck with less than 10 fathoms of water over it (See 6a)	**34**	uncov. uncovers
		35	Rep. reported
		(35a)	Shoal (rep. 1945) shoal reported
		36	Discol. discolored
(14a)	A number of sunken wrecks (wreckage)	**41**	P. A. position approximate
		42	P. D. position doubtful
		43	E. D. existence doubtful
(14b)	Obstruction of any kind (21 Obstr)	**44**	Pos. position
		(46)	
		(47)	

Figure 101. While the average mariner tries to aviod underwater dangers, the diver may seek them out, since they represent in many cases the most interesting bottom in an area. There are no secret 'best' places for fishing for the man who uses charts, since almost all discontinuities on the bottom are listed on charts, and these are usually the best for fish. (Courtesy of the U.S. Coast and Geodetic Survey)

Those who have never tried chart navigation should therefore acquaint themselves with methods of dead reckoning, taking cross bearings, and other such methods. These are best learned by obtaining one of the many books on the subject of inshore piloting and carefully studying it.

Aside from supplying bottom features, the charts give information on conditions along a coast, i.e. breakers, kelp, swampy, etc., the location of prominent landmarks, and all bouyage. There is also a certain amount of information on the land including streets, harbor basins, and prominent features of seacoast areas.

Most useful of all are the soundings which are the main reason for the charts as far as mariners are concerned. All water depths are given for mean low water, so if an accurate picture of depths is wanted a knowledge of tide rise and fall in the area is required. Generally, the diver will find the water somewhat deeper than specified on the charts, so that a recirculator user who sees depths of 35 and 40 feet should beware lest the actual depth be closer to 50 at high water. The charts are not, of course, a substitute for a depth gauge. Where depth lines are very close together, as on the offshore corner of the illustrative sample, the diver may generally expect to find an interesting bottom since such drop-offs have much activity and large fish.

For any diving work, the most detailed and large scale charts of an area are necessary which may mean that more than one chart will be necessary to cover a vacation region.

Obtaining Nautical Publications: Charts, tide and current tables, and "U.S. Coast Pilots" are obtained from the U.S. Coast and Geodedic Survey, Washington 25, D.C. or from local marine dealers. The office in Washington will send to interested parties a "Catalogue of Nautical Charts and Related Publications" which may be used for ordering.

"Sailing Directions", which relate to areas other than those noted at the beginning of this section are compiled by the U.S. Hydrographic Office and obtained from the Superintendent of Documents, Washington 25, D.C. The United States Government through its various agencies publishes a great deal of material related to the sea, navigation, oceanography, and related subjects. This material is listed in standard indexes of government publications which can be found in any large public library. The authors urge all readers to make full use of this valuable data.

CHECKLISTS

The following series of lists are suggested for those planning trips to one of the areas discussed previously. Several types of trips are con-

Figure 102. Frames from a 16 mm underwater movie taken in the Florida Keys. Here the diver investigates a cargo ship's wreckage in fifty feet of water.

sidered and the lists take into account the seriousness of the diving effort and the methods of transportation.

A—Viewing the undersea for short periods while in a warm water area.

1 pair of swim fins.
1 good diving mask (not air supplied).
1 snorkel.
1 Res-Q-Pac.
(will easily fit in part of a suitcase for flying or train travel)

B—Spearing fish (moderate size) in most American areas.
List A plus;
1 full length rubber suit (for cold water and where recommended previously).
1 rubber powered (two strand) gun or rubber driven hand spear.
1 half dozen spears for gun with 30 feet of good line.
1 Abalone or tire iron (for California).
1 ten or more pound weighted belt (only when suit is used).
1 knife.
1 one or two man rubber liferaft or inner tube.
Charts of area.
(all light equipment except weights which can be mailed if traveling by air)

C—Spearing fish near air charging facilities using diving equipment.
Lists A and B plus;
1 diving unit, rechargeable, giving two hours per day of surface breathing.
1 depth gauge.
1 decompression calculator or tables.
1 outboard motor, 7½ H.P. or larger (where using rented boat is necessary).
1 look box.
(if traveling by plane, diving gear will have to be expressed as will motor, although a small recirculator might fit in a suitcase)

D—Spearing fish and underwater investigation in areas more than one day away from populated regions and recharging facilites.
Lists A, B, and C plus;
Sufficient recharge for diving gear (see fishing chapter).
Outboard gasoline and container.
Four man or larger liferaft (for diving within a half mile of land).
Fittings to inflate raft and pump or gas cylinder to fill it.
Car top boat (for diving far out with self-contained equipment) or 15 foot or more car pulled boat (for diving with compressor).

E—Sport and investigation in completely non-populated areas.
Above four lists (A, B, C, D) including if possible the larger boat plus;
Tents.
Cook stove.
Sleeping bags.
Fresh water (at least two gallons per man per day).
Large (400 pounds or more) cake of ice with canvas cover.
Ice box.
Extra spears, gun elastics, line, etc.
General first aid supplies.
(a pick-up truck or jeep and trailor should prove most satisfactory
for a real expedition into the back country).

F—Spearing very large fish in any area.
All equipment needed in previous lists depending on area and transportation plus; CO_2 gun and recharge cylinders, four strand rubber
gun, or equally powerful unit.
A dozen spears with shock cord or equally strong line.
1 good gaff.
1 Mae West or inner tube for playing the fish.
Explosive spear heads (if available and fish very large).

G—Underwater photography.
Equipment depending on location of diving area and problem of
transportation plus; Camera, enclosure, films, filters, exposure meter,
etc., as specified in companion volume, "Underwater Photography".

H—Salvage and wreck investigation.
See chapter on Commercial Shallow Water Diving.

I—Scientific studies.
Equipment depends on scope of investigation. For securing live
specimens Dr. Beebe has used small explosive charges to stun fish.
A diving telephone will require use of full suit such as the Desco with
surface compressor, or more simply a helmet. Powerful flashlights are
available from Desco for close investigation of sea fauna, caves and
coral formations. A geologists hammer can crack off specimens of
undersea rocks and coral and a good sized pair of plyers will disloge
tough plants for study.

Appendix A

DECOMPRESSION TABLES

The following tables are for the use of anyone diving beyond the depth of 36 feet. If more than one dive is made during the day, add the time of the first dive to that of the second and decompress as indicated. The rate of ascent postulated in these tables is 25 feet per minute and should not be exceeded. The Thompson Engineering Company supplies this data on a handy rotating scale at slight cost.

Depth of Dive	Time Underwater from Surface to Beginning of Ascent	Stoppage at Different Depths in Minutes				Total Ascent Time
		40 Ft.	30 Ft.	20 Ft.	10 Ft.	
36 ft.	no limit	..	..	..	0	0-1½ min.
40 ft.	0-120 min.	..	..	..	0	2 min.
40 ft.	120-180 min.	..	..	..	2	4 min.
40 ft.	180-240 min.	..	..	..	4	6 min.
40 ft.	240-300 min.	..	..	..	6	8 min.
50 ft.	0- 78 min.	..	..	..	0	2 min.
50 ft.	78-120 min.	..	..	..	2	4 min.
50 ft.	120-150 min.	..	..	..	5	7 min.
50 ft.	150-190 min.	..	..	..	9	11 min.
50 ft.	190-300 min.	..	..	..	12	14 min.
60 min.	0- 55 min.	..	..	..	0	3 min.
60 min.	55- 75 min.	..	..	..	2	5 min.
60 min.	75-110 min.	..	..	..	13	16 min.
60 min.	110-150 min.	..	..	5	15	23 min.
60 min.	150-180 min.	..	..	7	16	26 min.
60 min.	180-210 min.	..	..	8	18	29 min.
70 ft.	0- 43 min.	..	..	..	0	3 min.
70 ft.	43- 60 min.	..	..	..	4	7 min.

Depth of Dive	Time Underwater from Surface to Beginning of Ascent	Stoppage at Different Depths in Minutes				Total Ascent Time
		40 Ft.	30 Ft.	20 Ft.	10 Ft.	
70 ft.	60- 75 min.	..	..	..	13	16 min.
70 ft.	75- 90 min.	..	..	4	16	23 min.
70 ft.	90-120 min.	..	..	13	16	32 min.
70 ft.	120-150 min.	..	..	18	21	42 min.
70 ft.	150-180 min.	..	..	21	32	56 min.
80 ft.	0- 35 min.	..	..	..	0	4 min.
80 ft.	35- 50 min.	..	..	..	6	10 min.
80 ft.	50- 70 min.	..	..	9	16	29 min.

Depth of Dive	Time Underwater from Surface to Beginning of Ascent	Stoppage at Different Depths in Minutes				Total Ascent Time
		40 Ft.	30 Ft.	20 Ft.	10 Ft.	
80 ft.	70-100 min.	..	..	20	16	40 min.
80 ft.	100-115 min.	..	..	22	26	52 min.
80 ft.	115-150 min.	..	..	28	29	61 min.
90 ft.	0- 30 min.	..	..	..	0	4 min.
90 ft.	30- 45 min.	..	...	..	6	10 min.
90 ft.	45- 60 min.	..	..	9	16	29 min.
90 ft.	60- 75 min.	..	..	18	14	36 min.
90 ft.	75- 95 min.	..	.2	27	21	54 min.
90 ft.	95-130 min.	..	9	27	29	69 min.
100 ft.	0- 25 min.	..	..	..	0	4 min.
100 ft.	25- 40 min.	..	..	..	12	16 min.

Depth of Dive	Time Underwater from Surface to Beginning of Ascent	Stoppage at Different Depths in Minutes				Total Ascent Time
		40 Ft.	30 Ft.	20 Ft.	10 Ft.	
100 ft.	40- 60 min.	..	..	18	16	38 min.
100 ft.	60- 75 min.	..	..	27	21	48 min.
100 ft.	75- 85 min.	..	6	28	21	59 min.
100 ft.	85- 90 min.	..	8	27	24	63 min.
100 ft.	90-120 min.	..	17	28	48	97 min.
110 ft.	0- 20 min.	..	..	..	0	5 min.
110 ft.	20- 35 min.	..	..	..	12	17 min.
110 ft.	35- 55 min.	..	..	22	21	48 min.
110 ft.	55- 75 min.	..	14	27	37	83 min.
110 ft.	75-105 min.	2	22	29	50	108 min.
120 ft.	0- 18 min.	..	..	..	0	5 min.
120 ft.	18- 30 min.	..	..	..	11	16 min.
120 ft.	30- 45 min.	..	..	18	21	44 min.
120 ft.	45- 65 min.	..	13	28	32	78 min.
120 ft.	65-100 min.	5	22	27	69	128 min.
130 ft.	0- 15 min.	..	..	..	0	6 min.
130 ft.	15- 35 min.	..	..	11	15	32 min.
130 ft.	35- 52 min.	..	6	28	28	68 min.
130 ft.	52- 60 min.	..	13	28	28	75 min.
130 ft.	60- 90 min.	9	22	28	69	134 min.
140 ft.	0- 15 min.	..	..	..	4	10 min.
140 ft.	15- 30 min.	..	..	8	21	35 min.
140 ft.	30- 45 min.	..	5	27	27	65 min.
140 ft.	45- 55 min.	..	15	28	32	71 min.
140 ft.	55- 85 min.	14	22	32	69	143 min.
150 ft.	0- 15 min.	..	..	..	7	13 min.
150 ft.	15- 30 min.	..	..	13	21	40 min.
150 ft.	30- 38 min.	..	..	28	30	64 min.
150 ft.	38- 50 min.	..	16	28	32	72 min.
150 ft.	50- 80 min.	18	23	32	69	148 min.

Appendix B

EQUIPMENT SOURCES

There are now a large number of firms making and selling diving equipment and other items related to diving. As newly designed equipment has come on the market, the surplus stocks have grown less and less easy to obtain. The novice diving enthusiast must therefore shop wisely and with full knowledge of the purposes to which he plans to put his equipment so as to avoid wasteful purchases. The following list is reasonably comprehensive. Every effort has been made to include all dealers in the United States who handle a major share of the underwater equipment sales at this time. Omissions are the result of lack of knowledge on the authors' part of the firms omitted.

(1) Diving Equipment and Supply Company (Desco) 234 North Broadway, Milwaukee 2, Wisconsin. Manufactures all the Desco gear mentioned in this book.

(2) U. S. Divers Company, 1045 Broxton Ave., West Los Angeles 24, Calif. Manufactures and distributes AQUA-LUNG in the North American Continent, also distributes Frogman Rubber Suits, Spear-Guns, Floating Knives, Snorkle Tubes, Water Tight Camera Cases, Imported Dive Masks, Swim Fins, Underwater Flashlights, etc.

(3) Fenjohn Underwater Photo and Equipment Co., 90 Crickett Ave., Ardmore, Penna. Manufacture and rent underwater cameras, distribute Aqua-Lung, suits, and related items.

(4) Morse Diving Equipment Co., 470 Atlantic Ave., Boston 10, Mass. Manufacture shallow water helmets and other shallow water diving equipment as noted in this book.

(5) Miller-Dunn Co., 2517 N.W. 21st Terrace, Miami, Fla. Manufacture helmets.

(6) Thompson Engineering Company, Grand Rapids, Mich., (Teco). Manufacture masks, pumps, compressors, etc.

(7) Byrd Commercial Diving, 3083 N.W. 59th St., Miami, Fla. Manufacture diving phones.

(8) Divers Supply, 1148 Wilmington Blvd., Wilmington, Calif. Manufacture lungs, distribute surplus gear (shallow water and deep) and other equipment.

(9) Mine Safety Appliances Co., Pittsburgh 8, Penna. Manufacture a self-contained recirculating lung.

(10) Bel-Aqua Water Sports Co., 3720 West 54th Street, Los Angeles, Calif. Manufacture suits, snorkels, and sell other equipment.

(11) The Spearfisherman, Box 388, Huntington Beach, California. Manufacture suits, masks and other items.

(12) W. J. Voit Rubber Co., Box 2529 Terminal Annex, Los Angeles 54, Calif. Manufactures fins and masks.

(13) Fisher Sporting Goods, 4135 West 182nd St., North Torrance, Calif. Manufacture CO_2 guns, explosive heads, spears, etc.

(14) Metal Formfab Corp., 3080 North Avon St., Burbank, Calif. Manufacture the Barracuda CO_2 gun.

(15) La Jolla Sporting Goods, 1051 Wall St., La Jolla, Calif. Sells self-contained equipment, guns, flippers, etc.

(16) Sports Exhibit Mart, 3722 San Fernando Road, Glendale, Calif. Sells divers supplies.

(17) Woody's Sporting Goods, 127 N. Tamarind, Compton, Calif. Sells guns, suits, flippers, masks, etc.

(18) Proctors Sporting Goods, 128 West Broadway, Long Beach, Calif. Sells fins, masks, guns, etc.

(19) The Florida Frogman, 5850 Sunset Drive, South Miami, Fla. Sell Cressi equipment, guns, masks, and all other material illustrated in this book in pictures credited to this distributer.

(20) Aqua-Lung Inc., 1329 Biscayne Blvd., Miami 39, Fla. Sell diving equipment, spear guns, lungs, etc.

(21) Aqua Sports, Inc., 348 South Pineapple, Sarasota, Fla. Sell lungs, fishing equipment, etc.

(22) The Aqua-Gun Company, 1121 No. Broadway, Yonkers 3, N. Y. Spearfishing guns, spears, sling spears, etc.

(23) M. & E. Marine Supply Co., P. O. Box 601, Camden, N. J. Sell new and surplus shallow and deep water equipment of all types.

(24) Sea Net Manufacturing Company, 1428 Maple Avenue, Los Angeles 15, Calif. Manufactures lungs, spears and heads, fins, masks, etc.

(25) Abercrombie & Fitch Co., 45th St. at Madison Ave., New York 17, N. Y. Sells diving and spearfishing equipment.

(26) Waterwear Company, Newport Beach, Calif. Rubber diving suits, underwater camera bags and rubber swim shirts and pants.

(27) Universal Sales Co., 1085 Peach Place, Concord, Calif. Cressi products and Japanese Tabe Socks.

Equipment Prices: Costs of diving equipment and spearfishing gear are quite variable. Here are presented the range of prices of the most often used items:

Helmets, (new) $100 and up, (used) $40 and up. Hose $12.50 per fifty foot lengths. Less for welding hose and surplus hose. Hand pumps (new) $80 and up, (used) $15 and up. One way valves $5 to $8 new. Volume tanks, $15 new, $8 surplus, $4 for oxygen tank of correct size.

Masks, (new) $18 to $55, (used) about half new price. Compressors, $50 and up with engines about the same. Suits, (new) $110 up, (surplus) $35 and up. Weighted belts, $15 to $40 depending on amount of weight. Homemade with lead runs, $3 to $4. Suitable gas masks under $5 apiece.

Recirculator, $80 for least expensive (Model A) up to $300 for largest units. Res-Q-Pac, $2. Depth gauge, $3.50. Soda Lime, $.75 a quart. Beralyme, 8 lbs for $6.75. Oxygen about three cents per cubic foot.

Throw-away, $100 for smallest model to $275 for largest (Navy Aqua-Lung). Air reserve device, $25. Bottle recharge, 70 cubic foot, $1 to $1.50.

Spear guns, (rubber) $20 and up, ($CO_2$), $50 and up. Knives, $3 and up. Rubber suits, (short) $20 to $50, (long) $60. Masks, $5 and up to $14 (not air supplied). Fins, $5 to $9.

Charts, $1 to $1.50. "Coast Pilots", $1.50 each. Welding regulators, $12.50 to $25 each. Torch, (underwater) $96.

Appendix C

DIVING BIBLIOGRAPHY

In an effort to consolidate the written data on diving, we have tried to collect as many references as possible in this one section which relate to deep and shallow diving practice, salvage, diving equipment, bells, and suits, small submarines, and related matters. Articles on diving written in popular periodicals have been omitted unless they contain sound information which will be useful to the diver. Generally, a popular article by a non-diver is filled with inaccurate and sometimes dangerous information which must be discounted. Historical references have been largely omitted and the reader will find a bibliography of these in "Half Mile Down", by Beebe. All written matter relating to undersea photography has been indexed in the companion volume, "Underwater Photography".

This list has been divided into two main categories, books and articles, and each category has been subdivided into popular and technical matter. This latter division is not too satisfactory in many cases, since some books and articles are by no means technical in the usual sense, but the division may assist the diver to select material of a how-to-do nature, even though it has no real engineering worth. A third list of special books, not actually written about diving, but containing useful information has been added at the end of the bibliography. No comment will be given on most references except where the title is in a foreign language or does not adequately express the content of the material. The following key will help to further identify the references.

(op)—out of print (refers to books)

(Juv.)—Juvenile (refers to books)

(es)—Available from Engineering Societies Library, 29 West 39th Street, New York, N. Y. in photostat. (refers to articles)

BOOKS

Technical:

(1) "Diving, Cutting, and Welding in Underwater Salvage Operations," F. E. Thompson, Jr., *Cornell Maritime Press.*

(2) "Deep Diving and Submarine Operations," Sir Robert Davis, *The Saint Catherine Press, Ltd.* (London) with 15 references.

(3) "L'Exploration Sous-Marine," D. Rebikoff (in French on equipment and diving methods), *B. Arthaud* (Paris) with 16 references.

(4) "Sub-Marine Spearfishing," I. S. Ivanovic', *A. S. Barnes*.

(5) "Underwater Blasting," R. Westwater and R. Haslam, *Imperial Chemical Industries, Ltd., Nobel Division* (British).

(6) "A Guide to Skin Diving and Underwater Spearfishing," Max L. Jones, *Universal Sales Company*.

(7) "The Compleat Goggler," Guy Gilpatrick, *Dodd, Mead and Company*. (op).

(8) "Shallow Water Diving for Pleasure and Profit," H. Schenck, Jr., and H. Kendall, *Cornell Maritime Press*. (first edition op).

(9) "Self-Contained Diving," Rene Bussoz, *U. S. Divers Company*. (booklet).

(10) "Military Diving, (T. M. 5-475)," from Superintendent of Documents, Washington, D. C. (booklet).

(11) "Diving Manual (1943)," U. S. Navy, from Supt. of Documents.

(12) "Bureau of Ships Manual, Chapter 94, Salvage, Section II, Diving," U. S. Navy, from Supt. of Documents.

(13) "Diving Manual" (1952), U. S. Navy, from Supt. of Documents.

Popular:

(1) "Arcturus Adventure," William Beebe, *Putnam and Sons* (op).

(2) "Beneath Tropic Seas," William Beebe, *Putnam and Sons* (op).

(3) "Half Mile Down," William Beebe, *Harcourt Brace*.

(4) "Nonsuch, Land of Water," William Beebe, *Harcourt Brace* (op).

(5) "On the Bottom," E. Ellsberg, *Dodd, Mead and Company*.

(6) "Men Under the Sea," E. Ellsberg, *Dodd, Mead and Company*.

(7) "Under the Red Sea Sun," E. Ellsberg, *Dodd, Mead and Company*.

(8) "Ocean Gold," E. Ellsberg, *Dodd, Mead and Company* (Juv.).

(9) "Spanish Ingots," E. Ellsberg, *Dodd, Mead and Company* (Juv.).

(10) "Thirty Fathoms Deep," E. Ellsberg, *Dodd, Mead and Company* (Juv.).

(11) "Treasure Below," E. Ellsberg, *Dodd, Mead and Company* (Juv.).

(12) "Deep Sea Divers," C. Zolotovsky, *Lippincotte* (Juv.).

(13) "Underseas Log," E. Bushnell and M. O'Moran, *Caxton Printers*.

(14) "Twenty Years Under the Sea," Williamson, *Branford* (op).

(15) "I Like Diving," Tom Eadie, *Houghton Miflin*.

(16) "Treasure Hunter," H. Riesberg, *Dodd, Mead and Company* (op).

(17) "Men Under the Sea," F. Meier, *Dell Books*.

(18) "Danger Is My Business," J. Craig, *Simon and Shuster* (op).

(19) "Diving to Adventure," H. Hass, *Doubleday*.

(20) "The Silent World," Cousteau and Dumas, *Harper and Brothers.*

(21) "Fun in the Water," R. Winston, *June, Osborn, Foster and Smith.*

(22) "Under Sea with Helmet and Camera," A. F. Dupont, *Dodd, Mead and Company* (op).

(23) "The Distant Shore," Jan de Hartog, *Harper and Brothers* (fiction).

(24) "Twenty Thousand Leagues Under the Sea," Jules Verne, *Grosset and Dunlap* (fiction).

PERIODICALS

Technical:

(1) "Salvage of H.M. Submarine 'Truculent'," C. L. Black, *Inst. of Engineers and Shipbuilders in Scotland (Transactions),* v. 94, 1950-51, pt. 3, pp. 160-184. (es)

(2) "Underwater Welding Aids Ship Salvage," R. H. Burke, *Welding Engineer,* v. 35, n. 4, Apr. 1950, pp. 20-22. (es)

(3) "Salvage of S.S. 'Steel Chemist'," *Pacific Marine Review,* v. 47, n. 5, May 1950, pp. 31-34. (es)

(4) "Les Operations de Renflouement a Bordeaux," A. Bron, *Annales des Ports et Chausees,* v. 118, n. 1, Jan.-Feb. 1948, pp. 41-82. (es) (on commercial diving)

(5) "Marine Salvage," W. A. Sullivan, *Society of Naval Architects and Marine Engineers,* advance paper n. 1, 1948, 39 p. (es)

(6) "Diving Bell for Underwater Gravimeter Operation," E. W. Frowe, *Geophysics,* v. 12, n. 9, Jan. 1947, pp. 1-2. (es)

(7) "Submersible Bolt Driving and Punching Gun," *Engineering,* v. 162, n. 4223, Dec. 20, 1946, pp. 597. (es)

(8) "Underwater Arc Cutting," L. Mills, *Welding Engineer,* v. 32, n. 4, Apr. 1947, pp. 55-57. (es)

(9) "Exploring Continental Shelf," C. J. Deegan, *Oil and Gas Journal,* v. 45, n. 6, June 15, 1946, pp. 98-101. (es) (on diving bells and tideland oil investigation)

(10) "Arc Welding and Cutting Underwater," L. Mills, *Transactions of the Institute of Welding,* v. 9, n. 4, Aug. 1945, pp. 128-130. (es)

(11) "Underwater Cutting and Welding," C. Kandel, *Welding Journal,* v. 25, n. 3, Mar. 1946, pp. 209-212. (es)

(12) "U.S. Navy Developments in Underwater Cutting," B. Ronay and C. D. Jensen, *Jour. American Society Naval Engineers,* v. 57, n. 4, Nov. 1945, pp. 456-480. (es)

(13) "Military Diver," R. R. Owen, *Military Engineer,* v. 37, n. 237, July 1945, pp. 280-281. (es)

(14) "How Wrecked and Sunken Ships are Salved," G. R. Critchey, *Journ. Royal Society of Arts*, v. 93, n. 4686, Mar. 2, 1945, pp. 164-172. (es)

(15) "How Navy Trains Salvage Divers," R. G. Skerrett, *Compressed Air Magazine*, v. 49, n. 1, 5, 6, Jan. pp. 2-7, May pp. 122-125, June pp. 156, 1944. (es)

(16) "Diving Amplifier," D. W. Gillerup, *Electronics*, v. 16, n. 9, Sept. 1943, pp. 170, 172, 174. (es)

(17) "Salvage of USS 'Lafayette'," B. E. Manseau and C. M. Hart, *Journ. American Society of Naval Engineers*, v. 55, n. 4, Nov. 1943, pp. 648-697. (es)

(18) "Human Life and Death at High Pressures," J. B. S. Haldane, *Nature* (London), v. 148, n. 3755, Oct. 18, 1941, pp. 458-460. (es)

(19) "Salvage of USS 'Squalus'," F. A. Tusler, *Journ. American Society of Naval Engineers*, v. 52, n. 2, May 1940, pp. 157-187. (es)

(20) "Les Probleme de l'exploration du Fond de la Mer," A. Piccard, *Societe' des Ingenieurs Civils de France, Memoires*, v. 91, n. 5, Sept.-Oct. 1938, pp. 673-685. (es) (on a deep diving sphere)

(21) "Salvage of HMS 'Thetis'," G. R. Critchley, *Journ. American Society of Naval Engineers*, v. 52, n. 4, Nov. 1940, pp. 658-671. (es)

(22) "Aero-otitis Media in Submarine Personnel," H. L. Maines, *Journ. Acoustical Society of America*, v. 17, n. 2, Oct. 1945, pp. 139-143. (es) (diving ear pain)

(23) "Underwater Blasting," R. Westwater and R. Haslam, *Civil Engineering* (London), v. 44, n. 517, 518, 519, 520, July 1949, pp. 374-376, Aug. pp. 436-439, Sept. pp. 519, 521, Oct. pp. 589-592. (es)

(24) "Note sur le Scaphandre Autonome, etc.," C. Beau, *Annales des Ponts et Chausees*, v. 106, n. 11, Nov. 1936, pp. 592-598. (es) (warmed self-contained gear)

(25) "Deep Diving and Underwater Rescue," R. H. Davis, *Indian Engineering*, v. 96, n. 16, Oct. 20, 1934, pp. 310-315, also *Journ. Royal Society of Arts*, v. 22, n. 4266, pp. 1032-1047, n. 4267, pp. 1049-1065, n. 4268, pp. 1069-1080, n. 4269, pp. 1083-1101, 1934. (es)

(26) "La Struttura s'ferica Galeazzi negli schafi resistenti dei Sommergibili," R. Galeazzi, *Rivisti Marittima*, v. 65, n. 6, June 1952, pp. 371-407. (es) (diving armour)

(27) "La technica de los buzos," R. Montero Azearraga, *Ingenieria y Construccion*, v. 9, n. 104 and 107, Aug. 1931, pp. 486-593, Nov. 1931, pp. 661-665. (es) (armour)

(28) "Diving," L. Hill, *Nature* (London), v. 125, n. 3150, Mar. 15, 1930, pp. 415-418. (es) (Davis escape lungs)

(29) "Un nuovo respiratore subacqueo ed antigas," A. Bellani, *Revista Marittime*, v. 62, n. 10, Oct. 1929. (es) (self-contained equipment)

(30) "Prevention of Freezing in Cold Weather Diving," W. C. Owen, and O. E. Grimm, *Journ. American Society of Naval Engineers*, v. 41, n. 2, May 1929, pp. 246-249. (es)

(31) "Submarine Escape," C. B. Momsen, *Journ. American Society of Naval Engineers*, v. 41, n. 2, May 1929, pp. 169-171. (es)

(32) "Le Scaphandre Autonome," *Nature*, (Paris), n. 2613, May 3, 1924, pp. 275-280. (es) (diving equipment)

(33) "Life at High Pressures," J. B. S. Haldane, *Science News*, v. 4, 1947. (England)

(34) "Underwater Noise due to Marine Life," D. P. Loye and D. A. Proudfoot, *Journ. Acoustical Society of America*, v. 18, n. 2, Oct. 1946.

(35) "Physics of Deep Sea Diving," L. E. Dodd, *American Journal of Physics*, v. 8, n. 3, March 1940.

(36) "Submarine Physics," G. P. Harnewell, *American Journal of Physics*, v. 16, n. 3, March 1948.

(37) "Physics and Physiology in Diving Decompression," H. Schenck, Jr., *American Journal of Physics*, v. 21, n. 4, April 1953.

(38) "Oxygen Poisoning in Man," K. W. Donald, *British Medical Journal*, May 17 and May 24, 1947.

Popular:

(1) "A Wonderer Under the Sea," W. Beebe, *The National Geographic Magazine*, Dec. 1932.

(2) "A Round Trip to Davy Jones's Locker," W. Beebe, *The National Geographic Magazine*, June 1931.

(3) "Goggle Fishing in California Water," *The National Geographic Magazine*, May 1949.

(4) "Fish Men Explore a New World Undersea," J. Cousteau, *The National Geographic Magazine*, Oct. 1952.

(5) "Hunters in the Sea," F. L. Harvey, *Argosy*, Sépt. 1952.

(6) "Under the Sea on a Glider," R. F. Dempewolff, *Popular Mechanics*, Oct. 1952.

(7) "Underwater Commandos," E. Smith, *Argosy*, Nov. 1950.

(8) "Quest for Galleon's Gold," *Popular Mechanics*, Oct. 1950.

(9) "Diver Battles Shark in Tunnel Under the Sea," *Popular Science*, Aug. 1950.

(10) "Diving to Spear Carp," R. T. Keagle, *Sports Afield*, July 1951.

(11) "Walking Under Water," Cross, *Popular Science Magazine*, July 1949.

The following list of references contains books and articles of interest to divers and includes material on oceanography, biology, physiology, and other matters. For the most part this data is of a technical or semi-technical nature and the reader will often have to extrapolate the information to the diving conditions.

Books:

(1) "Decompression Sickness," National Research Council, *W. B. Saunders Company*, with 545 references on high altitude and diving physiology.

(2) "The Sea Around Us," R. Carson, *Oxford University Press*, on popular oceanography.

(3) "Under the Sea Wind," R. Carson, *Oxford University Press*, on popular marine biology.

(4) "The Oceans," Sverdrup, Fleming, and Johnson, *Prentice Hall, Inc.*, the basic text on Oceanography.

(5) "Submerged Forests," C. Reid, *Cambridge University Press*, on bottom flora.

(6) "Submarine Geology," F. P. Shepard, *Harper and Brothers*, a standard work.

(7) "Marine Fishes of Southern California," P. S. Barnhart, *University of California Press*, a classic on this subject.

(8) "Marine Geology," Kennan, *John Wiley*.

(9) "Marine Shells of the West Coast of North America," *Stanford University Press*, in two volumes.

(10) "Oceanography," H. Bigelow, *Harper and Brothers*.

(11) "Field Book of Sea Shore Life," R. W. Miner, *Putnam*, a valuable handbook.

(12) "Fishes and Shells of the Pacific World," Nichols and Bartok, *Macmillan*.

(13) "The Book of Fishes," LaGorce, *National Geographic Society*.

(14) "The Tide," H. A. Marmer, *D. Appleton and Company*, a basic work on the subject.

(15) "Wind Waves at Sea, Breakers and Surf," Henry and Edmondson, *U. S. Navy, Hydrographic Office Publication no. 602* (op).

(16) "Self-Contained Oxygen Breathing Apparatus," G. W. Grove, *United States Government Printing Office* (from Supt. of Documents), a must for home equipment building, especially recirculators.

(17) "Respiration," J. S. Haldane, *Yale University Press* (op), the classic work on diving decompression is one chapter of this book.

(18) "Underwater Explosions," R. Cole, *Princeton University Press*.

(19) "A Dictionary of Fishes," R. Allen.

DIVER'S PERIODICALS

Two publications are currently available to the enthusiastic diver on a monthly subscription:

(1) "The Skin Diver," edited by Jim Auxier. $3.00 per year, 25 cents a copy. P. O. Box 128, Lynwood, California. This is a thin but valuable magazine for the goggle fisherman and shallow diver. It contains latest dope on laws, equipment, underwater accidents, and many hints on the sport. Originally a magazine for Californians, it is now considering the undersea problems everywhere in the U. S.

(2) "The Deep Sea Digest," edited by Lewis Maxwell. $1.00 per ten issues. Box 333, South Miami, Florida. A pamphlet which discusses many aspects of underwater life, lists books and equipment, and indulges in some philosophy as well. This publication considers many little known sea facts and may eventually act as a clearing house for divers' questions.

INDEX